THE ULTIMATE BOOK OF CHOCOLATE

*To Marie and Milan, for their unfailing support
in my quest for the finest flavours.*

MÉLANIE DUPUIS
RECIPES AND GUIDEBOOK

THE ULTIMATE BOOK OF CHOCOLATE

MAKING YOUR CHOCOLATE DREAMS COME TRUE

WITH CHOCOLATE SPECIALIST EMMANUELLE DE BEAUREGARD
PHOTOGRAPHS BY PIERRE JAVELLE
ILLUSTRATIONS BY YANNIS VAROUTSIKOS
ADDITIONAL MATERIAL BY ANNE CAZOR
DESIGN BY ORATHAY SOUKSISAVANH

Hardie Grant
BOOKS

CONTENTS

THE ESSENTIALS

Chocolate and how it is made 10
Basics 24
Chocolate sweets 32
Decorations 38
Creams and mousses 40
Pastries 54
Meringues 68
Glazing 70

RECIPES

Chocolate sweets 78
Moulding chocolate 110
Chocolate bars 124
Desserts 138
Log cakes 184
Choux pastry 192
Tarts 202
Great classics 222
Biscuits, cookies and cakes .. 242
Mousses and ice cream 260

ILLUSTRATED GLOSSARY

Utensils 268
Moulds 270
Products 272
Glossary 273
Tips for making 274
Choosing chocolate 275
Basic techniques: making 276
Basic techniques: preparing . 277
Basic techniques: piping 278
Basic techniques: finishing ... 279
Ingredients: cream, butter ... 280
Ingredients: eggs 281
Ingredients: sugar, honey 282
Ingredients: fruit, flavourings 283
Tips: dough 284
Tips: macarons & choux 285

HOW TO USE THIS BOOK

CHOCOLATE ESSENTIALS

Discover the main steps in chocolate-making.
Essential skills and basic recipes for making chocolates and pastries along with infographics and explanations of specific preparation techniques.

RECIPES

Use chocolate-making techniques to create sweets, cakes and desserts.
For each recipe there are cross-references to the essentials, infographics to demonstrate processes, and step-by-step photos illustrating stages of composition.

ILLUSTRATED GLOSSARY

Helps with the finer details of how to use utensils.
Illustrations of techniques and skills for making chocolates and pastries.

CHAPTER 1
CHOCOLATE ESSENTIALS

THE PRODUCT AND HOW IT IS MADE

THE CACAO POD 10
THE FRESH BEAN 11
3 VARIETIES OF COCOA 12
FERMENTATION 14
PROCESSING THE BEANS 15
GRINDING 16
CONCHING 17
COCOA MASS 18
COCOA POWDER 18
DISCOVERING THE ART OF
COCOA BUTTER 19
SUGAR 20
VANILLA & MILK 21
DARK CHOCOLATE 22
MILK & WHITE CHOCOLATE 23

CHOCOLATE BASICS

TEMPERING 24
MELTING 26
TEMPERING 1:
THE WORKTOP METHOD 27
TEMPERING 2:
THE SEEDING METHOD 28
TEMPERING 3
LEAVING TO STAND 29
TEMPERING 4:
MYCRYO COCOA BUTTER POWDER 30
KEEPING CHOCOLATE AT THE RIGHT
WORKING TEMPERATURE 31

CHOCOLATE SWEETS

COATING CHOCOLATES 32
MAKING MOULDED CHOCOLATES 34
DECORATING CHOCOLATES 36

DECORATIONS

CHOCOLATE DECORATIONS 38

CREAMS AND MOUSSES

50 PER CENT PRALINE & GIANDUJA 40
CREAMY GANACHE 42
WHIPPED WHITE GANACHE 44
EGG YOLK SYRUP MIXTURE 46
CHOCOLATE MOUSSE USING AN EGG
YOLK SYRUP MIXTURE 48
CHOCOLATE MOUSSE WITH
CRÈME ANGLAISE 50
DIPLOMAT PASTRY CREAM................................ 52

PASTRIES

CHOCOLATE PUFF PASTRY 54
SHORTCRUST PASTRY 58
FINGER BISCUITS 60
FLOURLESS CHOCOLATE BISCUIT 62
ALMOND BISCUIT BASE 64
CHOUX PASTRY 66

MERINGUES

SWISS MERINGUE 68
FRENCH MERINGUE.. 69

GLAZING

GLOSSY DARK GLAZE 70
ROCK GLAZE 72
MILK CHOCOLATE GLAZE 74
WHITE CHOCOLATE GLAZE 75

THE CACAO POD

Understand

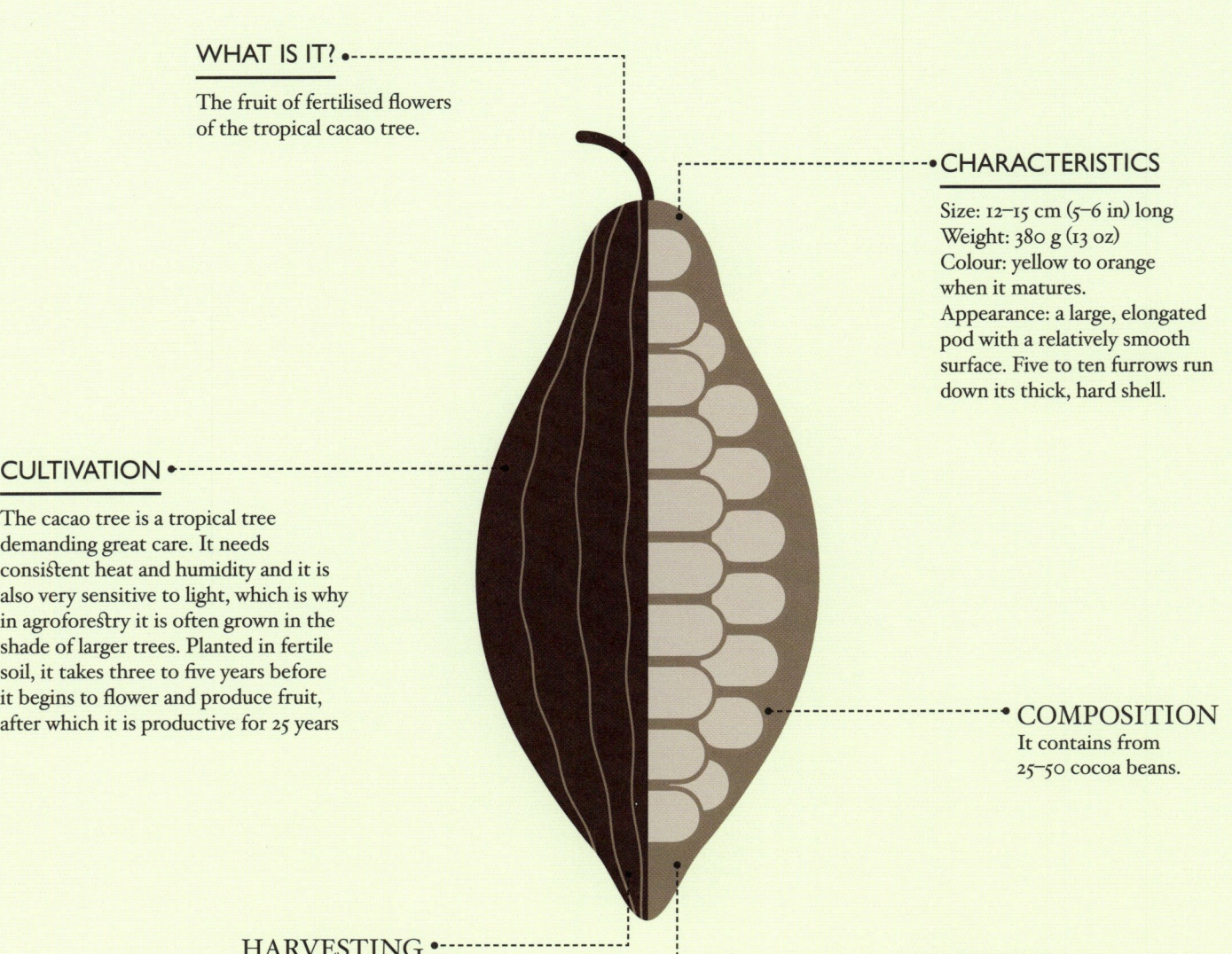

WHAT IS IT?

The fruit of fertilised flowers of the tropical cacao tree.

CHARACTERISTICS

Size: 12–15 cm (5–6 in) long
Weight: 380 g (13 oz)
Colour: yellow to orange when it matures.
Appearance: a large, elongated pod with a relatively smooth surface. Five to ten furrows run down its thick, hard shell.

CULTIVATION

The cacao tree is a tropical tree demanding great care. It needs consistent heat and humidity and it is also very sensitive to light, which is why in agroforestry it is often grown in the shade of larger trees. Planted in fertile soil, it takes three to five years before it begins to flower and produce fruit, after which it is productive for 25 years

COMPOSITION
It contains from 25–50 cocoa beans.

HARVESTING
Twice yearly. It takes four to five months for the pod to reach its final size.

MATURITY
The pod of the green variety turns yellow; the pod of the red variety turns orange.

THE FRESH BEAN

Understand

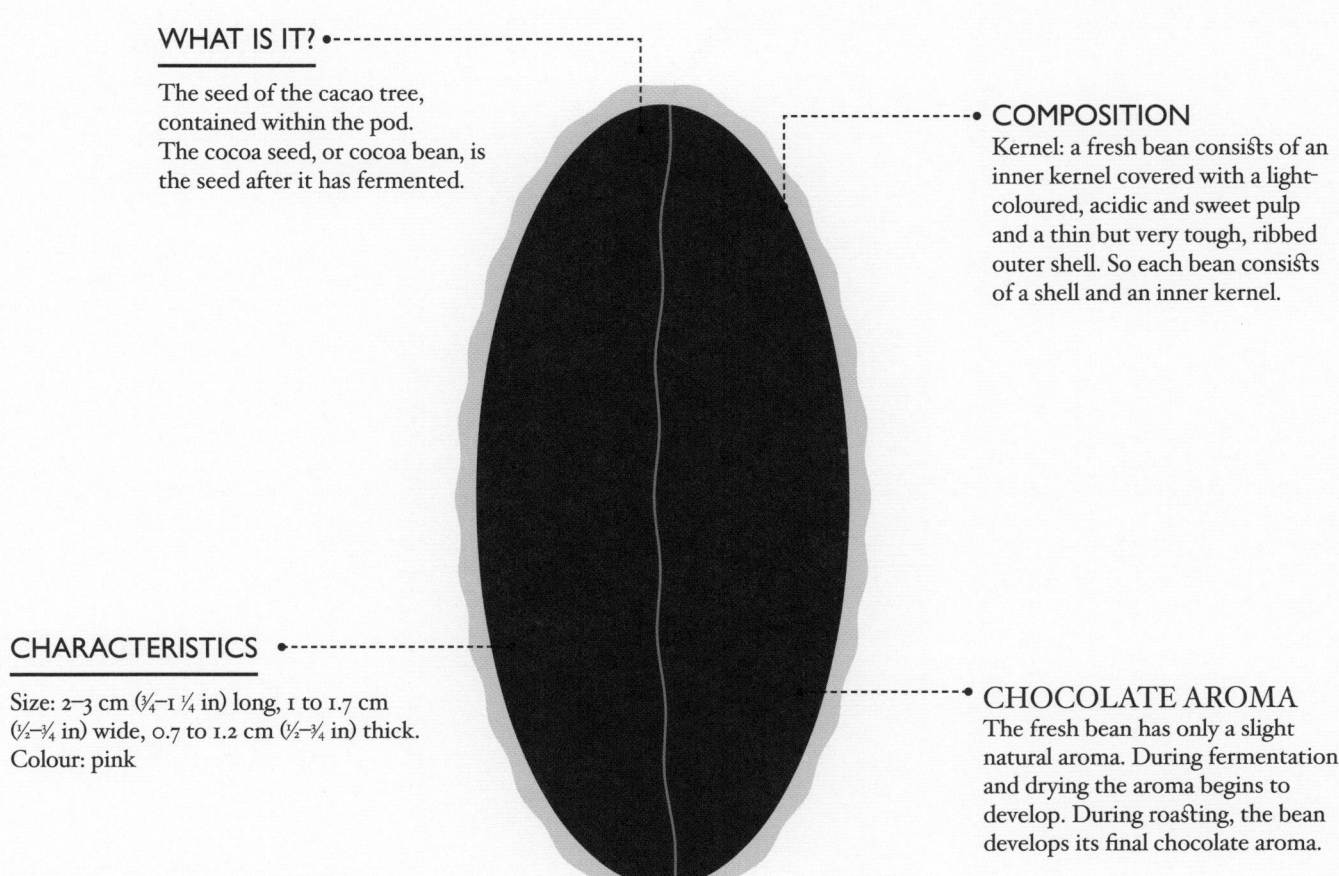

WHAT IS IT?
The seed of the cacao tree, contained within the pod. The cocoa seed, or cocoa bean, is the seed after it has fermented.

COMPOSITION
Kernel: a fresh bean consists of an inner kernel covered with a light-coloured, acidic and sweet pulp and a thin but very tough, ribbed outer shell. So each bean consists of a shell and an inner kernel.

CHARACTERISTICS
Size: 2–3 cm (¾–1 ¼ in) long, 1 to 1.7 cm (½–¾ in) wide, 0.7 to 1.2 cm (½–¾ in) thick.
Colour: pink

CHOCOLATE AROMA
The fresh bean has only a slight natural aroma. During fermentation and drying the aroma begins to develop. During roasting, the bean develops its final chocolate aroma.

HOW DOES THE CHOCOLATE FLAVOUR DEVELOP DURING FERMENTATION AND ROASTING?
During the various stages of processing, a number of reactions take place, which lead to the formation of aromatic molecules, giving a variety of aromatic notes to the different chocolate varieties.

3 VARIETIES
OF COCOA

Understand

FORESTARIO

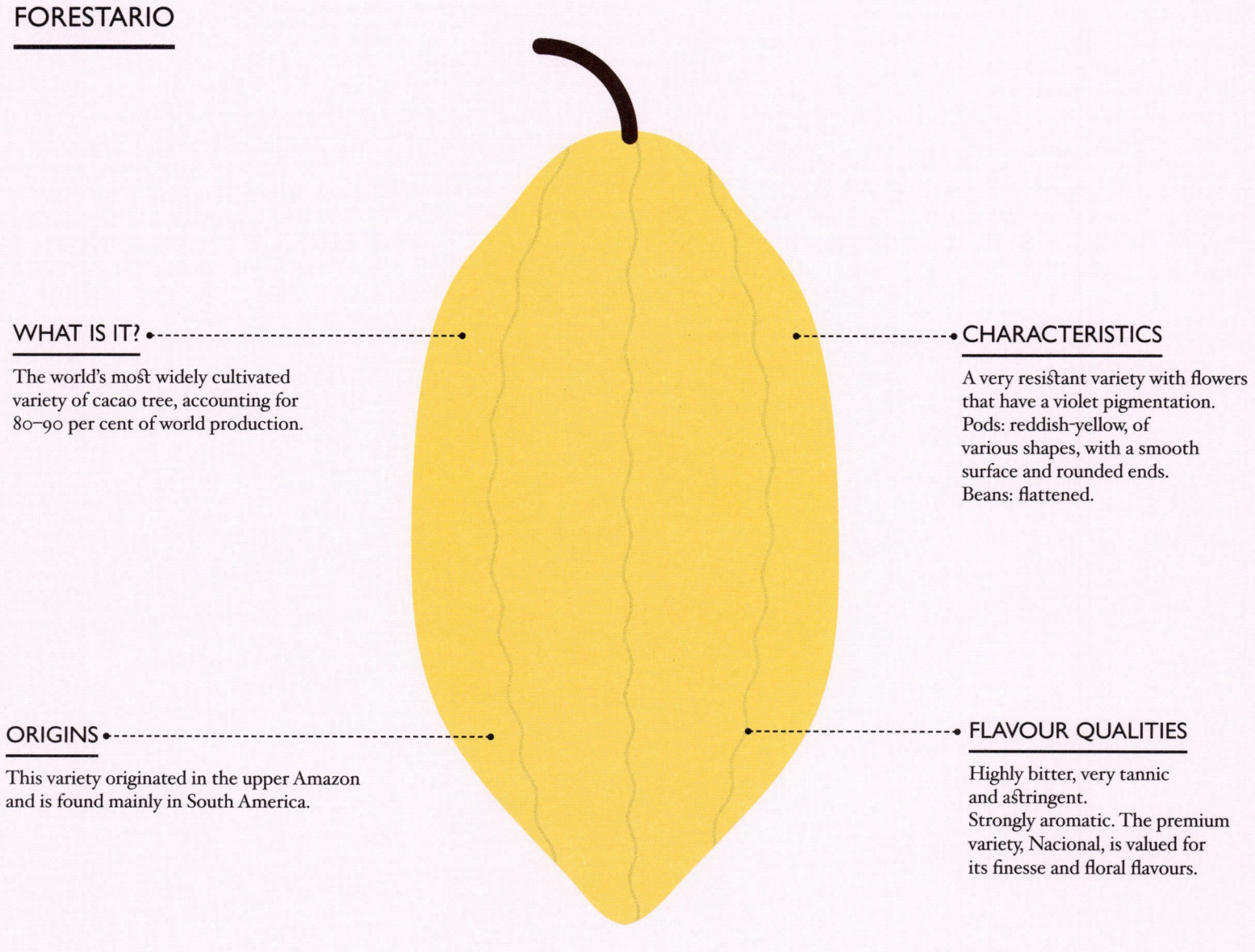

WHAT IS IT?

The world's most widely cultivated variety of cacao tree, accounting for 80–90 per cent of world production.

CHARACTERISTICS

A very resistant variety with flowers that have a violet pigmentation. Pods: reddish-yellow, of various shapes, with a smooth surface and rounded ends. Beans: flattened.

ORIGINS

This variety originated in the upper Amazon and is found mainly in South America.

FLAVOUR QUALITIES

Highly bitter, very tannic and astringent. Strongly aromatic. The premium variety, Nacional, is valued for its finesse and floral flavours.

CRIOLLO

WHAT IS IT?

The finest and rarest variety of cacao tree, much appreciated by chocolate lovers. Production is less than 5 per cent of total world production.

CHARACTERISTICS

This variety is particularly sensitive to disease and climatic variation. The pods are smooth, and large, elongated, pointed, reddish and yellow. The beans are light-coloured and rounded with very little tannin.

ORIGINS

The very first cultivated variety of cacao tree (by the Maya in Venezuela, but it is also grown in Central America and Mexico). Its name (Spanish for 'creole') was given by settlers in Venezuela, a country that already had a reputation as a high-quality producer.

TASTE QUALITIES

Low bitterness, highly aromatic, low in tannin and astringent. Very fine, delicate taste. The prremium variety is Porcelana from Venezuela.

TRINITARIO

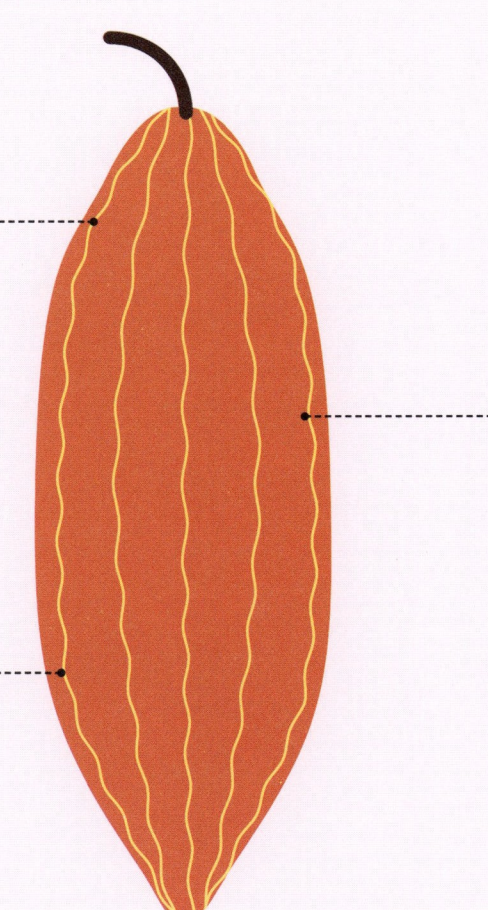

WHAT IS IT?

A cross of the Criollo and Forestario varieties. Cultivation of Trinitario represents 10–15 per cent of world production.

TASTE QUALITIES

With aromatic power and remarkable finesse, its qualities are somewhere between its parent varieties.

ORIGINS

Trinidad. The characteristics of the flowers, pods and beans are highly diverse and depend on the soil the tree is grown in.

FERMENTATION

Understand

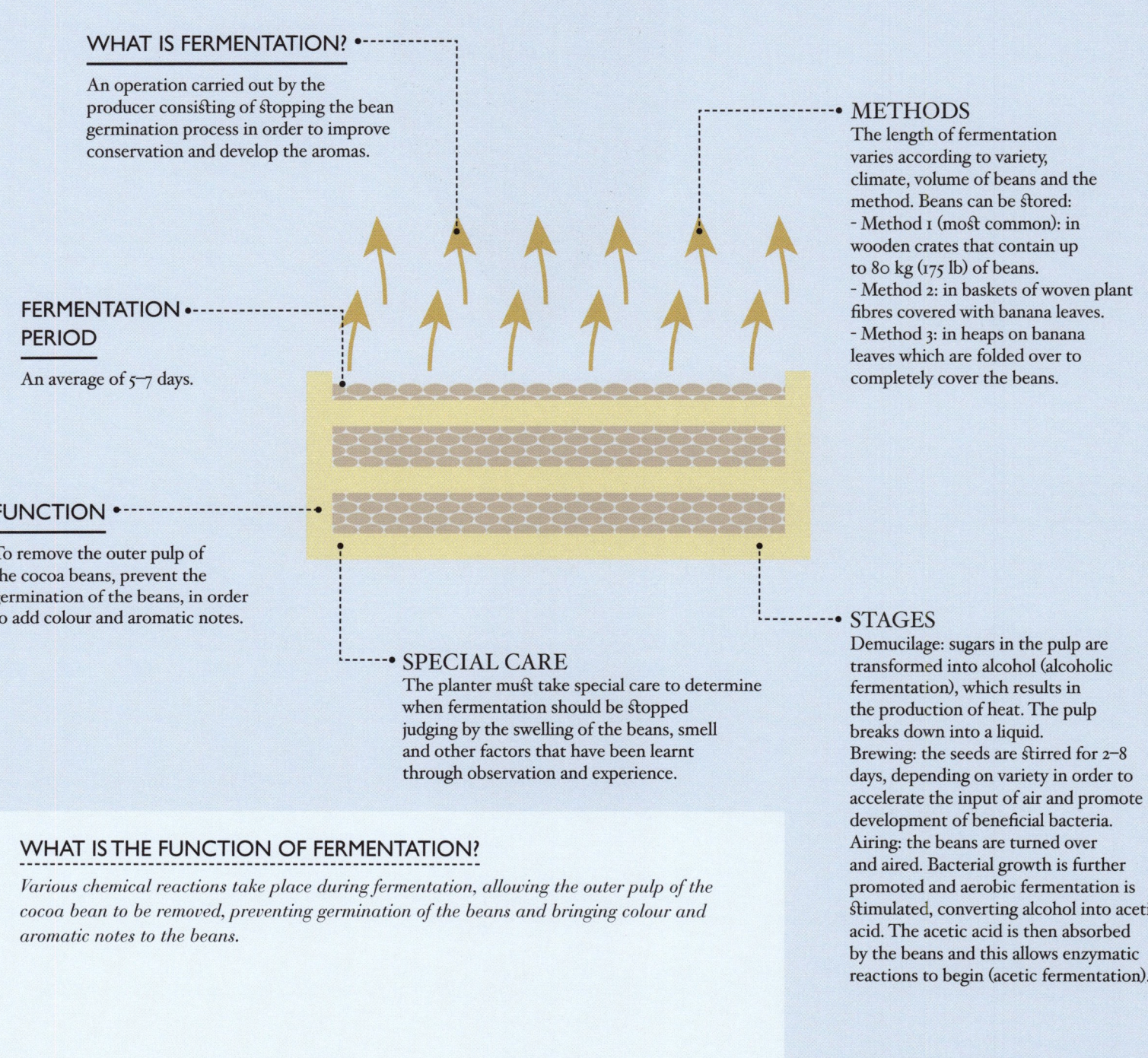

WHAT IS FERMENTATION?

An operation carried out by the producer consisting of stopping the bean germination process in order to improve conservation and develop the aromas.

FERMENTATION PERIOD

An average of 5–7 days.

FUNCTION

To remove the outer pulp of the cocoa beans, prevent the germination of the beans, in order to add colour and aromatic notes.

METHODS

The length of fermentation varies according to variety, climate, volume of beans and the method. Beans can be stored:
- Method 1 (most common): in wooden crates that contain up to 80 kg (175 lb) of beans.
- Method 2: in baskets of woven plant fibres covered with banana leaves.
- Method 3: in heaps on banana leaves which are folded over to completely cover the beans.

SPECIAL CARE

The planter must take special care to determine when fermentation should be stopped judging by the swelling of the beans, smell and other factors that have been learnt through observation and experience.

STAGES

Demucilage: sugars in the pulp are transformed into alcohol (alcoholic fermentation), which results in the production of heat. The pulp breaks down into a liquid.
Brewing: the seeds are stirred for 2–8 days, depending on variety in order to accelerate the input of air and promote development of beneficial bacteria.
Airing: the beans are turned over and aired. Bacterial growth is further promoted and aerobic fermentation is stimulated, converting alcohol into acetic acid. The acetic acid is then absorbed by the beans and this allows enzymatic reactions to begin (acetic fermentation).

WHAT IS THE FUNCTION OF FERMENTATION?

Various chemical reactions take place during fermentation, allowing the outer pulp of the cocoa bean to be removed, preventing germination of the beans and bringing colour and aromatic notes to the beans.

PROCESSING THE BEANS

Understand

DRYING

WHAT IS IT?
The producer dries the cocoa beans in the sun after fermentation.

DURATION
8–15 days.

PRINCIPLE
After fermentation, the beans are left to dry in the sun on planks or racks. They are turned over regularly with a rake. Moisture content is reduced from 80 per cent to 5 per cent. The dried beans are then packed in jute bags.

WHY DO THE BEANS NEED AIRING?
Turning the beans over regularly ensures homogeneous drying and optimises subsequent conservation by stopping fermentation reactions.

CRUSHING

WHAT IS CRUSHING?
When the chocolate maker separates the cocoa bean from the shell.

PRINCIPLE
The dried beans are crushed coarsely in a mill to remove the inedible outer shell.

THE ROASTER
A constantly rotating drum is used to roast cocoa. The regular movement of the drum allows the beans to be roasted evenly, without burning, in a process similar to that of roasting coffee beans.

ROASTING

WHAT IS ROASTING?
The chocolate maker roasts the cocoa beans to kill unwanted micro-organisms, reduce the water content (from 7 per cent to 2.5 per cent), improve separation between the shell and the kernel, eliminate mould and develop aromatic notes through various chemical reactions including the Maillard reaction and caramelisation.

PRINCIPLE
Roasting temperature: between 100°C and 140°C (212°F and 285°F)
Roasting time: 15–40 minutes. When the beans reach 140°C (285°F), the Maillard reaction, which gives the chocolate its characteristic taste and aromas occurs. The combined time and temperature variables will determine the main characteristics of the chocolate depending on the origin of the beans, their qualities, water content, size and the type of chocolate being made.

GRINDING

Understand

WHAT IS GRINDING?

The grain size of the cocoa beans is ground first into small fragments, or cocoa nibs, then further into a fine paste called cocoa mass is obtained.

PRINCIPLE

The cocoa beans pass through a grinder, then a milling machine. The resulting cocoa mass is mixed with the other raw materials (sugar, and sometimes milk) until a homogeneous paste is obtained. The granular size of the paste can be further reduced to between 20 and 25 microns using refining mills.

THREE GRINDING TECHNIQUES

Standard process
Roasted beans are hot-ground to produce coarse cocoa paste (also known as cocoa mass or cocoa liquor).

More recent process
The beans are lightly moistened then dried and shelled before being crushed to obtain small chips called 'green nibs'. These are roasted before being finely ground to produce cocoa mass or cocoa liquor.

Finer process
As above, the beans are lightly moistened then dried and shelled before being crushed to obtain green nibs, which are first crushed, and then roasted. This method reduces the grain size to a level that the palate can hardly detect, resulting in a soft and silky texture in the mouth.

THE MACHINE
Milling machines grind the cocoa fragments and refine the paste. Two granite grindstones rotate on a base made of the same granite, crushing the cocoa paste over and over again to give a very fine texture of between 20 and 30 microns.

HOW DOES THE FINENESS OF THE COCOA MASS AFFECT THE QUALITY OF THE CHOCOLATE?

Grinding is a particularly critical step in the process as the fineness of the cocoa mass is an important characteristic that determines the quality of the chocolate.

CONCHING

Understand

WHAT IS CONCHING?

A mechanical process carried out by the chocolate maker, which gives the cocoa paste a smoother, and silkier texture for a more refined taste. Conching also removes unpleasant volatile aromas, particularly acidity.

PRINCIPLE

The cocoa mass is poured into a large vat and stirred, backwards and forwards, with a roller, which moves in a similar way to a rolling pin. Under the granite slab at the base of the conching machine, heaters liquefy the chocolate, ensuring homogeneous conching. The more the chocolate is conched, the silkier and more intensely flavoured it becomes. Specialist chocolatiers conch their own chocolate for 72 hours to obtain the very best results.

THE EQUIPMENT

The conching machine was invented in 1879 by the Swiss chocolatier Rodolphe Lindt. Today's models are very similar to the first machines and consist of a tank with a concave, granite bottom that is heated from beneath. The continuous conching process is now done with a metal roller.

HOW DOES THE CHANGE IN TEXTURE COME ABOUT?

During conching, the sharp edges of the cocoa particles are worn away. The rounded particles improve the fluidity of the chocolate, which becomes smooth and shiny. Cocoa butter is also released, bringing velvety smoothness.

COCOA MASS

Understand

COCOA MASS

WHAT IS COCOA MASS?

It is the substance obtained after grinding the beans, also called cocoa liquor or cocoa paste. The chocolate maker will add other ingredients (sugar, vanilla, etc.) to make chocolate.

FUNCTION

It gives chocolate its aromatic qualities and characteristic taste.

COCOA POWDER

WHAT IS COCOA (UNSWEETENED CHOCOLATE) POWDER?

Powder obtained after grinding the kernels of fermented cocoa beans from the cacao tree. It is extremely fine and has a low fat content. It is produced in a press, and the residue of the pressing is a very compact cake several centimetres (1–2 in) thick containing only 10 per cent–20 per cent fat. Crushed, then finely pulverised, it becomes cocoa powder.

FUNCTION

Cocoa powder is a basic ingredient for all chocolate flavourings: biscuits, ice creams, dairy products, confectionery, etc. It is also a raw material for making spreads.

WHAT ARE THE DESIRED QUALITIES OF COCOA POWDER?

Cocoa powder must have good colouring properties, provide the desired flavouring (depending on the beans and the roasting process) and be very finely ground.

WHAT DOES THE PERCENTAGE OF COCOA MEAN?

It shows the total amount of cocoa bean in the chocolate. A 70 per cent cocoa chocolate is 70 per cent cocoa mass and 30 per cent sugar.

DISCOVERING THE ART OF
COCOA BUTTER

Understand

WHAT IS IT USED FOR?

Cocoa butter strongly influences the final texture of the chocolate. Its content varies greatly from one recipe to another.

WHAT TYPE SHOULD I CHOOSE?

Using chocolate chips makes weighing and melting easier.

WHAT HAPPENS WHEN COCOA BUTTER MELTS?

Solid cocoa butter is made up of different kinds of crystals which each melt at different temperatures. When tempering the chocolate, the chocolate maker carefully heats it to a temperature, which preserves the desired crystals and makes the others disappear.

SUGAR

Understand

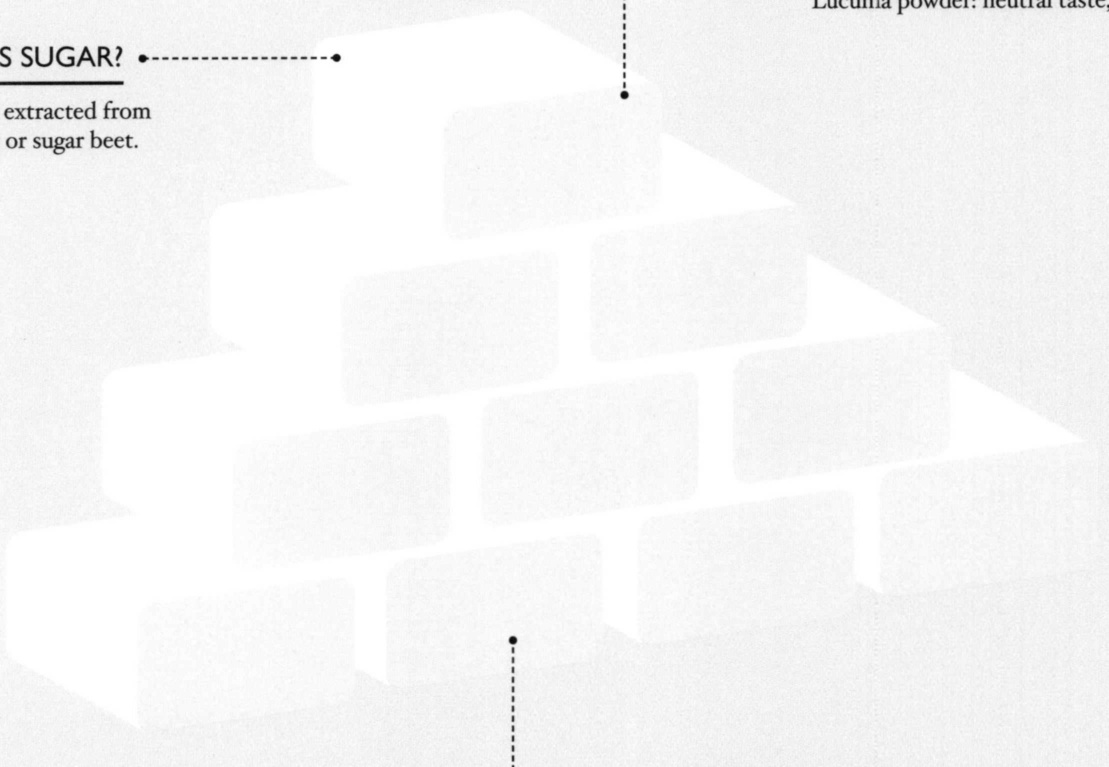

WHICH SUGAR SHOULD I CHOOSE?

Cane sugar: neutral taste (most chocolate).
Coconut sugar: neutral taste, low glycaemic index.
Lucuma powder: neutral taste, low glycaemic index.

WHAT IS SUGAR?

A product extracted from
sugar cane or sugar beet.

FUNCTION

It is the third main ingredient in
chocolate. It reduces bitterness,
enhances the powerful natural
flavour of the beans and
turns it into a delicacy.

VANILLA & MILK

Understand

VANILLA

WHAT IS VANILLA?

Vanilla is a standard ingredient in most white chocolate.

FUNCTION

Vanilla is a standard ingredient in chocolate recipes but it is not always included. It is used to flavour and mellow the taste. It is not present in dark chocolate but is often used in white chocolate.

MILK

WHAT SORT OF MILK IS USED?

Usually cow's milk. As well as fresh milk, milk powder, concentrated milk and sweetened condensed milk may also be used.

FUNCTION

An essential ingredient in milk chocolate and white chocolate, it makes chocolate smoother and mellower.

DARK CHOCOLATE

Understand

COMPOSITION

Dark or plain (baking, bittersweet or semi-sweet) chocolate must contain at least 35 per cent cocoa.

TASTE

Chocolate with less than 65 per cent cocoa has a sweet flavour and is often used in dessert chocolates for pastries. Chocolate with 65 per cent or 70 per cent cocoa is more bitter. It is used in cooking (baking chocolate) or for eating in bars. Chocolate with 80 per cent cocoa is much stronger in character. More bitter, it has a less of a melt-in-the-mouth texture. Chocolate with 90 per cent cocoa or more is very bitter, to be enjoyed in very small quantities.

ENERGY

Three squares, or 30g (about 1 oz) of 70 per cent cocoa dark chocolate provide: 160 calories, 12 g of fat (7 g of which are saturated), 8 g sugar and 2–4 g fibre. Three of 85 per cent cocoa dark chocolate provide the same amount of calories (160), more fat (14 g), less sugar (4 g) and 2–4g of fibre.

IS THE PERCENTAGE OF COCOA SYNONYMOUS WITH QUALITY?

No – quality is determined by other factors, above all by the variety of beans and the care taken during the processing stages. More chocolate makers are becoming more transparent about their processes and ingredients.

WHY DOES CHOCOLATE'S SURFACE TURN WHITE?

Chocolate contains fat crystals, some of which, over time, rise to the surface resulting in what's known as 'bloom'.

NOTE
When making a ganache (or a mousse) containing dark chocolate and cream, there is a risk of the fat separating out. If this happens, add milk gradually, in small amounts, until a smooth consistency is restored.

MILK & WHITE CHOCOLATE

Understand

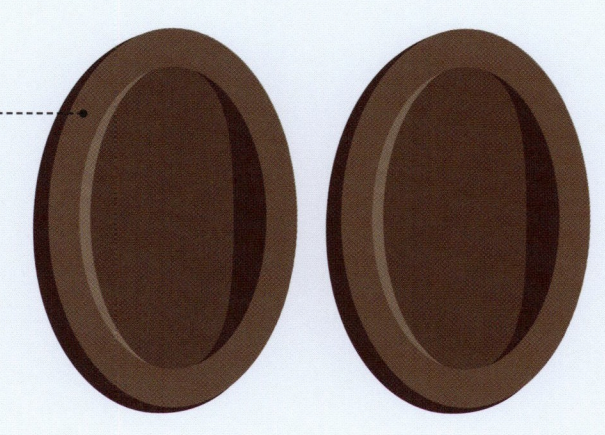

MILK CHOCOLATE

COMPOSITION

Good quality milk chocolate contains between 25 per cent and 40 per cent cocoa. It has less fat than dark chocolate but more sugar.

TASTE

A quality milk chocolate is a beautiful light brown. It should break with a 'snap' and melt in the mouth. Milk makes it smooth and sugar gives it a rounded flavour.

WHITE CHOCOLATE

COMPOSITION

It doesn't contain cocoa solids, but does contain cocoa butter, milk or milk powder and sugar, and often vanilla.

TASTE

Creamy, sweet, and often vanilla.

WHY ARE MILK AND WHITE CHOCOLATE SOFTER THAN DARK CHOCOLATE?

White and milk chocolates contain more cocoa butter, giving them softer textures. Dark chocolate contains less cocoa butter making it more brittle.

TEMPERING

Understand

WHAT IS TEMPERING?

Also called 'pre-crystallisation', tempering means subjecting the chocolate to a temperature curve so that it can be melted and worked on while retaining its taste and visual qualities. Use good quality chocolate with at least 32 per cent cocoa butter for tempering, ideally 'couverture'.

DARK COUVERTURE CHOCOLATE
1. Melts between 55° (131°F) and 58°C (136.5°F)
2. Lower the temperature to between 28° (82.4°F) and 29°C (84.2°F)
3. Increase the temperature to between 31° (87.8°F) and 32°C (89.6°F)

MILK COUVERTURE CHOCOLATE
1. Melts between 45° (113°F) and 48°C (118.4°F)
2. Lower the temperature to between 27° (80.6°F) and 28°C (82.4°F)
3. Increase the temperature to between 29° (84.2°F) and 30°C (86°F)

WHITE COUVERTURE CHOCOLATE
1. Melts between 45° (113°F) and 48°C (118.4°F)
2. Lower the temperature to between 26° (78.8°F) and 27°C (80.6°F)
3. Increase the temperature to between 28° (82.4°F) and 29°C (84.2°F)

WHAT IS THE PURPOSE OF TEMPERING?

It allows the chocolate to retain its crunchiness, brittleness, ability to melt and have a silky, shiny appearance. When correctly tempered, chocolate is more stable and less sensitive to moisture and heat.

WHAT HAPPENS DURING TEMPERING?

The chocolate mass is seeded with microcrystals. After melting, the chocolate is cooled to allow stable and unstable microcrystals to form. Then, by bringing the temperature back up, the unstable microcrystals are removed and only stable crystals remain.

Learn

PREPARE YOUR EQUIPMENT

Wipe the work surface clean with a moist cloth and cover with cling film (plastic wrap), which will then stick to the surface. This makes cleaning up easy: just peel away the film. Place a cloth near the double-boiler to prevent water splashing onto the work surface when taking the bowl out of the boiler. Placing the bowl of chocolate on a non-slip ring makes it more stable as you work and allows it to cool more slowly.

MELTING

Increasing the temperature makes all the fat molecules melt.

LOWERING THE TEMPERATURE

Once the couverture chocolate has reached its melting temperature (depending on the type of chocolate; see above), let the bowl cool down at room temperature until it reaches its working temperature.

The easiest way is just to let the melted couverture stand until it cools down to the required temperature.

You can speed up the process by placing the bowl in a cold-water bath, making sure that the water outside the bowl reaches the top level of the chocolate. Mix it regularly with a spatula to keep it at a constant temperature. Be careful not to splash water into the chocolate during mixing.

INCREASING THE TEMPERATURE

Bring the chocolate up to working temperature on the hot water double-boiler.

USING THE MELTED CHOCOLATE AND KEEPING IT AT THE RIGHT TEMPERATURE

Regularly check the temperature of the chocolate: when it goes down more than 2°C (3.6°F) below its working temperature, bring the temperature back up on the double-boiler heating it in 10-second stages, but being careful not to overheat it.

MELTING

Understand

WHAT IS IT?

Transforming solid chocolate
(in pieces) into liquid.

EQUIPMENT YOU WILL NEED

Cutting board
Serrated knife
Double-boiler
Microwavable mixing bowl

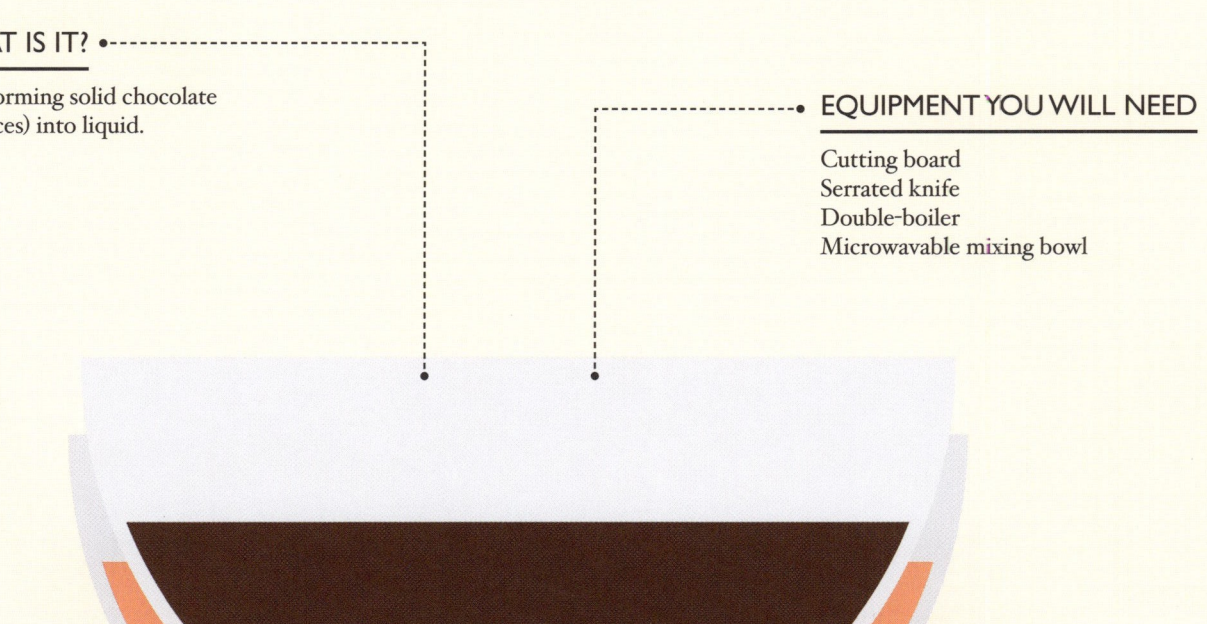

TIP

When melting in a double-boiler, make sure
the bowl containing the chocolate does
not touch the bottom of the pan or the
surface of the water, or the chocolate may
overheat or burn. It is the steam that melts
the chocolate, not a direct heat source.
Chop the chocolate into regular-sized pieces
or use good-quality chocolate chips.

HOW TO DO IT

In a double-boiler (page 276): half fill a
saucepan with hot water, put the chocolate
in a bowl and place it on the saucepan
above the hot water. Let the chocolate
melt slowly, stirring with a spatula until
a smooth, even texture is reached.

In the microwave: put the chocolate in
a microwave-safe (non-metallic) double-
boiler. Heat for 1 minute at 500 W, then
stir with a spatula. Repeat the operation
in 30-second stages stirring each time.
Check the temperature (depending on
the chocolate you are making, page 24).

TEMPERING METHOD 1:
THE KITCHEN WORKTOP METHOD

Understand

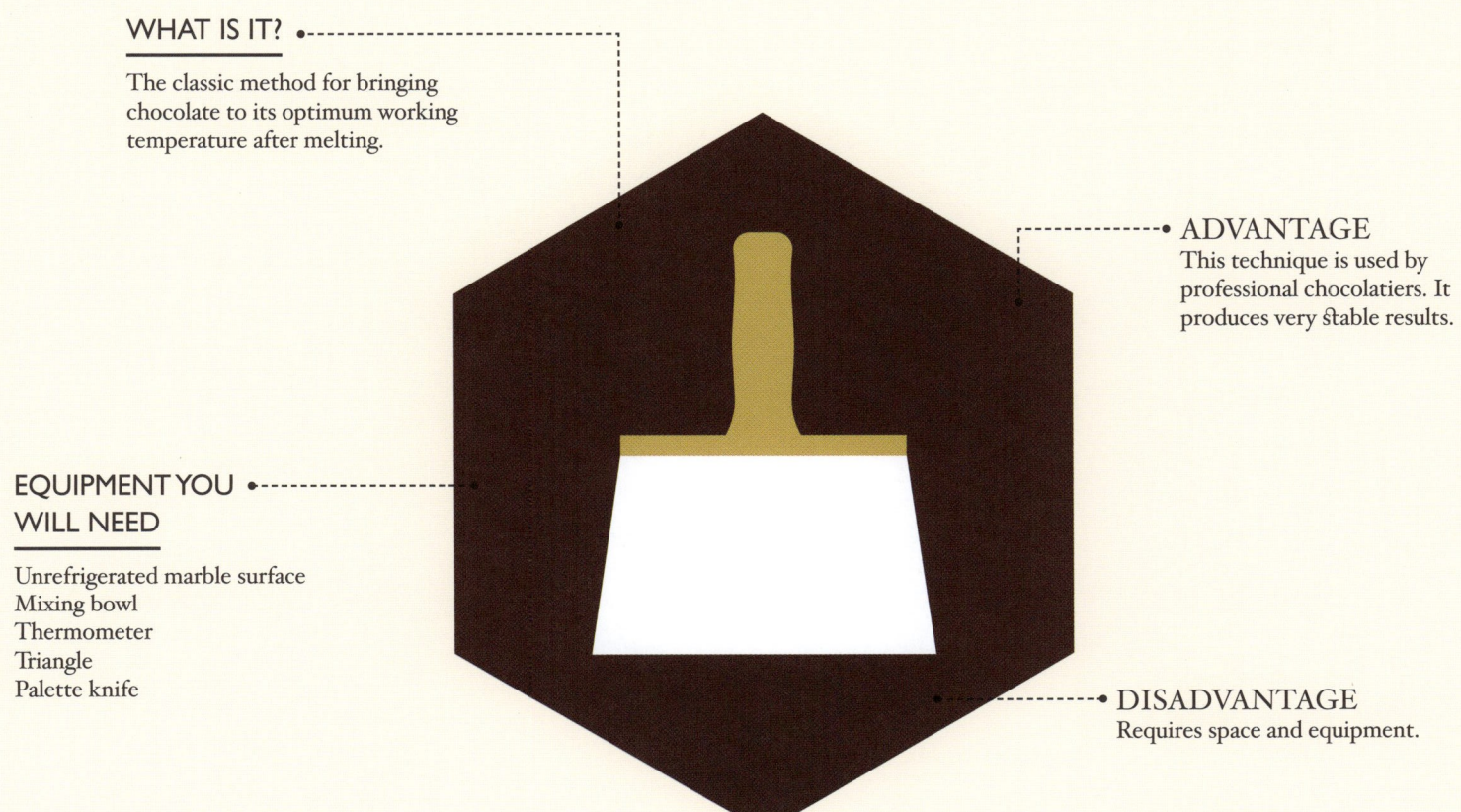

WHAT IS IT?
The classic method for bringing chocolate to its optimum working temperature after melting.

ADVANTAGE
This technique is used by professional chocolatiers. It produces very stable results.

EQUIPMENT YOU WILL NEED
Unrefrigerated marble surface
Mixing bowl
Thermometer
Triangle
Palette knife

DISADVANTAGE
Requires space and equipment.

ADVICE

Avoid stainless steel worktops, which retain too much heat. Also avoid working on refrigerated marble, which is extremely moist and too cold, and will cause the chocolate to thicken irreversibly.
Once the couverture chocolate has melted, pour out three quarters of it onto the worktop.

Spread the chocolate on the worktop and mix by folding it back on itself using a triangle and a palette knife. The temperature must remain constant depending on the chocolate you are making (see page 24), so you should check it regularly with a thermometer.

Put half of the warm couverture chocolate back into the double-boiler bowl to halt the cooling process immediately and mix well. Gradually add the rest of the hot couverture until it reaches its correct optimum working temperature (see page 24).

TEMPERING METHOD 2:
THE SEEDING METHOD

Understand

WHAT IS IT?

A quick method for bringing chocolate to its optimum working temperature after melting.

ADVANTAGES
Handy and fast, requires little equipment.

EQUIPMENT YOU WILL NEED

Double-boiler bowl
Spatula
Thermometer

DISADVANTAGE
Suitable only for small quantities.

HOW TO DO IT

When the couverture chocolate has melted, add 30 per cent of the chocolate chips using a spatula. Stir continuously to produce the seeding effect and to ensure a constant temperature, depending on the chocolate you are making (page 24). Check the temperature and gradually add more chocolate chips until the working temperature is reached depending on the chocolate you are making (see page 24).

WHAT DOES 'SEEDING' MEAN?

Using the properties of the stable cocoa butter molecules in the chocolate chips to seed other molecules and make them stable. Unstable crystals tend to align themselves to the stable crystals as if by imitation.

TEMPERING METHOD 3:
LEAVING TO STAND

Understand

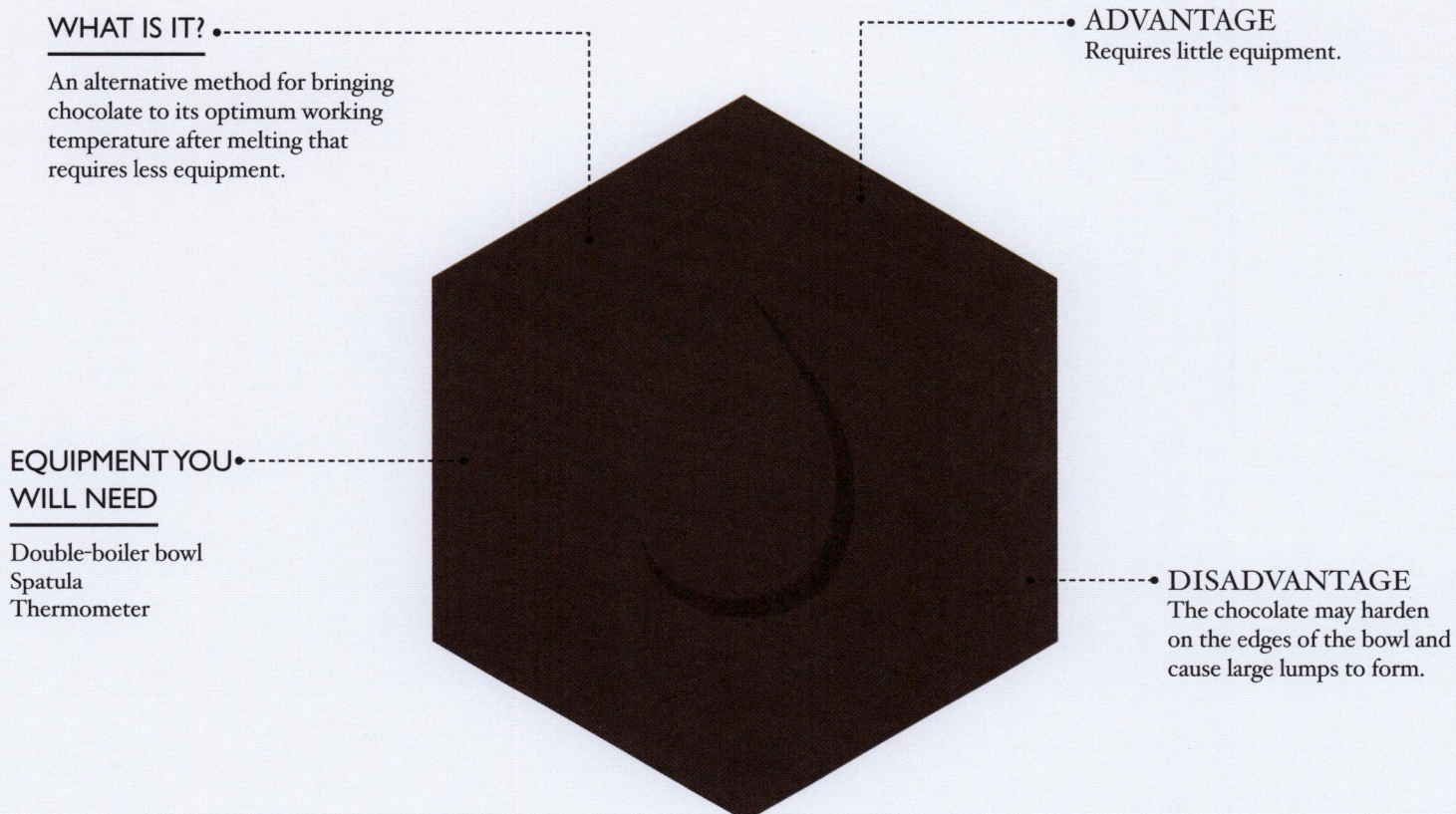

WHAT IS IT?
An alternative method for bringing chocolate to its optimum working temperature after melting that requires less equipment.

ADVANTAGE
Requires little equipment.

EQUIPMENT YOU WILL NEED
Double-boiler bowl
Spatula
Thermometer

DISADVANTAGE
The chocolate may harden on the edges of the bowl and cause large lumps to form.

HOW TO DO IT

When the couverture chocolate has reached its melting temperature (depending on the chocolate you are making, see page 24), at room temperature, let the bowl cool down until the chocolate reaches its working temperature.

You can speed up the process by placing the bowl in a cold-water bath, making sure that the water in the outer bowl reaches the top level of the chocolate in the inner bowl. Mix regularly with a spatula to maintain a constant temperature.

Take care not to splash water into the chocolate during mixing. To do this, stabilise the base of the bowl by placing a non-slip ring under the bowl containing the cold water. Then bring it back up to working temperature on a hot water double-boiler.

TEMPERING METHOD 4:

USING MYCRYO COCOA BUTTER POWDER

Understand

WHAT IS IT?
An easy method for bringing chocolate to its optimum working temperature after melting that's ideal for small quantities.

ADVANTAGE
Allows small quantities to be prepared quickly.

DISADVANTAGES
Suitable only for small quantities. Shorter shelf life: chocolate may develop a white 'bloom' more quickly.

EQUIPMENT YOU WILL NEED
Bowl
Spatula
Thermometer

ADVICE
If you have no Mycryo, chop up pure cocoa butter very finely.

TYPICAL USE
Decoration for which a very small quantity is needed (for example, the wings and eyes of a chocolate hen).

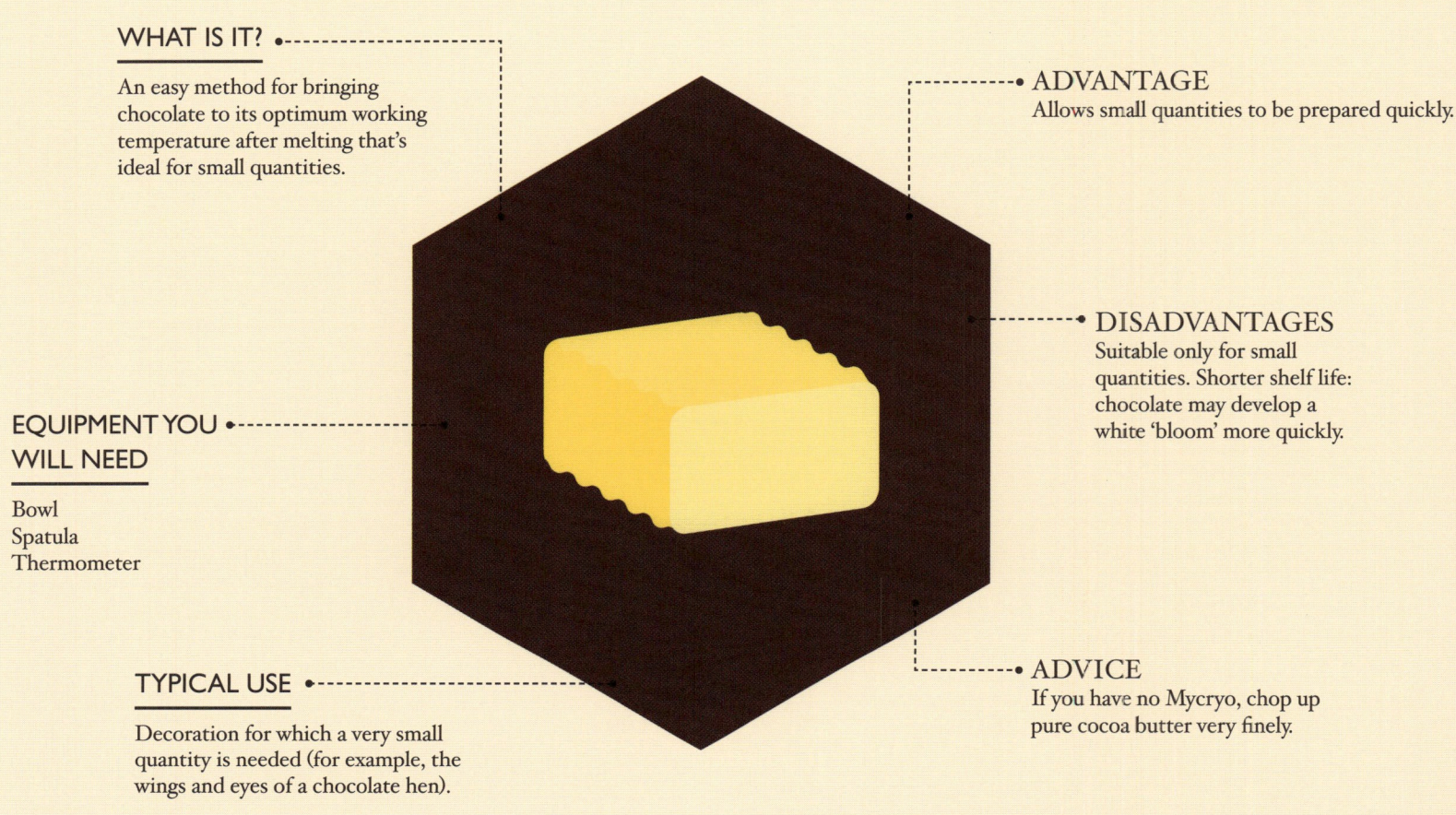

HOW TO DO IT
Start by melting the couverture chocolate in a double-boiler. When about 10 per cent of the chocolate chips still aren't melted, remove from the heat. The couverture will be at around 40°C (104°F). Stir in the remaining chips until the chocolate has melted completely, so that the couverture is at around 35°C (95°F). Add the Mycryo, folding in gently with a spatula. Allow the temperature to drop to working temperature, depending on the chocolate selected (see page 24).

WHAT IS THE FUNCTION OF MYCRYO
Mycryo, a brand of powdered cocoa butter, is used to seed the chocolate. It provides stable crystals that seed the tempering process.

KEEPING CHOCOLATE AT THE RIGHT WORKING TEMPERATURE

Understand

WHAT IS IT?

Three ways to keep couverture chocolate at the right working temperature or reheat for use.

EQUIPMENT YOU WILL NEED

Saucepan
Thermometer

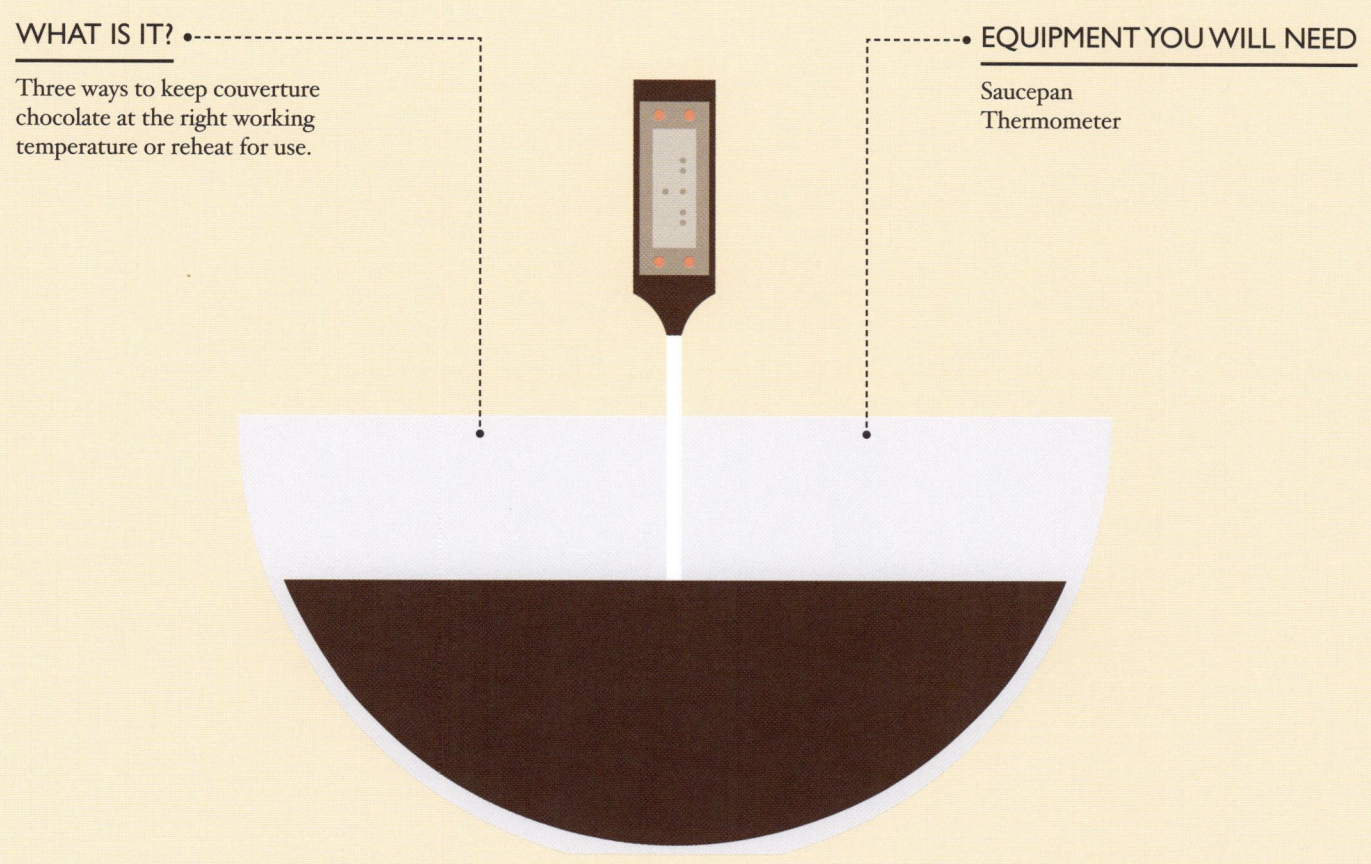

TIPS

If the correct working temperature is exceeded, you should go back to the beginning and repeat the tempering process.

Method 1: Heat in a double-boiler bowl, removing it regularly from the heat to check the temperature depending on the chocolate you have chosen (page 24). Care must be taken as the bowl keeps its heat and transfers it to the chocolate even when it is out of the hot water.
Method 2: keep some couverture warm and add it to the cooled chocolate in order to reheat it.
Method 3: use a professional tempering machine, these are designed to keep couverture chocolate at just the right temperature.

COATING
CHOCOLATES

Understand

WHAT DOES IT MEAN?

Giving chocolates a fine, crisp outer coating.

TRICKY POINT

Tempering the couverture chocolate.

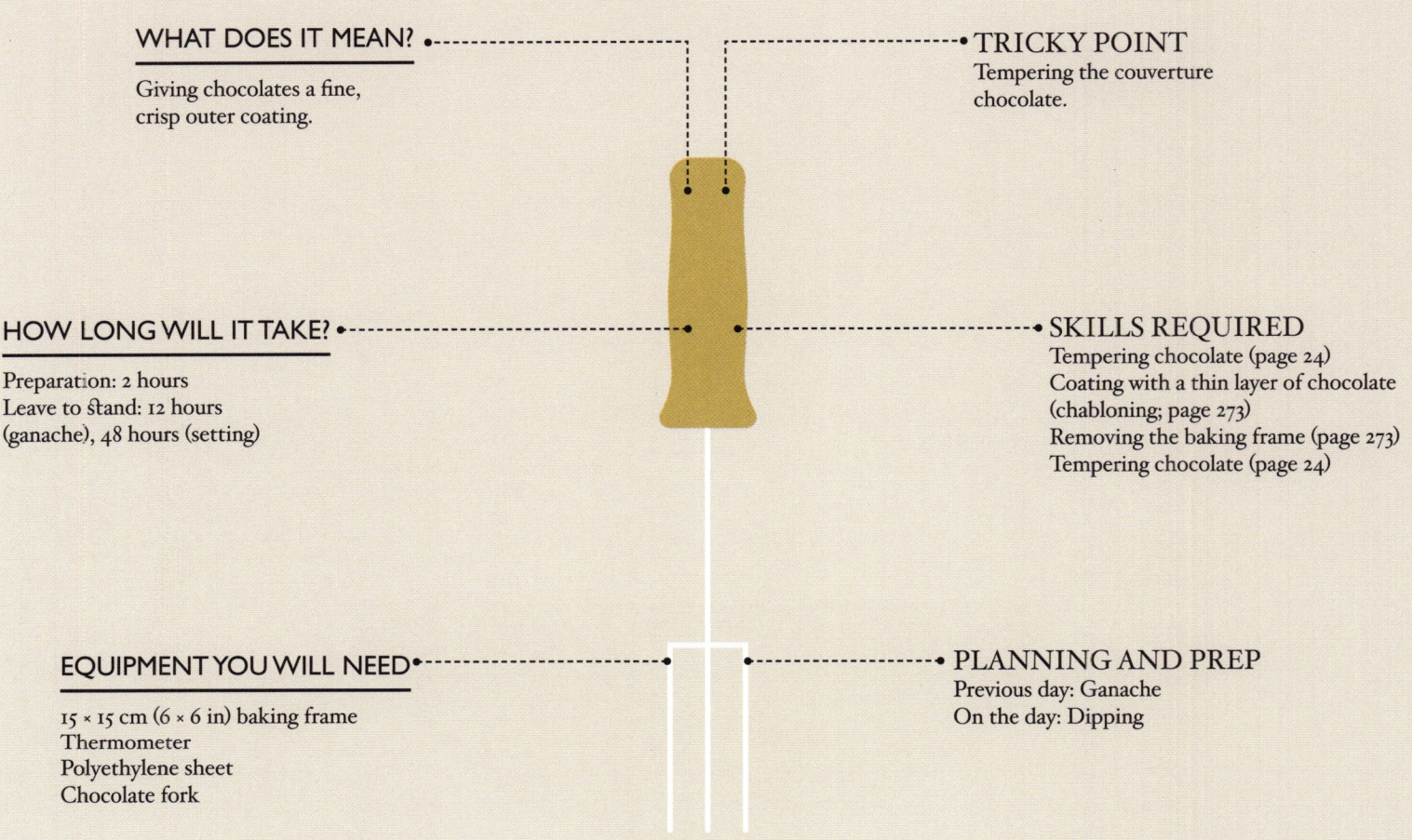

HOW LONG WILL IT TAKE?

Preparation: 2 hours
Leave to stand: 12 hours (ganache), 48 hours (setting)

SKILLS REQUIRED

Tempering chocolate (page 24)
Coating with a thin layer of chocolate (chabloning; page 273)
Removing the baking frame (page 273)
Tempering chocolate (page 24)

EQUIPMENT YOU WILL NEED

15 × 15 cm (6 × 6 in) baking frame
Thermometer
Polyethylene sheet
Chocolate fork

PLANNING AND PREP

Previous day: Ganache
On the day: Dipping

WHY DOESN'T THE GANACHE MELT WHEN IT IS DIPPED IN COUVERTURE CHOCOLATE?

The ganache is at 17°C (62.6°F) when it is immersed in the 28-35°C (82.4-95°F) couverture. This temperature difference means that the ganache does not melt or only does so slightly, on the surface.

TIP

When all the sweets have been dipped, pour the remaining chocolate onto a baking sheet, let it harden and keep in a dry place. Use it to make chocolate mousse, ganache or fondants. Do not re-temper as the chocolate will lose its fluidity. Coveringthe underside and top of the ganache with a fine layer of chocolate first (chabloning; page 273) makes it easier to handle during coating.

Learn

METHOD

1 Temper 200 g (7 oz) of couverture chocolate (page 24). Put a polyethylene sheet on a baking tray and coat with a thin layer of tempered chocolate using a brush (page 273), then put the frame on the sheet.

2 To make the ganache, pour it into the frame when it is at the right temperature: 35°C (95°F) for dark chocolate, 32°C (89.6°F) for milk chocolate and 27/28°C (80.6/82.4°F) for white. Smooth it out then leave to set for 10 to 12 hours at 15 to 17°C (59 to 62.6°F).

3 Temper the remaining couverture. Remove the frame (page 273). Lightly coat the top surface with chocolate (page 273) using a spatula. Before the thin chocolate layer has cooled completely, cut the sweets to size using a knife.

4 Coat in the couverture chocolate. Using a chocolate fork, dip it into the melted chocolate, moving it up and down. Lift it out: the melted chocolate should stick to the outside but should not run off when it is put on the polyethelene sheet. Leave to sit at 15° to 17°C (59 to 62.6°F) for 48 hours to ensure the cocoa fat has fully set.

MAKING MOULDED
CHOCOLATES

Understand

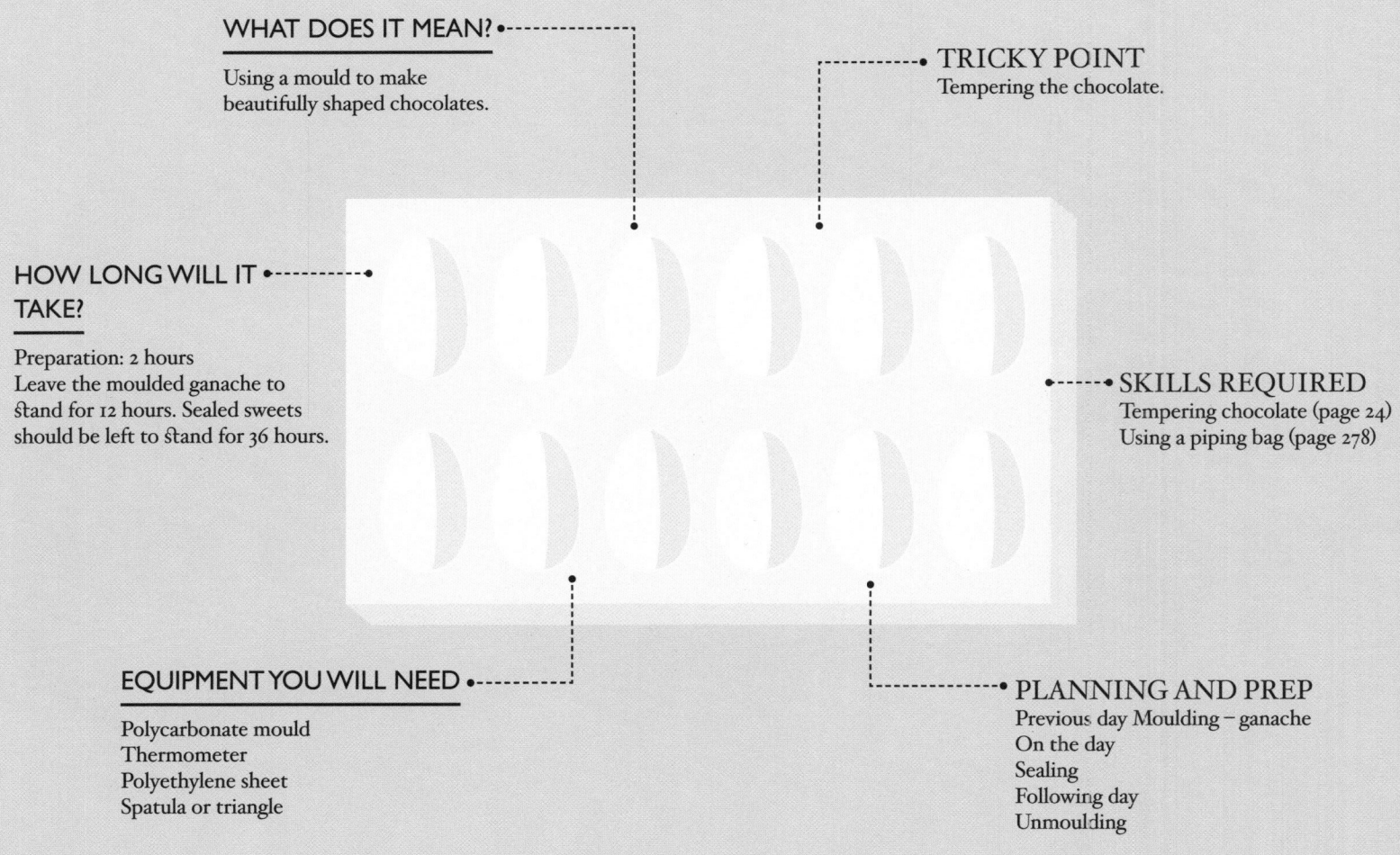

WHAT DOES IT MEAN?

Using a mould to make
beautifully shaped chocolates.

TRICKY POINT
Tempering the chocolate.

**HOW LONG WILL IT
TAKE?**

Preparation: 2 hours
Leave the moulded ganache to
stand for 12 hours. Sealed sweets
should be left to stand for 36 hours.

SKILLS REQUIRED
Tempering chocolate (page 24)
Using a piping bag (page 278)

EQUIPMENT YOU WILL NEED

Polycarbonate mould
Thermometer
Polyethylene sheet
Spatula or triangle

PLANNING AND PREP
Previous day Moulding – ganache
On the day
Sealing
Following day
Unmoulding

ADVICE
Make sure that the moulds are clean and
wipe the imprints carefully with cotton wool
to remove any trace of moisture or grease.
Be careful not to leave any fingermarks.
When handling the mould, hold it by its edges
and avoid prolonged hand contact with the
mould imprints as body heat is higher than
the temperature at which the couverture
chocolate is used and white marks ('bloom')
may appear after crystallisation. Do not wait
too long between layers so that they adhere
well to each other and not separate on eating.

TIPS
Spray the first layer into the moulds with a
chocolate spray gun, if you have one, instead
of using a brush. Ideally you should leave
to stand for 48 hours, but the chocolates
can be unmoulded in four to six hours.
If unmoulding is not going well, place the
mould in the freezer for 15 minutes.

Learn

1. Temper two-thirds of the coating chocolate (page 24). Apply a thin layer in the mould using a dry brush. Wait a few minutes for this first coat to begin to set.

2. Fill the mould imprints completely using a ladle, tap on the side of the mould with the handle of a spatula in order to allow air bubbles to escape.

3. Turn the mould over and tap to remove excess chocolate. Leave the mould upside-down and place it on spacers so that the excess chocolate runs out.

4. When the couverture begins to set, scrape the mould with a triangle or spatula. If the previous coat is too thin, apply a second coat, following steps 3 and 4. Allow to set for about 2 hours. During that time, make the soft or semi-liquid filling and allow it to cool down to a temperature of 27°C (80.6°F). Using a piping bag (page 278) fill the moulds stopping 2 or 3 mm from the top. Leave to set for 10 to 12 hours at 15 to 17°C (59 to 62.6°F).

5. When the chocolates have set, temper the rest of the couverture to seal the sweets. Fill the remaining space in each mould, pat, scrape, and put on a polyethylene sheet.

6. To unmould the chocolates, twist the mould slightly, turn it over and tap on the side.

DECORATING CHOCOLATES

Understand

WHAT HAS HAPPENED TO A CHOCOLATE THAT HAS LOST ITS SHINE?

A dull, matt surface means that the chocolate has not been tempered properly. It will taste fine, but will melt too easily in your hand and will tend to whiten over time.

Learn

1

2

3

4

5

1 FORK
After coating, place the chocolate on a polyethylene sheet and immediately use the prongs of a fork to trace a decoration on the surface. Then lift off the fork and leave to set.

2 CONE
When the chocolate has set, fill a cone (page 274) with melted couverture and, working quickly, run fine threads of chocolate onto the surface. Leave the decoration to set.

3 TOPPING
After coating, put a few crushed seeds or nuts on the surface and leave to set.

4 GOLD LEAF
After coating, add a fragment of gold leaf using a toothpick and allow to set.

5 PAINTBRUSH DECORATION
Prepare a decorating paste with 70 g (2 ½ oz) white couverture chocolate, 10 g (½ oz) cocoa butter and a very small amount of fat-soluble food colouring. Brush each mould imprint with the paste before coating it with chocolate.

DECORATING CHOCOLATE

1 FLAKES

Temper 150 g (5 oz) couverture chocolate (page 24), pour onto the back of a baking tray and spread out a thin layer using a palette knife. Wait a few minutes for the chocolate to begin to set and then, using a dessert ring or a pastry cutter, scrape off flakes of chocolate.

2 CHOCOLATE DISCS

Temper 150 g (5 oz) couverture chocolate (page 24), pour onto a polyethylene sheet and spread out a thin layer using a palette knife. Wait a few minutes for the chocolate to begin to set then, using pastry rings or cutters of various diameters, cut out discs. Place a baking sheet and a baking tray on top to prevent them from curling as they set and the couverture shrinks.

3 CHOCOLATE SQUARES

Temper 150 g (5 oz) couverture chocolate (page 24), pour onto a polyethylene sheet and spread out a thin layer using a palette knife. Wait a few minutes for the chocolate to begin to set then, using a ruler and a paring knife, cut out 3 cm (1 ¼ in) strips crosswise and lengthwise into squares. Place a baking sheet and a baking tray on top to prevent them from curling as they set and the couverture shrinks.

4 COCOA NIB DISCS

Temper 150 g (5 oz) couverture chocolate (page 24), pour onto a polyethylene osheet and spread out a thin layer using a palette knife. Sprinkle with cocoa nibs. Wait a few minutes for the chocolate to begin to set then, using dessert rings or pastry cutters of various diameters, cut out discs. You can also put the couverture in a piping bag (page 278) and pipe out discs to the desired size on a polyethylene sheet. Tap on the sheet so that the chocolate spreads out evenly.

5 DECORATIVE CAKE SURROUND

Put a baking tray in the freezer for 30 minutes. Melt the chocolate in a double-boiler at about 40°C (104°F). Take the baking tray out of the freezer and, working quickly, spread out a thin layer of chocolate using a palette knife. Using a paring knife, cut a strip of chocolate to the required size, using a ruler. Gently peel the strip off the tray with the knife and put it immediately around the cake.

DECORATING CHOCOLATE

6 LATTICE EFFECT DECORATIONS

Temper 150 g (5 oz) couverture chocolate (page 24), put in a piping bag, make a very small hole in the bag, then press out thin chocolate hoops onto a polyethylene sheet, overlapping them (page 278). Leave to set, then break off to make decorative pieces.

7 CIGARETTE SHAPES AND MINIATURE FANS

Temper 150 g (5 oz) couverture chocolate (page 24), pour onto the back of a cooking tray and spread out thinly using a palette knife. Wait a few minutes for the chocolate to begin to set then, using a triangle, scrape off a few centimetres (a couple of inches) to roll into cigarette shapes. Slightly change the angle to produce small fans, score the surface in one direction across the width of a strip, then scrape off flakes.

8 CHOCOLATE SWIRLS

Temper 150 g (5 oz) couverture chocolate (page 24), pour onto a polyethylene sheet and spread out a thin layer using a palette knife. Holding the top end of the sheet, pull a chocolate comb towards you to score lines on the chocolate. Now twist the strip into a swirl shape, put a weight on each end and leave it weighted while the chocolate hardens, so that the strip does not unroll.

9 WOLF FANGS

Temper 150g (5 oz) couverture chocolate, pour onto a polyethylene sheet and spread out a thin layer using a palette knife. Wait a few minutes for the chocolate to begin to set then, using a ruler and a paring knife, cut strips 8 cm (3 1/4 in) wide and 3 cm (1 1/4 in) long to make rectangles, then cut diagonally to make triangles.

Put a baking sheet and a tray on top to prevent them from curling up as they set and the couverture shrinks.

10 CHOCOLATE FEATHERS

Temper 150 g (5 oz) couverture chocolate (page 24), dip the blade of a paring knife into the chocolate and place the chocolate-filled blade on a strip of polyethylene sheet or transparent acetate strip. Lift the blade of the knife up slightly and pull it towards you to produce a feather. Put in a round mould to shape the decorations.

50% PRALINE &
GIANDUJA

Understand

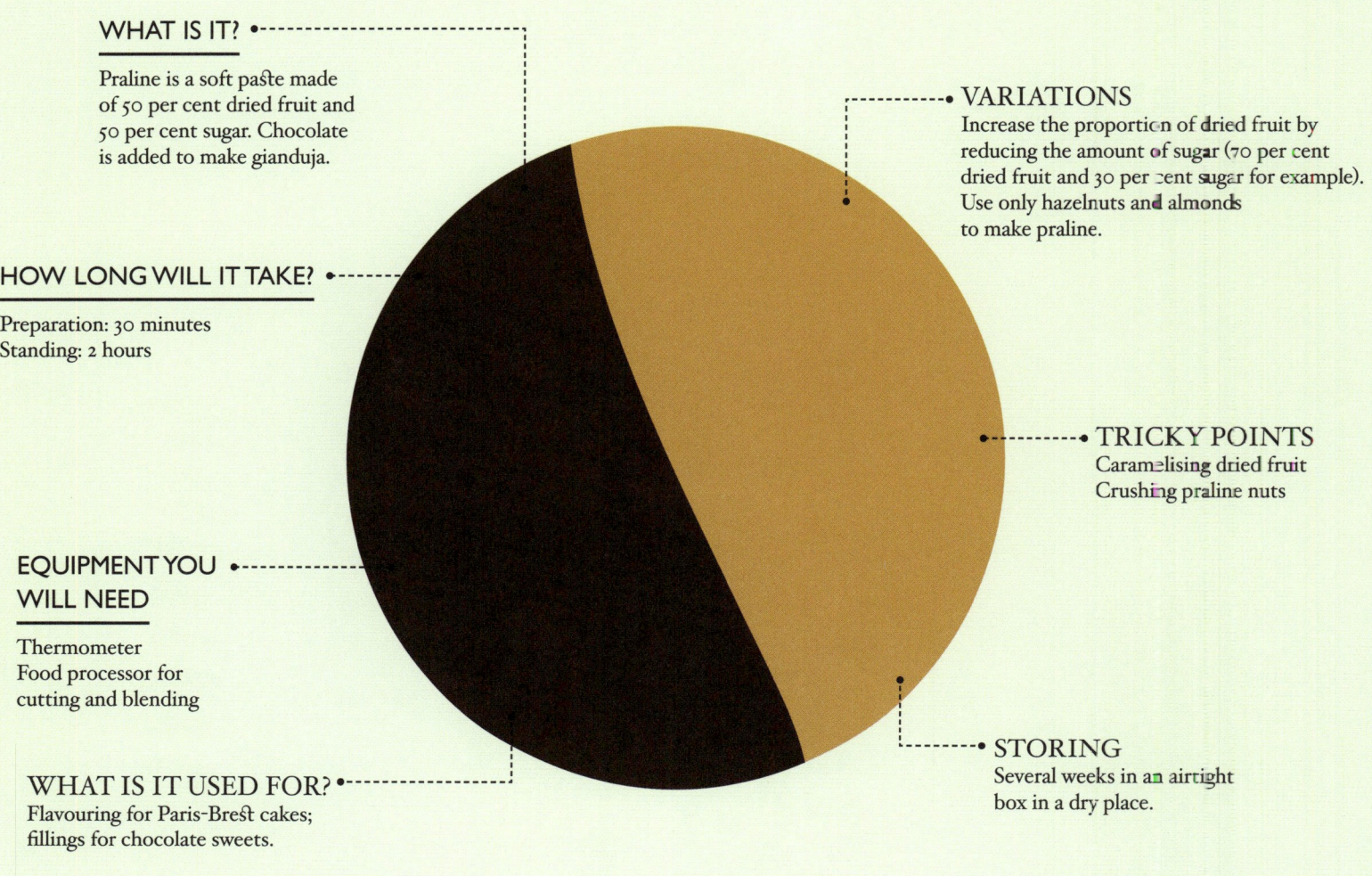

WHAT IS IT?

Praline is a soft paste made of 50 per cent dried fruit and 50 per cent sugar. Chocolate is added to make gianduja.

HOW LONG WILL IT TAKE?

Preparation: 30 minutes
Standing: 2 hours

EQUIPMENT YOU WILL NEED

Thermometer
Food processor for cutting and blending

WHAT IS IT USED FOR?

Flavouring for Paris-Brest cakes; fillings for chocolate sweets.

VARIATIONS

Increase the proportion of dried fruit by reducing the amount of sugar (70 per cent dried fruit and 30 per cent sugar for example). Use only hazelnuts and almonds to make praline.

TRICKY POINTS

Caramelising dried fruit
Crushing praline nuts

STORING

Several weeks in an airtight box in a dry place.

WHY IS THE DRIED FRUIT ROASTED?

Roasting reduces the water content and develops the aromas.

ADVICE

Process in small quantities if needed, depending on the how powerful the mixer is. If the mixture starts to get hot, stop and wait a few minutes. To prevent the sugar from burning during caramelisation, remove the pan from the heat from time to time and mix well.

TIPS

Make sure that the dried fruit is fresh so that the praline can be kept for some time without going rancid. To check if the dried fruits are cooked, cut one in half: it should be a golden colour inside.

Learn

FOR 600 G (1 LB 5 OZ) PRALINE

150 g (5 oz) shelled almonds
150 g (5 oz) shelled hazelnuts
120 g (4 oz) water
300 g (10 ½ oz) white caster (superfine) sugar

FOR 320 G (11 OZ) GIANDUJA

200 g (7 oz) praline
120 g (4 oz) dark couverture chocolate (66% cocoa)

MAKING THE PRALINE

1 Preheat the oven to 170°C (340°F/gas 5). Put the almonds and hazelnuts on a tray covered with baking paper and bake for 15 to 20 minutes.

2 Put the water and then the sugar in a saucepan and bring to a boil over a medium-high heat. When it boils, put the thermometer into the mixture, taking care not to let it touch the bottom or sides of the pan and heat until the temperature reaches 110°C (230°F).

3 Once this temperature is reached, remove from the heat and add the roasted dried fruit. Stir with a spatula until the sugar crystallises. Return to medium heat then, stirring continuously, cook until the white sugar caramelises around the dried fruit.

4 Transfer immediately to a baking tray covered with baking paper (lay it as flat as possible) and leave to cool to room temperature. Coarsely crush, then put in a food mixer fitted with a blade and blend until smooth. Put aside in an airtight tin.

FOR THE GIANDUJA

1 Melt the chocolate in a double-boiler (page 276).

2 Mix it with the praline. Use immediately or spread on a sheet and leave to harden for later use.

CREAMY GANACHE

Understand

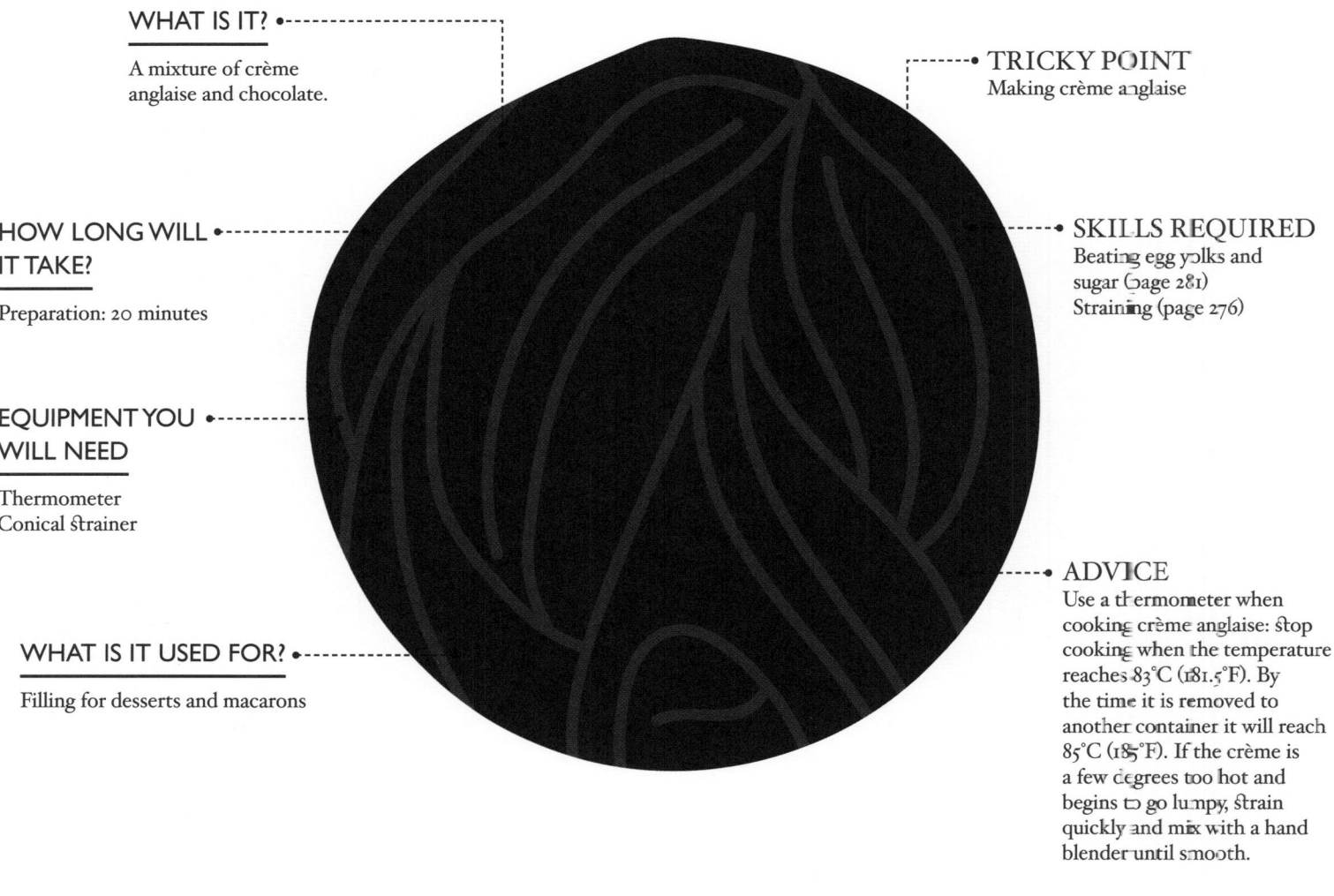

WHAT IS IT?

A mixture of crème anglaise and chocolate.

HOW LONG WILL IT TAKE?

Preparation: 20 minutes

EQUIPMENT YOU WILL NEED

Thermometer
Conical strainer

WHAT IS IT USED FOR?

Filling for desserts and macarons

TRICKY POINT
Making crème anglaise

SKILLS REQUIRED
Beating egg yolks and sugar (page 281)
Straining (page 276)

ADVICE
Use a thermometer when cooking crème anglaise: stop cooking when the temperature reaches 83°C (181.5°F). By the time it is removed to another container it will reach 85°C (185°F). If the crème is a few degrees too hot and begins to go lumpy, strain quickly and mix with a hand blender until smooth.

WHY IS CRÈME ANGLAISE LIKELY TO GO LUMPY IF IT OVERHEATS?

Crème anglaise contains egg protein. If overheated, the proteins coagulate and give the crème a lumpy texture.

Learn

FOR 450 G (1 LB) GANACHE

50 g (2 oz) egg yolk (3 or 4 yolks)
50 g (2 oz) white caster (superfine) sugar
250 g (9 oz) milk
150 g (5 oz) plain, dark chocolate
60% cocoa (minimum)

1 Beat the yolks with the sugar (page 281).

2 Bring the milk to the boil. Just before it boils, pour half of it onto the egg yolk and sugar mixture. Mix with a whisk. When the mixture is evenly blended, pour back into the saucepan.

3 Return to medium heat, stirring all the time with a spatula, until a thin layer of cream coats the spautla when it is removed (85°C) (185°F).

4 Take off the boil, add the chocolate immediately, mix together and blend. Strain the mixture (page 276). Cover with cling film (plastic wrap). Keep refrigerated until ready to use.

WHIPPED WHITE
GANACHE

Understand

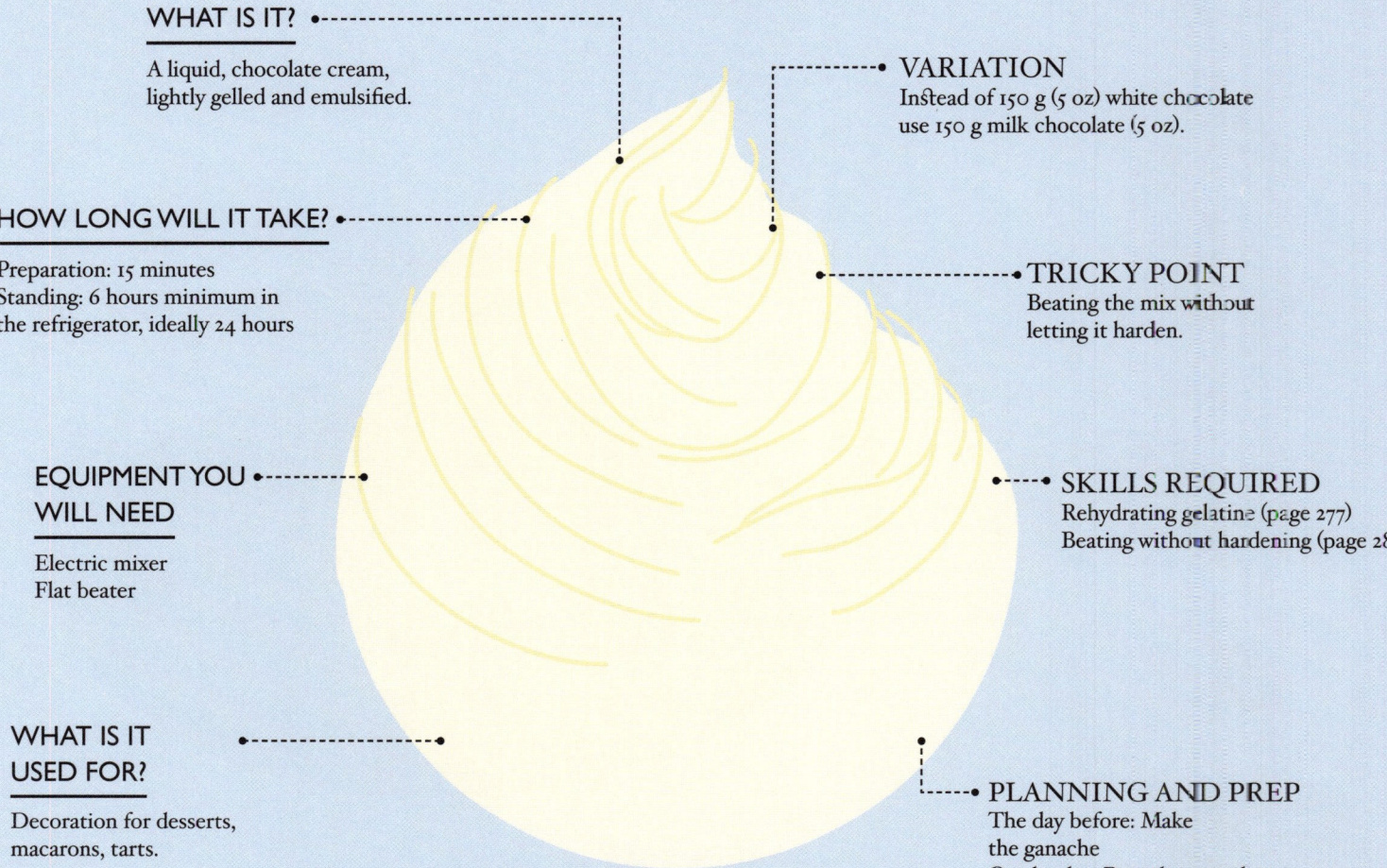

WHAT IS IT?

A liquid, chocolate cream, lightly gelled and emulsified.

HOW LONG WILL IT TAKE?

Preparation: 15 minutes
Standing: 6 hours minimum in the refrigerator, ideally 24 hours

EQUIPMENT YOU WILL NEED

Electric mixer
Flat beater

WHAT IS IT USED FOR?

Decoration for desserts, macarons, tarts.

VARIATION

Instead of 150 g (5 oz) white chocolate use 150 g milk chocolate (5 oz).

TRICKY POINT

Beating the mix without letting it harden.

SKILLS REQUIRED

Rehydrating gelatine (page 277)
Beating without hardening (page 280)

PLANNING AND PREP

The day before: Make the ganache
On the day: Beat the ganache

WHAT HAPPENS WHEN GANACHE HARDENS?

If the ganache has not cooled enough before whipping, it may heat up in the mixer and the gelatine will melt. As it melts, the gelatine will become unstable and the ganache will harden.

WHY DOES GANACHE BECOME MATT AFTER WHIPPING?

Ganache becomes matt for two reasons: the white chocolate crystallises and air is incorporated into the ganache.

ADVICE

The higher the chocolate content in the ganache, the thicker the consistency. If the ganache contains less chocolate, heat only half of the cream and pour the rest in cold; use it more quickly. Make sure you allow ganache to cool well before beating to prevent it from hardening.

Learn

FOR 350 G (12 OZ) GANACHE

230 g (8 oz/8 fl oz/scant 1 cup) whipping cream
2 g (1 sheet) sheet gelatine
150 g (5 oz) white chocolate

1 Rehydrate the gelatine (page 277) in cold water.

2 Heat the cream until it begins to boil. Remove from the heat and add the gelatine. Mix, then pour over the white chocolate into a heatproof bowl. Wait 1 minute, then whisk. Pour into a bowl or container, cover with cling film (plastic wrap) and leave to chill in the refrigerator for at least 6 hours, ideally overnight.

3 Put the cold ganache into a stand mixer fitted with a flat whisk attachment (see above) and beat on slow or medium speed until the ganache takes on a matt finish.

EGG YOLK SYRUP
MIXTURE

Understand

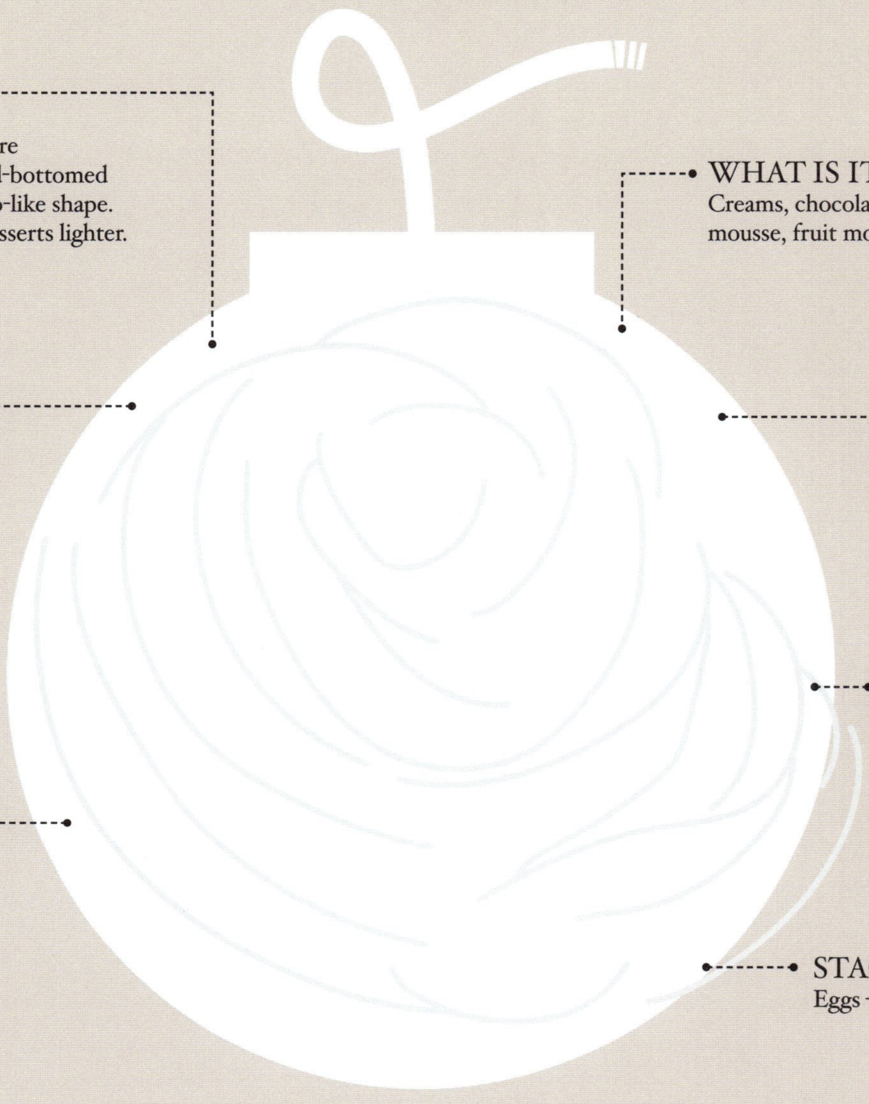

WHAT IS IT?

An egg yolk and syrup mixture traditionally made in a round-bottomed bowl with a distinctive bomb-like shape. It is used to make mousse desserts lighter.

HOW LONG WILL IT TAKE?

Preparation: 15 minutes

EQUIPMENT YOU WILL NEED

Thermometer
Electric mixer

WHAT IS IT USED FOR?

Creams, chocolate mousse, fruit mousse

TRICKY POINTS

Heating the sugar
Incorporating the syrup

SKILLS REQUIRED

Making syrup (page 282)

STAGES

Eggs – syrup – mix

WHY MUST THE SIDES OF THE PAN STAY PERFECTLY CLEAN WHEN MAKING THE SYRUP?

Keeping the sides of the pan clean prevents the sugar from crystallising. If there are any impurities, sugar tends to crystallise around it and form lumps.

ADVICE

Do not mix the syrup after boiling as it may crystallise.

VARIATION

For a lighter mixture, use both the egg whites and the yolks.

Learn

TO MAKE 150 G (5 OZ)

40 g (1 ½ oz) water
100 g (3 ½ oz) white caster (superfine) sugar
80 g (3 oz) egg yolks (5 or 6)

1 Put the egg yolks in the mixer bowl and whisk at maximum speed for about 3 minutes, until they triple in volume. Make a syrup: weigh the water and then the sugar into a small saucepan being careful to keep the sides of the pan clean. Bring to the boil, then clean the sides again with a damp brush. Bring the temperature up to 115°C (240°F).

2 Stop boiling the syrup. When it stops bubbling, drizzle a thin stream into the egg yolks, continuing to whisk briskly with a mixer until it is warm or cool depending on use.

CHOCOLATE MOUSSE USING AN EGG YOLK SYRUP
MIXTURE

Understand

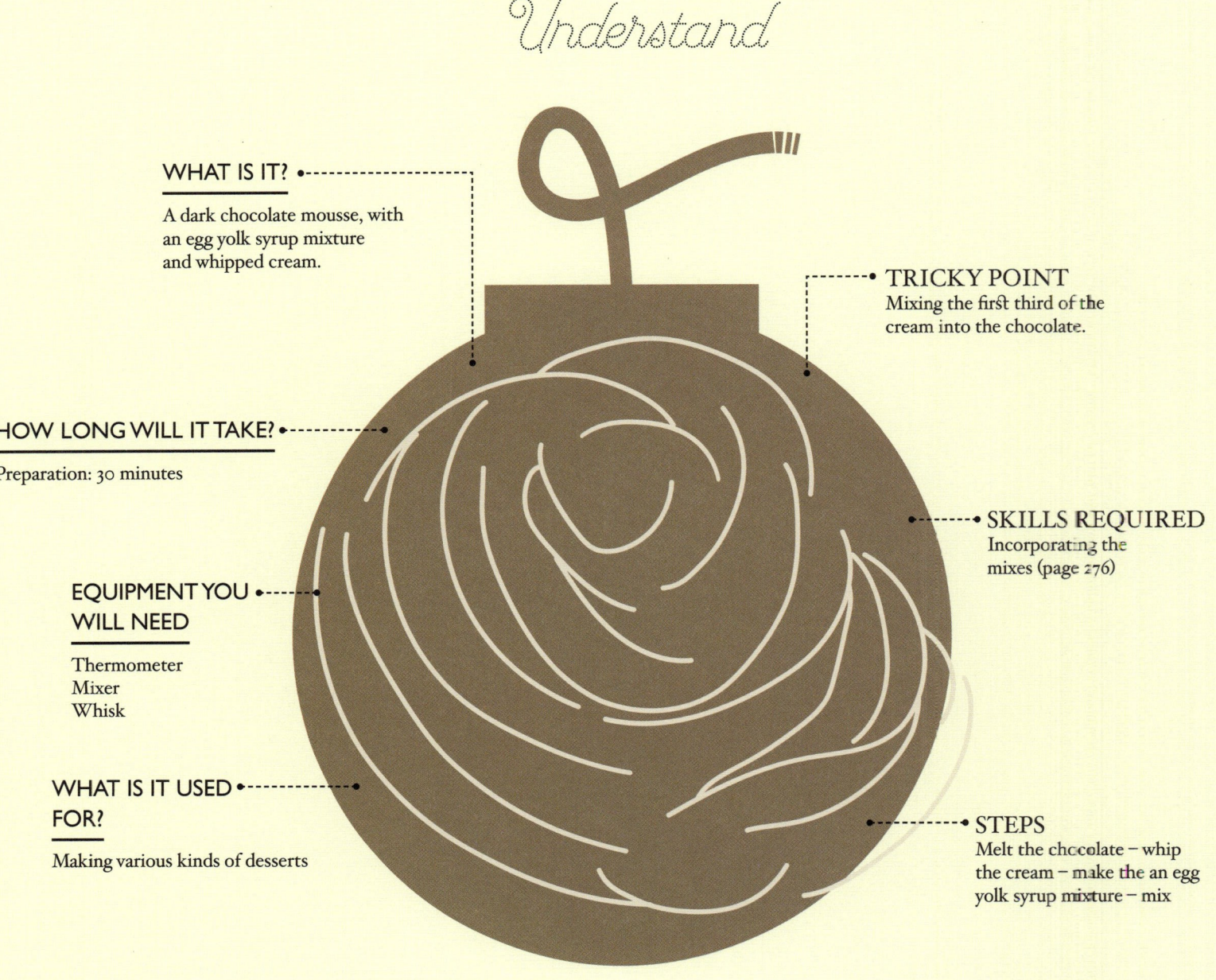

WHAT IS IT?
A dark chocolate mousse, with an egg yolk syrup mixture and whipped cream.

HOW LONG WILL IT TAKE?
Preparation: 30 minutes

EQUIPMENT YOU WILL NEED
Thermometer
Mixer
Whisk

WHAT IS IT USED FOR?
Making various kinds of desserts

TRICKY POINT
Mixing the first third of the cream into the chocolate.

SKILLS REQUIRED
Incorporating the mixes (page 276)

STEPS
Melt the chocolate – whip the cream – make the an egg yolk syrup mixture – mix

WHY SHOULD THIS MOUSSE BE USED IMMEDIATELY AFTER MAKING?
It is best to use the mousse immediately, when its texture is light, fluffy and easy to work with. If kept in a cool place before use as a dessert, the chocolate crystallises too much, making the texture firmer.

ADVICE
Stop whipping the cream when it takes on a matt finish.

TIP
For a slightly richer result, add 5 per cent mascarpone.

Learn

FOR 700 G (1 LB 9 OZ)

CHOCOLATE MOUSSE

200 g (7 oz) dark chocolate
(minimum 60% cocoa)
350 g (12 oz) whipping cream

EGG YOLK SYRUP MIXTURE

40 g (1 ½ oz) water
100 g (3 ½ oz) white caster (superfine) sugar
80 g (3 oz) egg yolk (5 to 6 yolks)

1 Melt the chocolate in a double-boiler (page 276). After melting, remove the boiler bowl and allow the chocolate to cool down to room temperature.

2 Whip the cream (page 280), transfer to a bowl and set aside in the refrigerator.

3 Make the egg yolk syrup mixture (page 46). Add one-third of the whipped cream to the melted chocolate and whip briskly.

4 Once the egg yolk syrup mixture is warm, add it to the cream-chocolate mixture. Mix gently using the spatula.

5 Add the remaining whipped cream and mix gently until smoothly blended. Use immediately.

CHOCOLATE MOUSSE WITH CRÈME
ANGLAISE

Understand

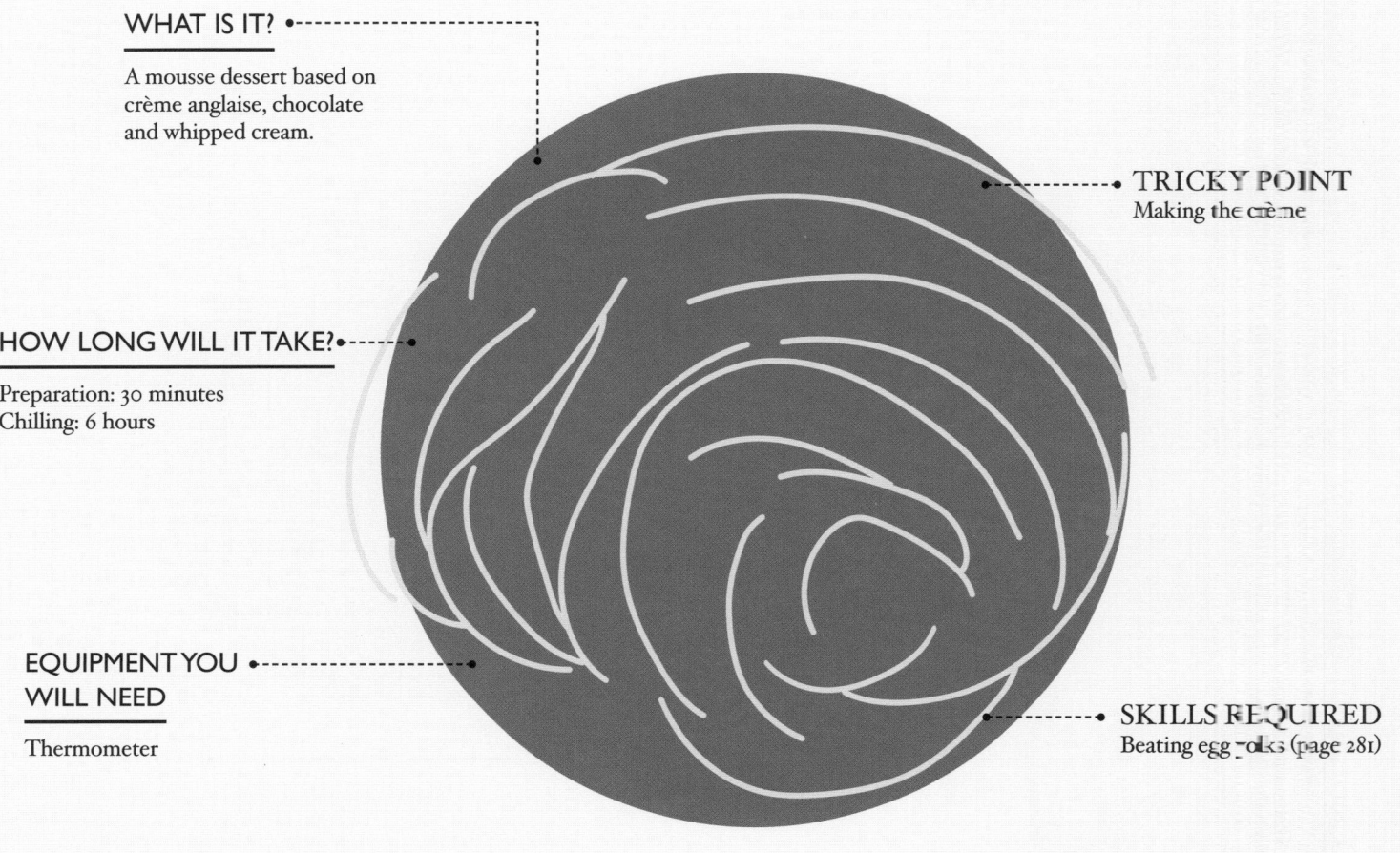

WHAT IS IT?

A mousse dessert based on crème anglaise, chocolate and whipped cream.

HOW LONG WILL IT TAKE?

Preparation: 30 minutes
Chilling: 6 hours

EQUIPMENT YOU WILL NEED

Thermometer

TRICKY POINT
Making the crème

SKILLS REQUIRED
Beating egg yolks (page 281)

WHY MUST THE CREAM BE REALLY COLD BEFORE IT IS WHIPPED?

When cream is whipped to make a mousse, the fat forms globules around the incorporated air bubbles. When the cream is cold, it more easily forms a network of fat to trap the air. Using too-warm cream will result in grainy whipped cream.

ADVICE

When making a mousse to pour into a dessert, it is best not to whip the cream up too firmly, so that the mousse can be poured out easily without it setting too quickly.

Learn

FOR 550 G (20 OZ) MOUSSE

CRÈME ANGLAISE BASE

60 g (2 oz) whipping cream
60 g (2 oz) milk
25 g (1 oz) egg yolks (2 yolks)
10 g (½ oz) white caster (superfine) sugar

FOR DARK CHOCOLATE MOUSSE

175 g (6 oz) dark chocolate 66% cocoa
225 g (8 oz) whipping cream

FOR MILK CHOCOLATE MOUSSE

150 g (5 oz) crème anglaise base
275 g (10 oz) milk chocolate
225 g (8 oz) whipping cream

FOR WHITE CHOCOLATE MOUSSE

150 g (5 oz) crème anglaise base
250 g (9 oz) white chocolate
225 g (8 oz) whipping cream
4 g sheet gelatine (to be added to the milk for making the crème anglaise base)

1 Whip the cold cream until it froths. Make the crème anglaise: bring the milk to the boil while beating the yolks and the sugar with a whisk (page 281). Just before the milk boils, pour half of it into the whisked yolk mixture. Whisk until evenly blended then pour back into the saucepan. Return to medium heat, stirring continuously until the cream is thick enough to coat the spatula (85°C (185°F) maximum).

2 In the meantime, melt whichever type of chocolate you are using chocolate in a double-boiler (page 276).

3 Pour the cream over the chocolate and mix.

4 Put a third of whipped cream in this mixture and whip. Add the rest of the cream and mix gently with the whisk, then finish using a spatula.

DIPLOMAT PASTRY CREAM

Understand

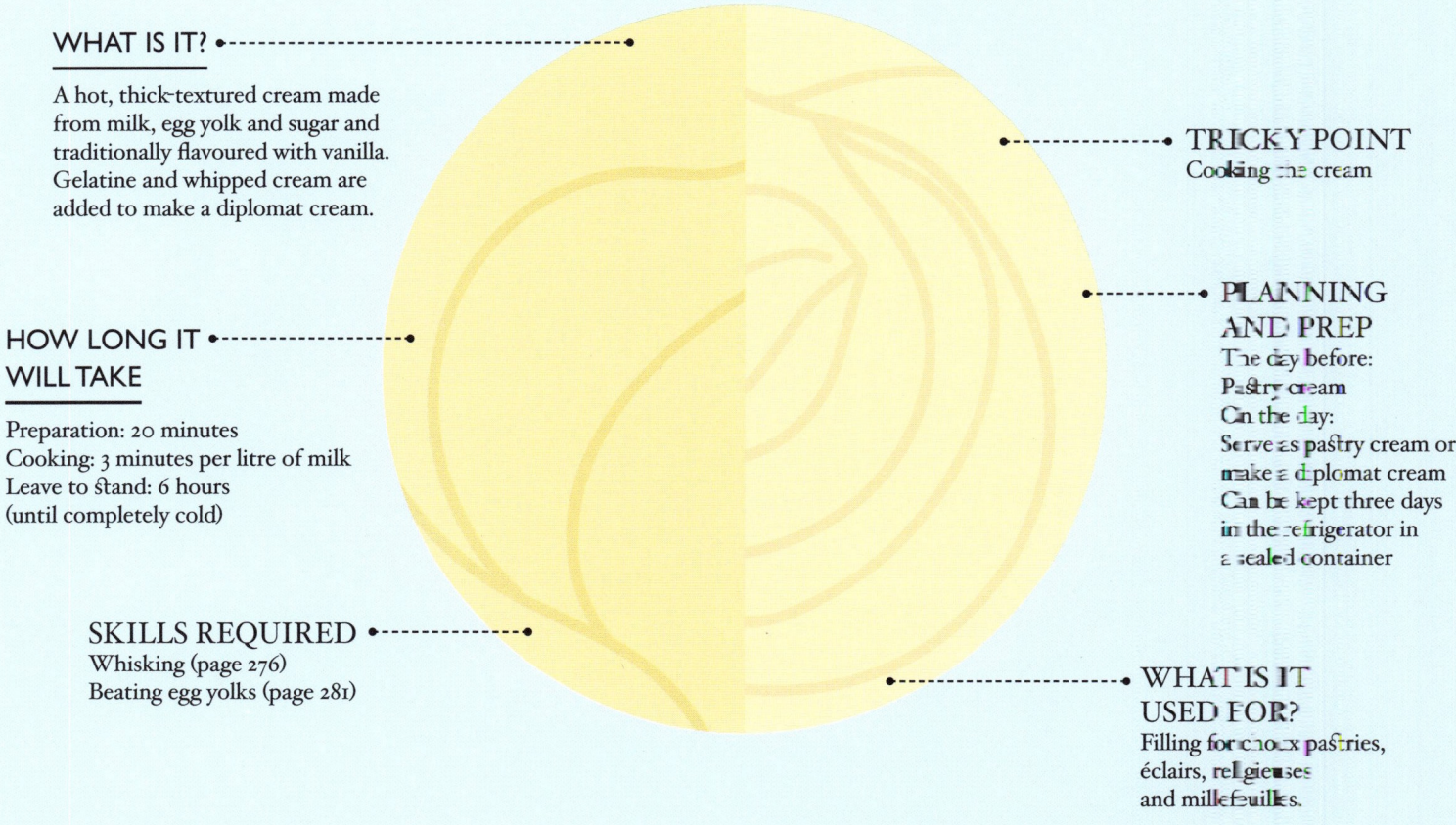

WHAT IS IT?

A hot, thick-textured cream made from milk, egg yolk and sugar and traditionally flavoured with vanilla. Gelatine and whipped cream are added to make a diplomat cream.

HOW LONG IT WILL TAKE

Preparation: 20 minutes
Cooking: 3 minutes per litre of milk
Leave to stand: 6 hours
(until completely cold)

SKILLS REQUIRED
Whisking (page 276)
Beating egg yolks (page 281)

TRICKY POINT
Cooking the cream

PLANNING AND PREP
The day before:
Pastry cream
On the day:
Serve as pastry cream or make a diplomat cream
Can be kept three days in the refrigerator in a sealed container

WHAT IS IT USED FOR?
Filling for choux pastries, éclairs, religieuses and millefeuilles.

HOW DOES A MIXTURE THICKEN WHEN COOKED?

During cooking, the starch in the flour thickens the mix through gelatinisation. Egg yolk proteins also play a role in thickening by coagulating the mixture.

WHY USE CORNFLOUR (CORNSTARCH) AND NOT WHEAT FLOUR?

Cornflour (cornstarch) is perfect for the thickening we are after because it does not contain gluten. Using wheat flour would produce thickening but also elasticity because of its gluten content.

Learn

FOR 400 G (14 OZ) PASTRY CREAM

250 g (9 oz) milk
50 g (2 oz) egg yolk (3 to 4 yolks)
60 g (2 oz) white caster (superfine) sugar
25 g (1 oz) cornflour (cornstarch)
25 g (1 oz) unsalted butter

1 Heat the milk in a saucepan.

2 Meanwhile, beat the yolks with the sugar (page 281) in a bowl and add the cornflour (cornstarch).

3 When the milk begins to boil, pour half of it onto the yolk-sugar-cornflour (cornstarch) mixture. Put everything back into the saucepan, put on a high heat and stir briskly.

4 When the mixture begins to thicken, continue cooking, stirring constantly. Once it starts to boil, the rule is to allow 3 minutes cooking time per litre (34 fl oz/4 cups) of milk. For 250 g (9 oz) milk, it will take about 30 seconds.

5 When the cooking time is up, take off the heat and add the butter. Mix, then transfer to a large, shallow dish to cool quickly then cover with cling film (plastic wrap). Allow to cool completely before using.

FOR 500 G (1 LB 2 OZ) DIPLOMAT CREAM

400 g (14 oz) pastry cream (see above)
4 g (2 sheets) sheet gelatine
100 g (3 ½ oz) whipping cream

1 To make a diplomat cream: rehydrate the gelatine in cold water (page 280). After adding the butter to the pastry cream, stir in the drained gelatine, mix and cool.

2 Whip the cream (page 280), then set aside in the refrigerator. Whip the pastry cream briskly to make it smooth, add a third of the whipped cream and whisk thoroughly.

3 Add the rest of the cream and mix gently using a spatula.

CHOCOLATE
PUFF PASTRY

Understand

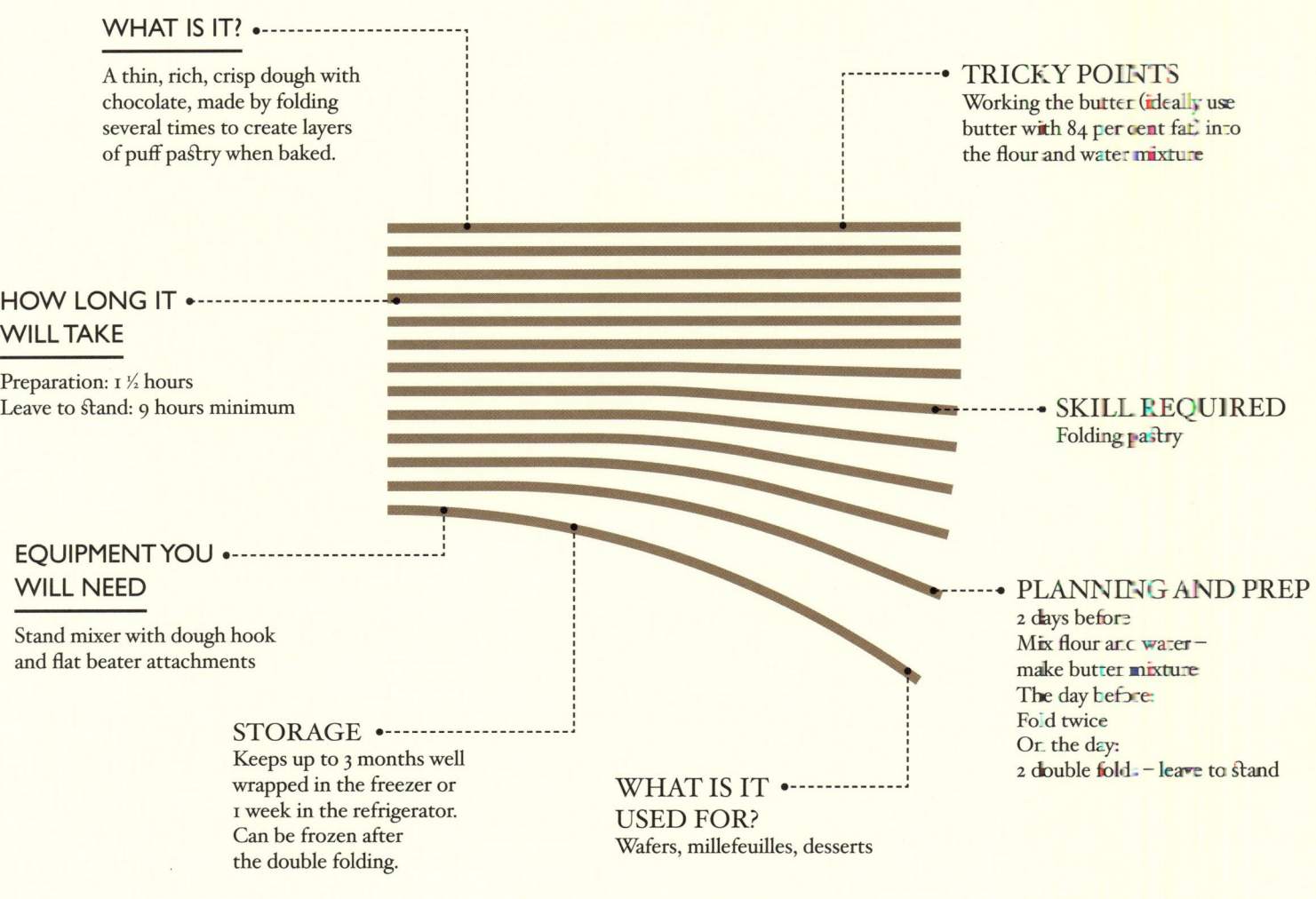

WHAT IS IT?

A thin, rich, crisp dough with chocolate, made by folding several times to create layers of puff pastry when baked.

TRICKY POINTS

Working the butter (ideally use butter with 84 per cent fat) into the flour and water mixture

HOW LONG IT WILL TAKE

Preparation: 1 ½ hours
Leave to stand: 9 hours minimum

SKILL REQUIRED

Folding pastry

EQUIPMENT YOU WILL NEED

Stand mixer with dough hook and flat beater attachments

PLANNING AND PREP

2 days before
Mix flour and water –
make butter mixture
The day before:
Fold twice
On the day:
2 double folds – leave to stand

STORAGE

Keeps up to 3 months well wrapped in the freezer or 1 week in the refrigerator. Can be frozen after the double folding.

WHAT IS IT USED FOR?

Wafers, millefeuilles, desserts

WHAT IS THE VINEGAR FOR?

Vinegar acidifies the dough, which improves its keeping qualities but also affects the gluten structure and the texture of the dough.

WHY DO YOU NEED TO LEAVE IT TO STAND?

Standing time allows the fat to solidify and also stabilises the gluten structure.

ADVICE

It is important to let the dough stand for the two periods, otherwise it will become too soft and break up when you fold it, or it will shrink when rolled. 20 to 30 minutes before rolling and folding, take the dough out of the refrigerator to make it easier to work and prevent it from crumbling. Do not exceed 6 folds otherwise the layering effect will be lost.

Learn

**TO MAKE ABOUT 1.2 KG
(2LB 11 OZ) PASTRY**

1   FLOUR AND WATER MIXTURE

170 g (6 oz) water
10 g (2 ⅓ teaspoons) salt
10 g (½ oz) white vinegar
360 g (12 oz) flour

2   DOUGH FOR FOLDING

450 g (1 lb) unsalted butter (ideally with 84% fat)
115 g (3 ½ oz) flour
30 g (1 oz) cocoa (unsweetened
chocolate) powder

To make chocolate puff pastry

1   Make the flour and water mix: to the bowl of a stand mixer fitted with the dough hook, add the water, salt, white vinegar and flour, in that order. Knead until fully homogenised (page 284), shape into a ball, wrap tightly and store in the refrigerator for at least 4 hours.

2   Prepare the butter mixture: cut the butter into the mixing bowl in small cubes and mix until it has a creamy consistency. Add the flour and cocoa, scraping down the sides of the bowl with a spatula carefully during kneading (page 284). Mix until blended, remove, flatten the mix and store in cling film (plastic wrap) in the refrigerator for at least 4 hours.

3   After 4 hours, roll out the butter mixture into a rectangle measuring about 50 × 20 cm (20 × 8 in), tapping it lightly with the rolling pin to softening the butter without heating it. Roll the flour and water mixture into a rectangle measuring approximately 35 × 20 cm (14 × 8 in).

4   Put the flour and water mixture on top of the butter mixture. Bring the upper part of the mixtures halfway down, taking care to keep them as square as possible. Fold the lower part (butter and flour) up over the previous fold. The first single fold is now complete.

5   Roll out slightly with the rolling pin from the centre outwards.

6   Make the second single fold: turn the dough a quarter of a turn so that the opening is on the right, press down with the rolling pin 3 cm (1 1/4 in) from each end to seal them off, then, working towards the centre, press down similarly every few centimetres (inches) to make it easier to roll. Always roll straight in front of you until you have made a strip about 60 cm (2 feet) long and fold in the same way as in step 4. Refrigerate for at least 3 hours.

7   Take the dough out of the refrigerator, put the opening on the right and roll out the dough in the same way as before to make a layer of pastry about 80 cm (2 1/2 feet) long.

8   Make a double fold: fold 10 cm (4 in) from the bottom towards the top, then seal by pressing down lightly with the rolling pin. Bring the upper part down to the previous one without overlapping, taking care to keep the edges square, and press down with the rolling pin to seal.

9   Bring the upper part back down again to cover the lower part completely widen by rolling slightly from the center to the outside, then give it a quarter turn so that the opening is on the right. Repeat the previous method to obtain a second double fold. Put in the refrigerator for 2 hours before rolling out.

SHORTCRUST PASTRY

Understand

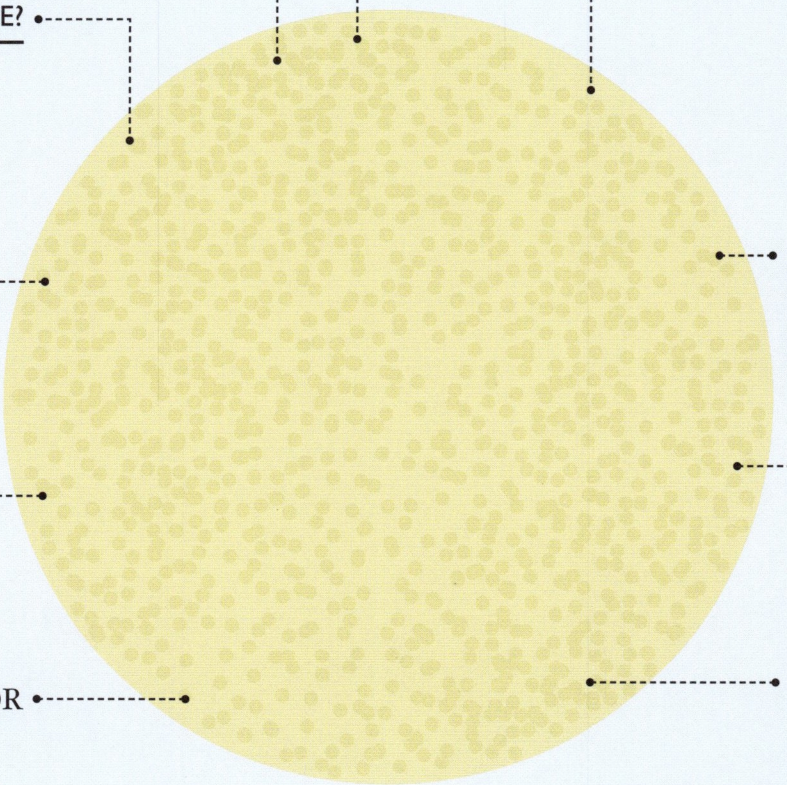

WHAT IS IT?
A very crumbly dough used to make pastry bases.

TRICKY POINT
The pastry is fragile

HOW LONG WILL IT TAKE?
Preparation: 15 minutes
Standing: 6 to 24 hours in the refrigerator

VARIATIONS
Chocolate dough: replace 20 g (³/₄ oz) flour with 20 g (³/₄ oz) cocoa (unsweetened chocolate) powder.
Hazelnut dough: replace 20 g (³/₄ oz) flour with 40 g (1 ¹/₂ oz) ground hazelnuts.

EQUIPMENT YOU WILL NEED
Stand mixer
Flat beater attachment

SKILLS REQUIRED
Making shortcrust (page 284)
Kneading (page 284)
Rolling out (page 284)
Lining a mould (page 284)

WHAT IS IT USED FOR?
Pie and tart bases

PLANNING AND PREP
The day before:
Make the dough
On the day:
Line the mould and bake

ALSO USED FOR
Small biscuits

STORAGE
The uncooked dough will keep for 3 months wrapped in cling film (plastic wrap) in the freezer, or roll out and cut into small discs and keep in an airtight container. Sprinkle flour between the discs when putting them one on top of the other to prevent sticking, and store for up to 3 months.

HOW IS THE CRUMBLY CONSISTENCY OBTAINED?
Kneading the dough just a little prevents the gluten structure from developing. As it has very little binding agent, it remains crumbly.

WHY SHOULD THE DOUGH NOT BE KNEADED TOO MUCH?
Avoid over-kneading when rolling the dough so that it does not lose its crumbly texture and stop it from shrinking when baked.

TIPS
To soften the dough and roll it out more easily without heating it, lay it out on a work surface and tap it lightly with a rolling pin. Buttering the tart rings stops the dough from sticking to them during baking (so the edges do not collapse), and also makes it easy to unmould the tart after baking.

Learn

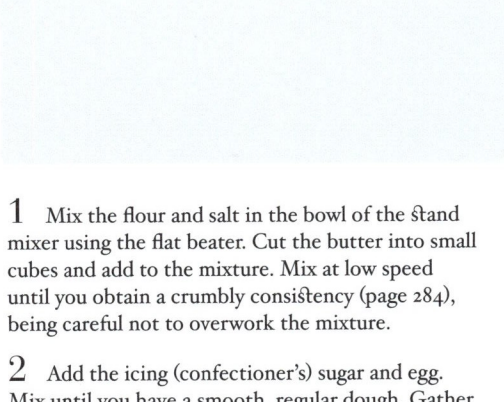

FOR 12 × 8 CM (8 × 3 IN) PASTRY BASES OR 1 × 24 CM (1 × 9 ½ IN) PASTRY BASE

200 g (7 oz) flour
70 g (2 ½ oz) unsalted butter
1 g (¼ teaspoon) salt
70 g (2 ½ oz) icing (confectioner's sugar
60 g (2 oz) egg (1 egg)

1 Mix the flour and salt in the bowl of the stand mixer using the flat beater. Cut the butter into small cubes and add to the mixture. Mix at low speed until you obtain a crumbly consistency (page 284), being careful not to overwork the mixture.

2 Add the icing (confectioner's) sugar and egg. Mix until you have a smooth, regular dough. Gather into a ball and knead gently if necessary (page 284).

3 Lay out flat on a sheet of cling film (plastic wrap) and leave to rest for at least 6 hours, ideally overnight. When rolling the dough, be gentle and do not knead it too much.

FINGER BISCUITS

Understand

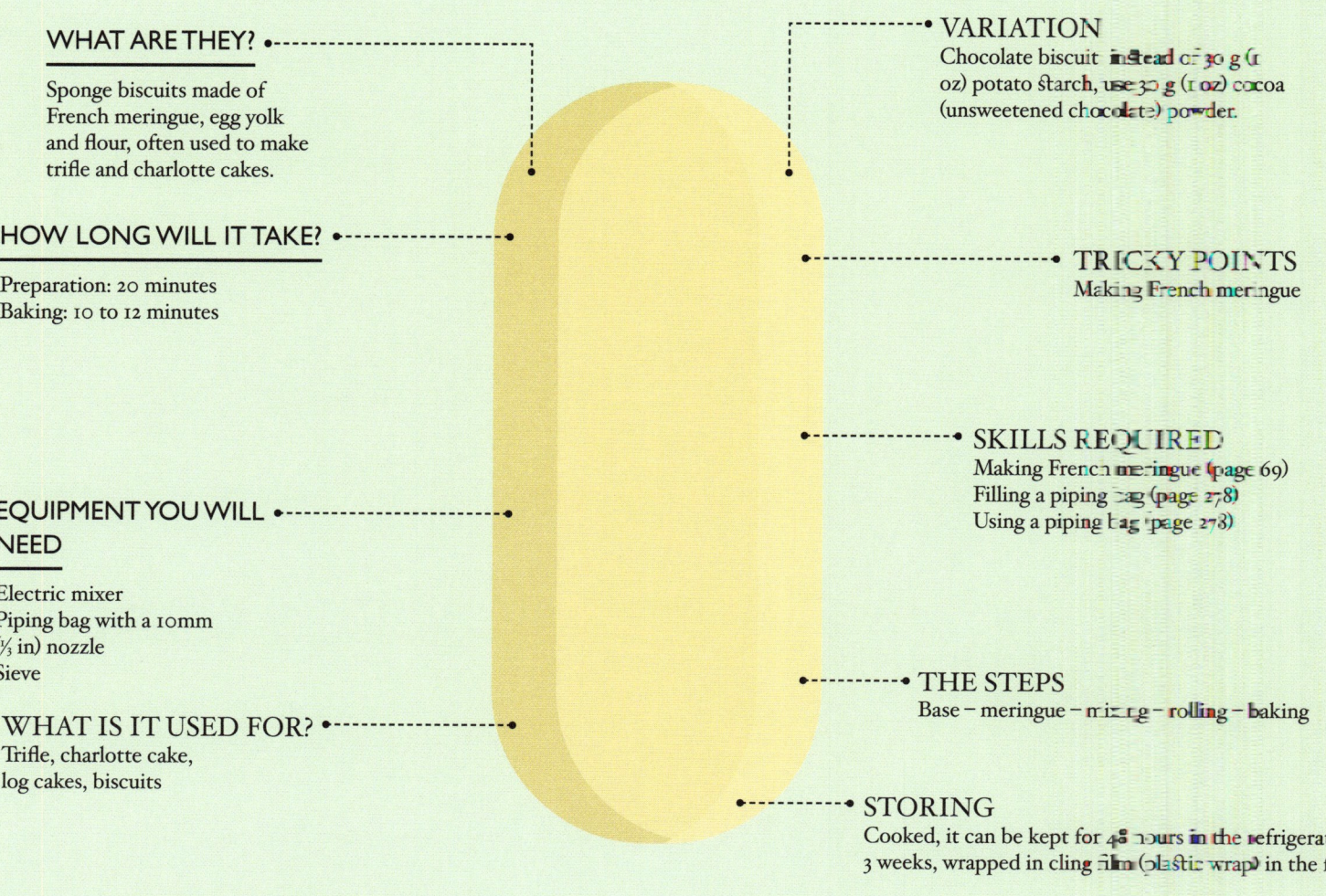

WHAT ARE THEY?

Sponge biscuits made of
French meringue, egg yolk
and flour, often used to make
trifle and charlotte cakes.

HOW LONG WILL IT TAKE?

Preparation: 20 minutes
Baking: 10 to 12 minutes

**EQUIPMENT YOU WILL
NEED**

Electric mixer
Piping bag with a 10mm
(⅓ in) nozzle
Sieve

WHAT IS IT USED FOR?

Trifle, charlotte cake,
log cakes, biscuits

VARIATION

Chocolate biscuit instead of 30 g (1
oz) potato starch, use 30 g (1 oz) cocoa
(unsweetened chocolate) powder.

TRICKY POINTS

Making French meringue

SKILLS REQUIRED

Making French meringue (page 69)
Filling a piping bag (page 278)
Using a piping bag (page 278)

THE STEPS

Base – meringue – mixing – rolling – baking

STORING

Cooked, it can be kept for 48 hours in the refrigerator, or
3 weeks, wrapped in cling film (plastic wrap) in the freezer.

WHY IS THE BAKING TIME IMPORTANT?

*The flour in the biscuit contains starch but no gluten, so the biscuit has very little elasticity.
If the biscuit is baked for too long it becomes dry and brittle.*

ADVICE

To spread the mixture without overworking
it, fill a piping bag and using a 10 mm
(⅓ in) plain nozzle (page 278) and pipe out
(page 278) tightly packed rolls of dough
over the entire surface of the baking tray.

TIP

For individual biscuits pipe out 6 cm
(2 ½ in) lengths, spacing them out well.

Learn

TO MAKE ONE 40 × 30 CM (15 × 12 IN) BISCUIT OR 750 G (1 LB 10 OZ) INDIVIDUAL BISCUITS

BASE

200 g (7 oz) egg yolks (14 to 15 yolks)
90 g (3 ¼ oz) white caster (superfine) sugar
90 g (3 ¼ oz) flour
90 g (3 ¼ oz) potato starch

FRENCH MERINGUE

220 g (8 oz) egg whites (7 to 8 whites)
90 g white caster (superfine) sugar

1 Preheat the oven to 190°C (375°F/gas 6 ½). Make the base: beat the yolks with the sugar in a mixing bowl bowl until the mixture doubles in volume. Set aside. Sieve the flour and potato starch onto a baking sheet.

2 Make a French meringue (page 69). Add one-third of the meringue to the egg yolks and mix well. Add the flour and potato starch, mix together, then gently fold in the rest of the meringue.

3 Line a baking tray with baking paper (baking parchment). Working widthwise with the piping bag, pipe out tightly packed rolls with a 10 mm (¾ in) nozzle over the entire baking tray (page 278). Bake in the oven for 10 to 12 minutes. Remove the biscuit by running your finger under the baking sheet.

FLOURLESS CHOCOLATE
BISCUIT

Understand

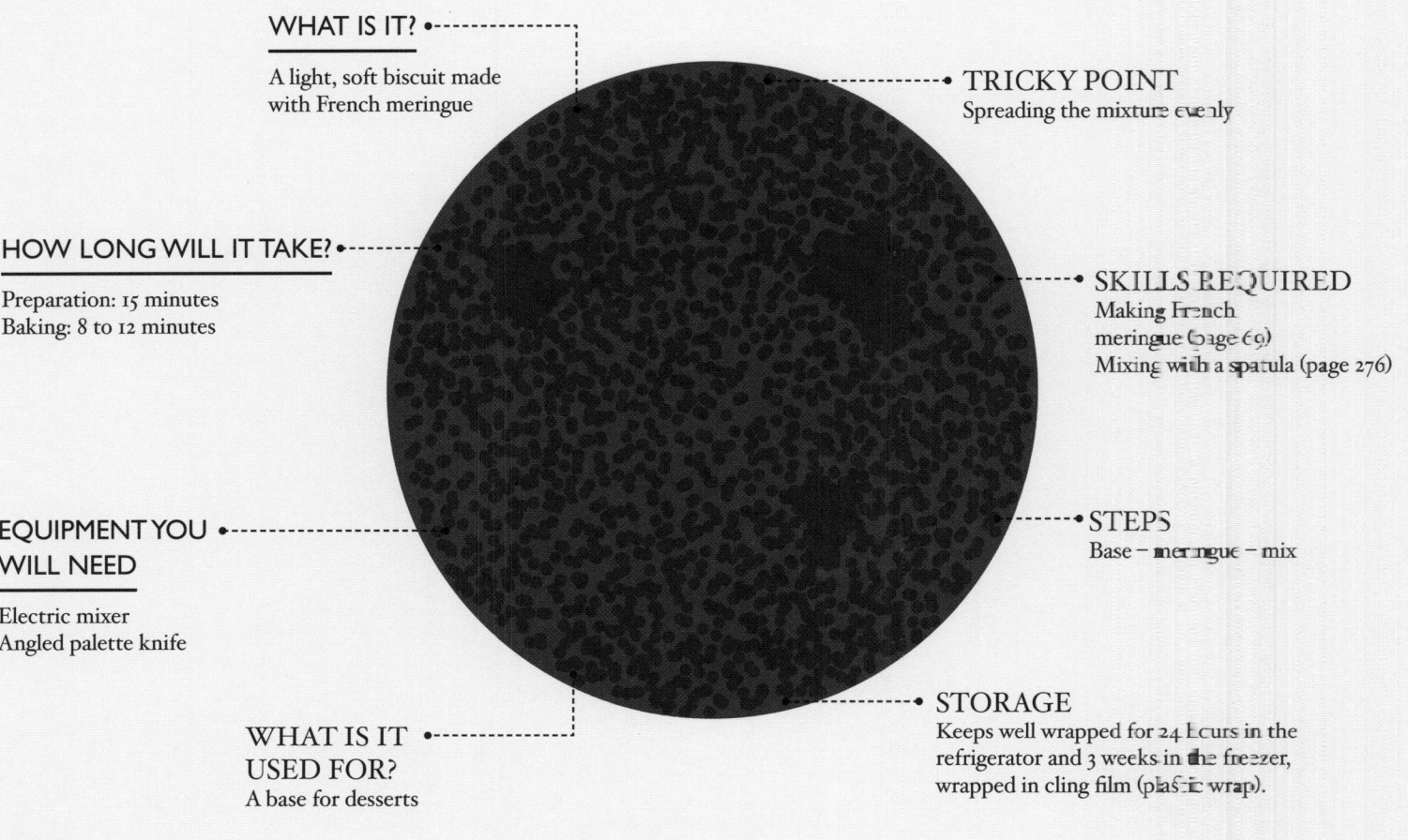

WHAT IS IT?

A light, soft biscuit made
with French meringue

TRICKY POINT

Spreading the mixture evenly

HOW LONG WILL IT TAKE?

Preparation: 15 minutes
Baking: 8 to 12 minutes

SKILLS REQUIRED

Making French
meringue (page 69)
Mixing with a spatula (page 276)

**EQUIPMENT YOU
WILL NEED**

Electric mixer
Angled palette knife

STEPS

Base – meringue – mix

STORAGE

Keeps well wrapped for 24 hours in the
refrigerator and 3 weeks in the freezer,
wrapped in cling film (plastic wrap).

**WHAT IS IT
USED FOR?**

A base for desserts

**WHY DO YOU NEED
TO BE CAREFUL NOT TO
OVERWORK THE DOUGH?**

*This recipe contains no flour, which
makes the biscuit mixture more fragile
before baking, because there is no gluten.
The dough is also quite dry and contains
little air. To prevent any more air from
escaping, and to try to keep the biscuit soft,
it is best not to overwork it.*

ADVICE

Use eggs that are not super-fresh. The albumen
in slightly older eggs is less thick, so it is easier
to whip up. Do not overwork the biscuit to
prevent it collapsing and to keep it soft.
To remove the biscuit more easily, sprinkle
icing (confectioner's) sugar on another baking
sheet, turn the biscuit over onto it, place
the grill on the sheet which is stuck to the
biscuit, hold the grill with one hand and pull
the sheet with the other. Holding the grill on
the sheet prevents the biscuit from breaking.

TIP

Grease the baking tray with softened
butter to prevent the baking sheet moving
when the biscuit is being spread out.

Learn

MAKES A 40 × 30 CM (15 × 12 IN) BASE

CHOCOLATE BISCUIT BASE
90 g (3 ¼ oz) egg yolks (5 or 6 yolks)
70 g (2 ½ oz) white caster (superfine) sugar
40 g (1 ½ oz) cocoa (unsweetened chocolate) powder

FRENCH MERINGUE
125 g (4 oz) egg whites (4 whites)
70 g (2 ½ oz) white caster (superfine) sugar

1 Preheat the oven to 180°C (350°F/gas 6). Beat the yolks and 70 g (2 ½ oz) sugar in the bowl of a stand mixer on full power until the mixture doubles in volume. Set the mixture aside in a bowl.

2 Make a French meringue (page 69). Add one-third of the meringue to the egg yolk and sugar mixture and sieve the cocoa powder over it. Mix gently using a spatula. When the mixture is well blended, add the rest of the meringue and mix gently using a spatula.

3 Spread the mixture out evenly on a baking tray lined with baking paper (baking parchment).

4 Bake for 8 to 12 minutes. Check if the biscuit is cooked by running your finger under the baking sheet. If the biscuit begins to separate from the paper (parchment), it is ready.

5 Transfer the biscuit to a baking rack. Leave to cool.

ALMOND
BISCUIT BASE

Understand

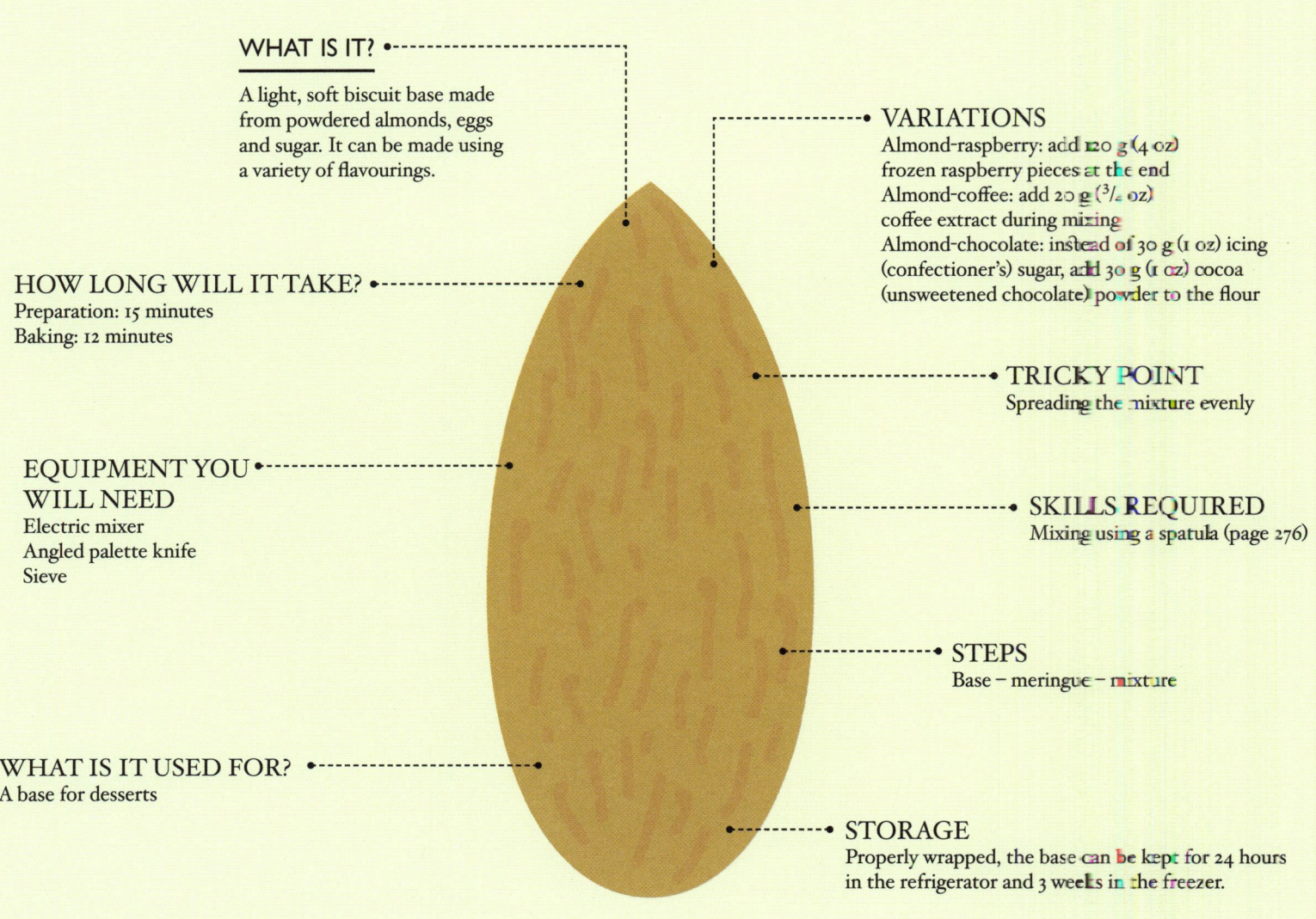

WHAT IS IT?
A light, soft biscuit base made from powdered almonds, eggs and sugar. It can be made using a variety of flavourings.

HOW LONG WILL IT TAKE?
Preparation: 15 minutes
Baking: 12 minutes

EQUIPMENT YOU WILL NEED
Electric mixer
Angled palette knife
Sieve

WHAT IS IT USED FOR?
A base for desserts

VARIATIONS
Almond-raspberry: add 120 g (4 oz) frozen raspberry pieces at the end
Almond-coffee: add 20 g (³/₄ oz) coffee extract during mixing
Almond-chocolate: instead of 30 g (1 oz) icing (confectioner's) sugar, add 30 g (1 oz) cocoa (unsweetened chocolate) powder to the flour

TRICKY POINT
Spreading the mixture evenly

SKILLS REQUIRED
Mixing using a spatula (page 276)

STEPS
Base – meringue – mixture

STORAGE
Properly wrapped, the base can be kept for 24 hours in the refrigerator and 3 weeks in the freezer.

WHY IS IT IMPORTANT NOT TO OVERWORK THE MIXTURE?
It contains little flour, so overworking the biscuit base may cause it to collapse. Treating it gently will also keep it soft.

TIP
Grease the baking sheet with softened butter to stop it moving when the biscuit is being spread.

Learn

MAKES A 40 × 30 CM (15 × 12 IN) BISCUIT BASE

ALMOND BASE

40 g (1 ½ oz) egg yolks (3 yolks)
70 g (2 ½ oz) eggs (1 or 2 yolks and whites)
75 g (2 ½ oz) icing (confectioner's) sugar
75 g (2 ½ oz) ground (powdered) almonds
65 g (2 ½ oz) flour

FRENCH MERINGUE

115 g (3 ½ oz) egg whites (4 whites)
50 g (2 oz) white caster (superfine) sugar

1 Preheat the oven to 180°C (350°F/gas 6). Beat the eggs (yolks and whites), egg yolks, icing sugar and ground almonds for a few minutes, gradually accelerating to maximum speed until the mix has a light and airy consistency. Set aside in a bowl.

2 Sieve the flour. Make a French meringue (page 69).

3 Add half of the flour and one-third of the meringue to the egg and sugar mixture. Mix with a spatula (page 276) working from the centre outwards and turning the bowl gradually until well blended. Add the remaining flour and mix lightly. Add the remaining meringue and mix using a spatula. Stop as soon as the mixture is completely blended.

4 Spread the mixture out evenly on a baking tray covered with baking paper (baking parchment) using the angled palette knife. Cook in the oven for 12 minutes. Transfer to a cooling rack and allow to cool for 20 minutes.

CHOUX PASTRY

Understand

WHAT IS IT?

A dough made from eggs, butter, flour, milk and water. It is piped into shapes and puffs up when baked.

HOW LONG WILL IT TAKE?

Preparation: 30 minutes

WHAT IS IT USED FOR?

Choux pastries, éclairs, Paris-Brest cake, St-Honoré cake

TRICKY POINTS

Incorporating the flour
Drying the dough
Stirring in the eggs

STORAGE

Keeps for 3 weeks in an airtight container in the freezer.

WHY DOES THE WET PASTRY MIX TO BE DRIED IN THE PAN FIRST?

To remove some of the water. If it is too moist, it will spread when placed on the baking tray and during cooking.

WHAT IS THE CRUNCHY 'CRAQUELIN' LAYER FOR?

This crispy outer layer helps the choux to develop evenly during baking.
Baked choux pastries should have a very smooth, even finish.

ADVICE

Be sure to use the right amount of egg: the weight of the liquid (water plus milk) must be equal to that of the eggs (ie for every 200 g (7oz) liquid, there must be 200 g (7oz) egg). If you have egg left over, weigh it and set aside the excess to use as egg wash. Drying the choux pastry is very important, because when the cream filling is added and the choux is put in the refrigerator, the additional moisture would make the choux pastry soft and spongy.

Learn

FOR 400 G (14 OZ) DOUGH

100 g (3 ½ oz) milk
100 g (3 ½ oz) water
90 g (3 ¼ oz) unsalted butter
2 g (½ teaspoon) salt
120 g (4 oz) flour
200 g (7 oz) eggs (4 eggs)

CRUNCHY OUTER 'CRAQUELIN' LAYER

75 g (2 ½ oz) unsalted butter
100 g (3 ½ oz) brown sugar
100 g (3 ½ oz) flour

1 Put the milk, water, salt and butter in a saucepan and bring to the boil. Make sure that the butter has completely melted.

2 When the mixture begins to rise, remove the pan from the heat, pour in all the flour and mix thoroughly with a spatula. This is called a 'wet pastry' mix.

3 When the wet pastry mix is well blended, flatten it out on the bottom of the saucepan and heat it up again without stirring. When the mixture begins to crackle, shake the mixture and check the bottom of the pan. If a thin film of dough is clinging evenly to the pan, it is dry enough (see page 285).

4 Remove the pan from the heat and stir the dough with a spatula until most of the steam has evaporated. Whisk the eggs and fold half of them into the mixture. Once smooth, fold in the remaining egg in two stages.

5 To make the crispy outer 'craquelin': mix the softened butter and brown sugar. Add the flour then, once the mixture is well blended, transfer it to a baking sheet. Place a second sheet on top and roll out a thin, 2 mm layer. Freeze for at least 1 hour before use.

SWISS MERINGUE

Understand

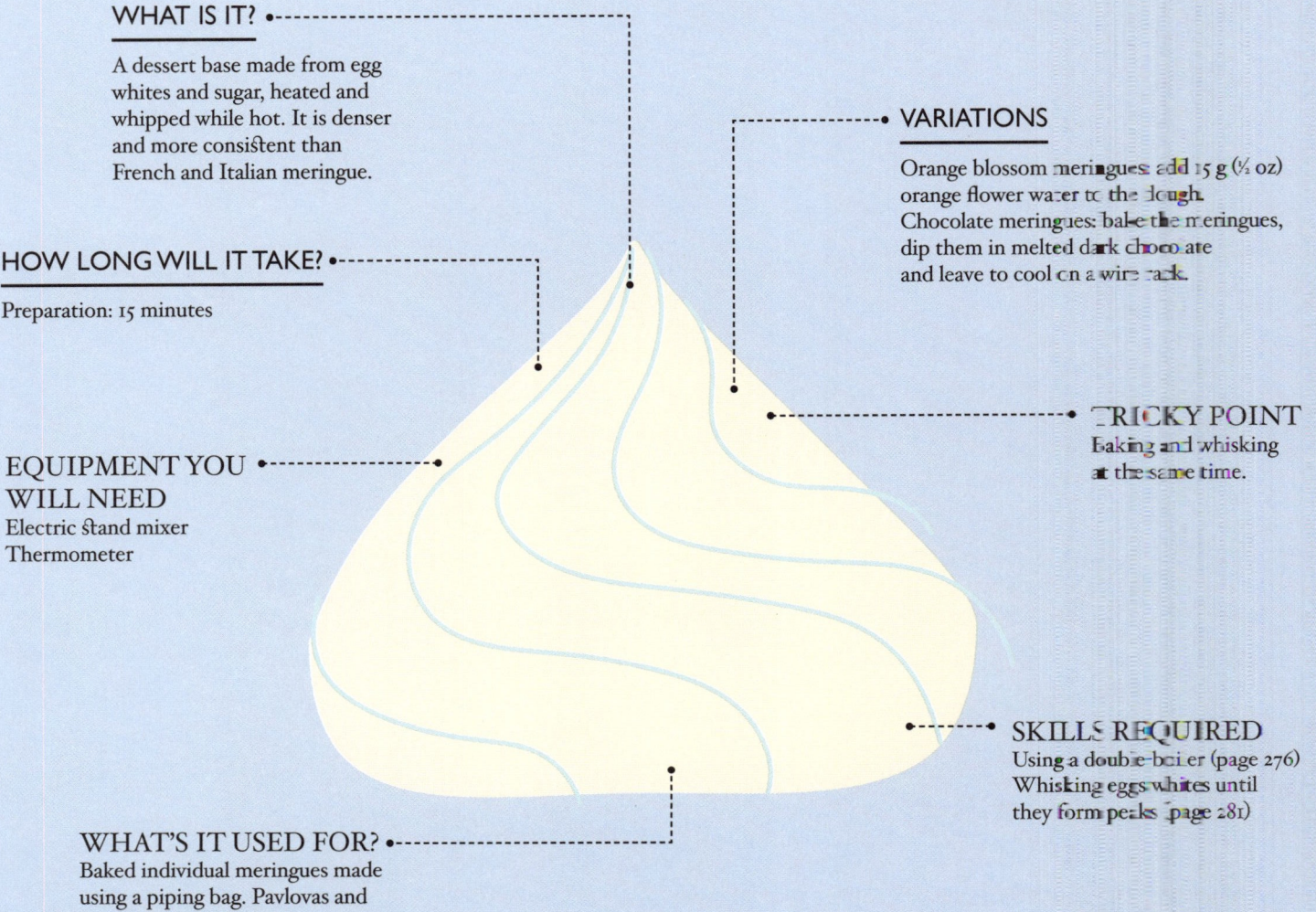

WHAT IS IT?
A dessert base made from egg whites and sugar, heated and whipped while hot. It is denser and more consistent than French and Italian meringue.

HOW LONG WILL IT TAKE?
Preparation: 15 minutes

EQUIPMENT YOU WILL NEED
Electric stand mixer
Thermometer

WHAT'S IT USED FOR?
Baked individual meringues made using a piping bag. Pavlovas and other meringue-based desserts.

VARIATIONS
Orange blossom meringues: add 15 g (½ oz) orange flower water to the dough. Chocolate meringues: bake the meringues, dip them in melted dark chocolate and leave to cool on a wire rack.

TRICKY POINT
Baking and whisking at the same time.

SKILLS REQUIRED
Using a double-boiler (page 276)
Whisking eggs whites until they form peaks (page 281)

WHY USE A DOUBLE-BOILER?

Depending on the temperature, egg proteins may curdle. A temperature of 40°C (104°F) limits the risk of the protein curdling. The double-boiler ensures constant temperature.

TIP
Whisking the egg whites in a double-boiler at 40°C (104°F) allows the proteins in the egg to develop more fully, so that more air can be incorporated, and forms smaller bubbles. This is why Swiss meringue is denser and more compact than other meringues.

FOR 300 G (10 ½ OZ) MERINGUE
100 g (3 ½ oz) egg whites (3 to 4 whites)
100 g (3 ½ oz) white caster sugar
100 g (3 ½ oz) icing (confectioner's) sugar

1   Prepare a double-boiler (page 276). Put the egg whites and caster sugar in the boiler bowl and, whisking gently, heat up to about 40°C (104°F).

2   Transfer to the bowl of a stand mixer and whisk at full power until the mixture is cool.

3   Sieve the icing sugar, add it into the bowl, mix on low power to begin, then finish mixing with the spatula.

FRENCH MERINGUE

Understand

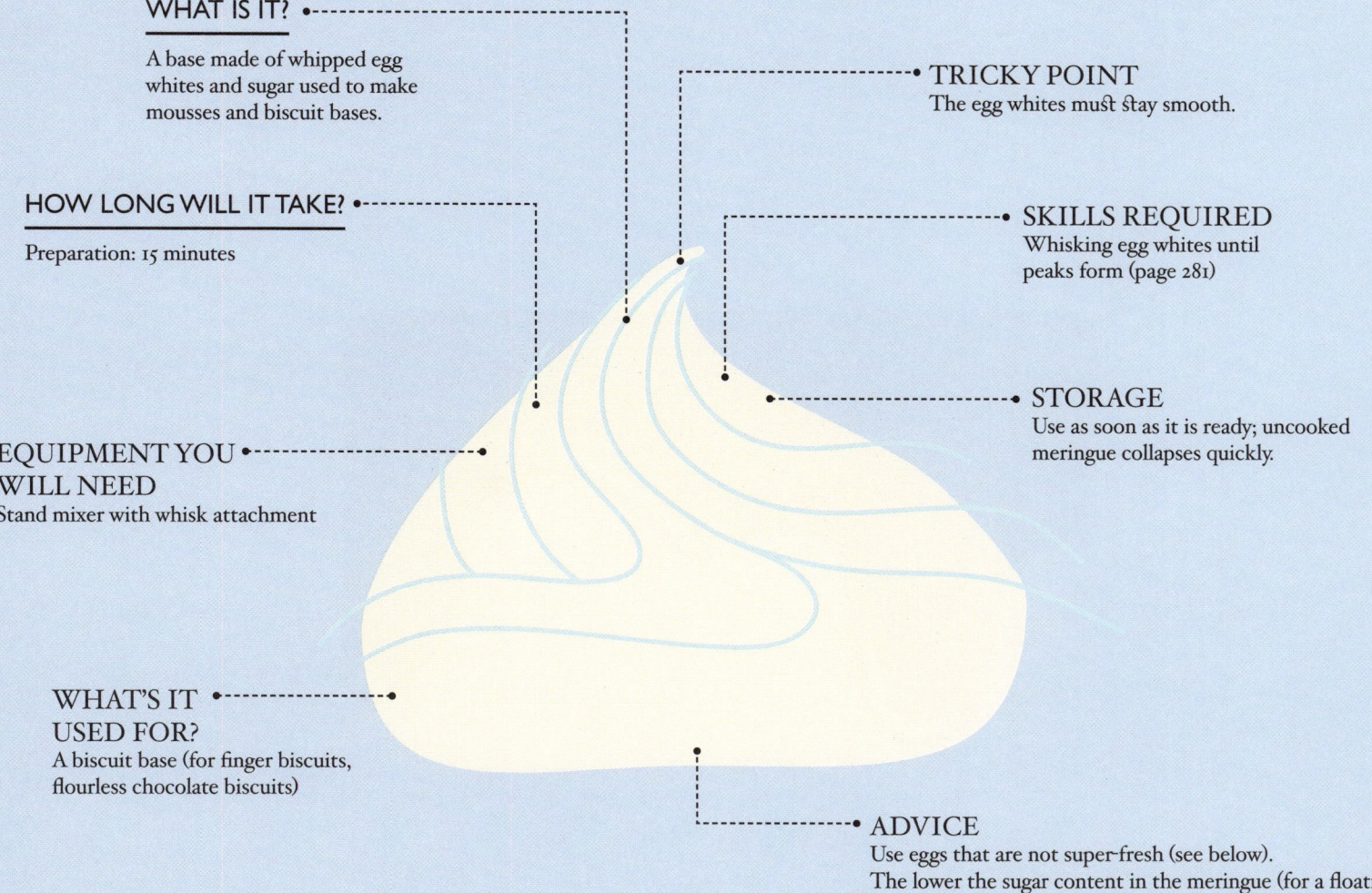

WHAT IS IT?
A base made of whipped egg whites and sugar used to make mousses and biscuit bases.

HOW LONG WILL IT TAKE?
Preparation: 15 minutes

EQUIPMENT YOU WILL NEED
Stand mixer with whisk attachment

WHAT'S IT USED FOR?
A biscuit base (for finger biscuits, flourless chocolate biscuits)

TRICKY POINT
The egg whites must stay smooth.

SKILLS REQUIRED
Whisking egg whites until peaks form (page 281)

STORAGE
Use as soon as it is ready; uncooked meringue collapses quickly.

ADVICE
Use eggs that are not super-fresh (see below). The lower the sugar content in the meringue (for a floating island dessert, for example), the more unstable it will be.

WHY USE EGGS THAT ARE NOT SUPER-FRESH?

As eggs age, their pH value changes slightly, resulting in a change in protein structure, which makes the incorporated air more stable.

FOR 275 G (10 OZ) MERINGUE

150 g (5 oz) egg whites (5 whites)
125 g (4 oz) white caster (superfine) sugar

1 Put the egg whites in the bowl of the stand mixer fitted with the whisk. Begin with mixer at a quarter of its power: the mixture should become frothy as you mix. Add a quarter of the sugar.

2 Increase the mixer speed, continue mixing and when you see ripples forming on the surface of the whites, add another quarter of the sugar.

3 Increase the mixer speed again. When the whites start to thicken around the whisk, add the remaining half of the sugar and set the mixer to maximum power for about 2 minutes. Peaks should form when the whisk is removed from the mix.

GLOSSY DARK
GLAZE

Understand

WHAT IS IT?
A thin, glossy cocoa glaze used to coat cakes and to glaze desserts.

HOW LONG WILL IT TAKE?
Preparation: 15 minutes
Standing: 1 ½ to 2 hours for use (at around 40°C (104°F); see below

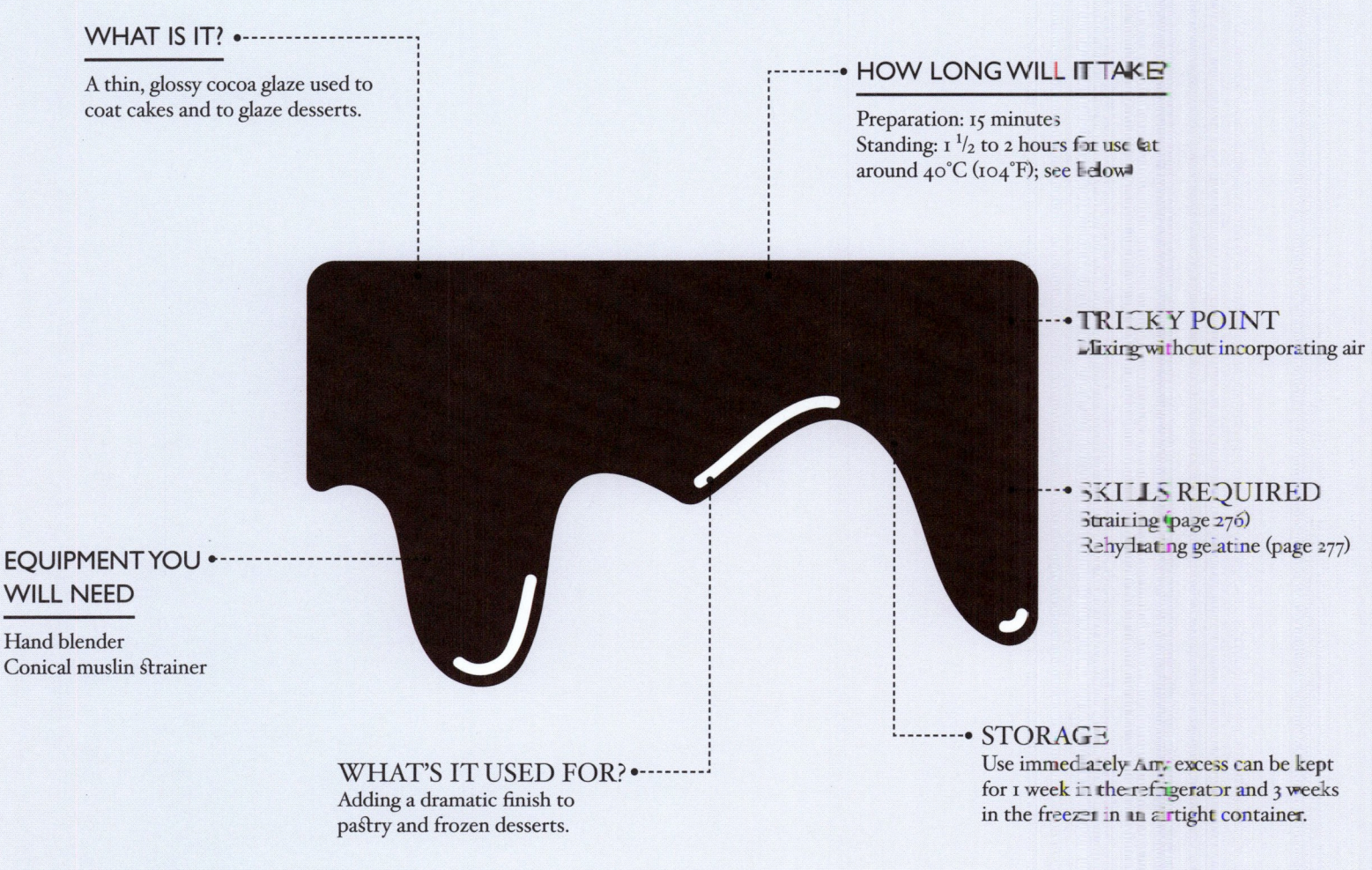

TRICKY POINT
Mixing without incorporating air

SKILLS REQUIRED
Straining (page 276)
Rehydrating gelatine (page 277)

EQUIPMENT YOU WILL NEED
Hand blender
Conical muslin strainer

WHAT'S IT USED FOR?
Adding a dramatic finish to pastry and frozen desserts.

STORAGE
Use immediately. Any excess can be kept for 1 week in the refrigerator and 3 weeks in the freezer in an airtight container.

ADVICE
Glaze should be used at around 40°C (104°F). The cake you are coating must be completely frozen for the glaze to adhere well to the surface. Always have more glaze to hand than required.
If the glaze is too hot when poured out, the layer will be too thin. If this happens, put the pastry back in the freezer for 15 minutes and pour the glaze from the baking tray back into the remaining glaze. Take the pastry from the freezer once again and re-glaze. Immediately check how well the glaze is running to avoid unwanted streaks; the glaze on a frozen product sets very quickly.

TIP
Allowing as little air as possible to get in while mixing: put the blender head into the glaze without turning it on, move it around gently to let any air bubbles escape, then turn on the blender without moving it for about 30 seconds to 1 minute.

Learn

TO MAKE 750 G (1LB 9 OZ) GLAZE

180 g (6 ½ oz) water
150 g (5 oz) whipping cream
330 g (11 oz) white caster (superfine) sugar
14 g (7 sheets) gelatine
120 g (4 oz) cocoa (unsweetened chocolate) powder

1 Rehydrate the gelatine (page 277) in cold water. Bring the water, cream and sugar to the boil in a saucepan.

2 Remove the pan from the heat and add the gelatine and cocoa powder. Whisk thoroughly. Pour into a measuring glass, mix well, then pour through the strainer into a bowl. Cover with cling film (plastic wrap), then cool at room temperature down to 40°C (104°F) before using.

ROCK
GLAZE

Understand

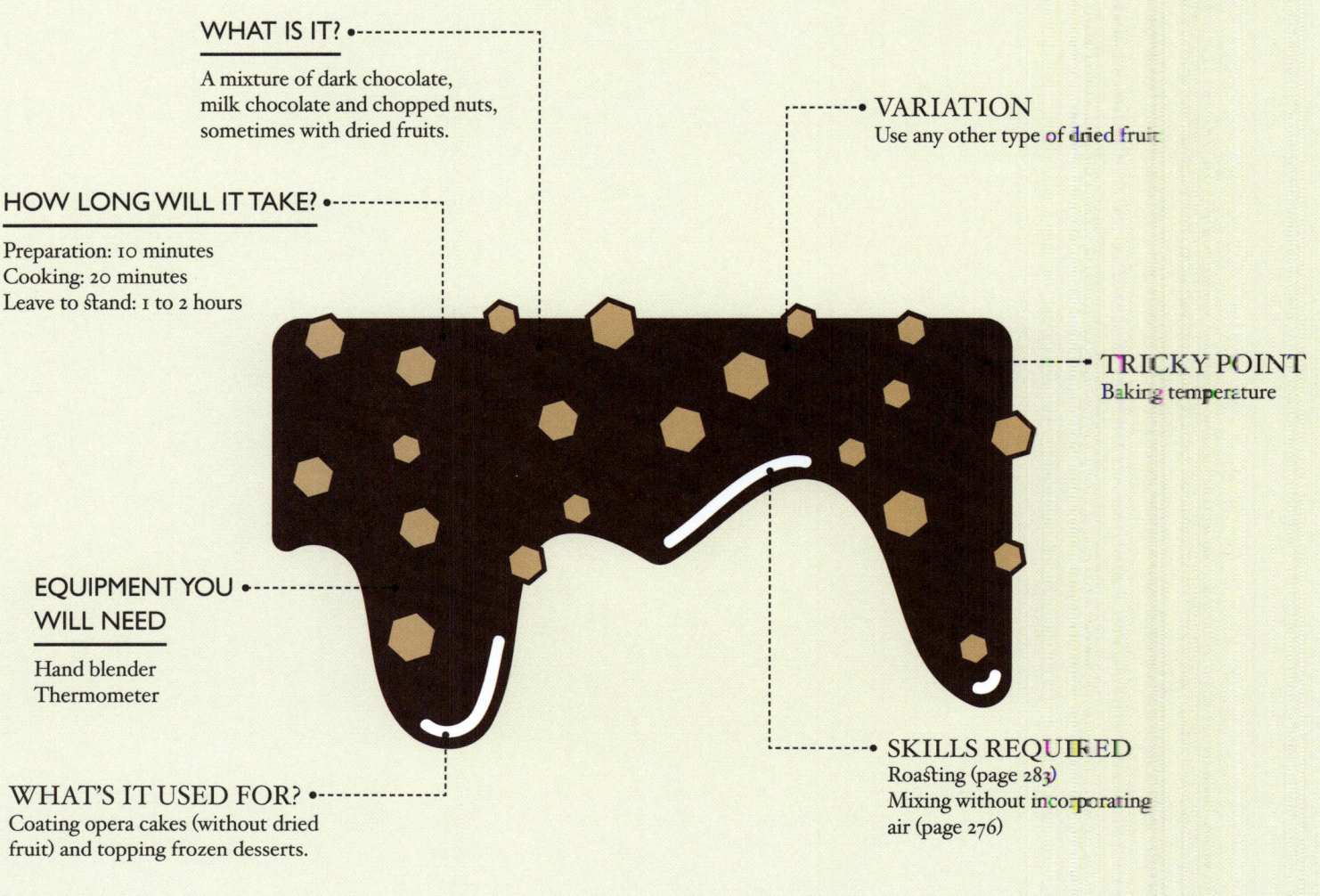

WHAT IS IT?
A mixture of dark chocolate, milk chocolate and chopped nuts, sometimes with dried fruits.

HOW LONG WILL IT TAKE?
Preparation: 10 minutes
Cooking: 20 minutes
Leave to stand: 1 to 2 hours

EQUIPMENT YOU WILL NEED
Hand blender
Thermometer

WHAT'S IT USED FOR?
Coating opera cakes (without dried fruit) and topping frozen desserts.

VARIATION
Use any other type of dried fruit

TRICKY POINT
Baking temperature

SKILLS REQUIRED
Roasting (page 283)
Mixing without incorporating air (page 276)

TIP
When pouring out the rock glaze, use a spatula to remove the excess from the rack.

ADVICE
Store remaining glaze in a container at room temperature for up to 1 month. To use, melt gently in a double-boiler.

72

Learn

TO MAKE 300 G (10 ½ OZ) GLAZE

130 g (4 oz) milk chocolate
150 g (5 oz) dark chocolate (66% cocoa)
25 g (1 oz) grapeseed oil
80 g (3 oz) chopped almonds

1 Roast the chopped almonds for 20 minutes in a 160°C (320°F/gas 4) oven (page 283). Melt the 2 chocolates together in a double-boiler.

2 Remove the bowl from the double-boiler, pour in the oil and mix gently using a spatula, without incorporating any air. Let the temperature drop to around 40°C (104°F). Add the chopped almonds, mix well and use immediately.

MILK CHOCOLATE
GLAZE

Understand

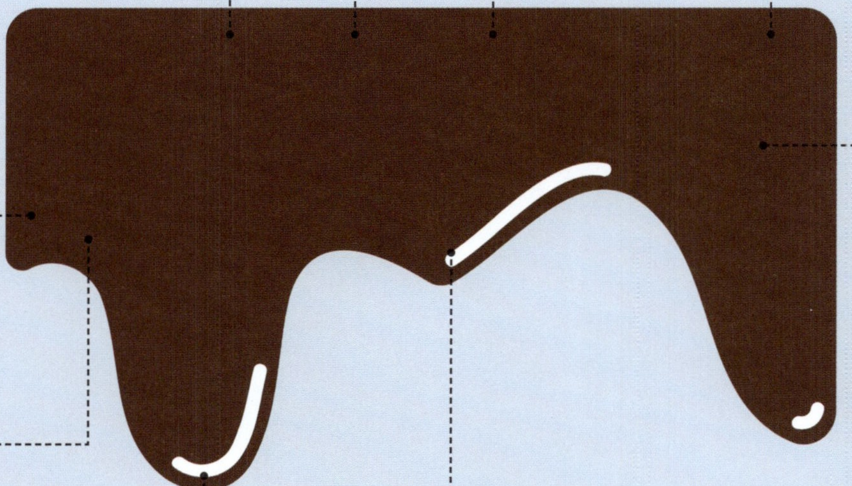

WHAT IS IT?
A versatile chocolate glaze topping.

SKILL REQUIRED
Using a double-boiler (page 276)

**HOW LONG
WILL IT TAKE?**
Preparation: 15 minutes

STORAGE
Store in an airtight
container for up to
1 week in the refrigerator,
1 month in the freezer.

ADVICE
The glaze should be used at around
40°C (104°F). The cake you are coating
must be completely frozen for the glaze
to adhere well to the surface. Always
have more glaze to hand than required.
If the glaze is too hot when it is poured,
the coating will be too thin. If this
happens, put the cake back in the
freezer for 15 minutes, remove the hot
glaze from the baking tray and mix it
with the remaining glaze. Take the cake
out of the freezer and glaze again.

**EQUIPMENT YOU
WILL NEED**
Hand blender
Conical strainer

WHAT'S IT USED FOR?
A finish for log cakes,
tarts and desserts.

TIP
To mix without adding air: put the blender into
the glaze without turning it on, stir gently to allow
the air bubbles to escape, then turn on the blender
without moving it for about 30 seconds to 1 minute.

TRICKY POINTS
Mixing without incorporating air

HOW DOES THE GLAZE
STICK TO THE CAKE?

*On contact with a frozen cake, the cocoa
butter crystallises. The glaze becomes
stickier, adheres to the cake, and then
hardens as it cools.*

TO MAKE 550 G (1 LB 3 OZ) GLAZE

250 g (9 oz) milk chocolate
90 g (3 1/4 oz) dark chocolate
225 g whipping cream
40 g (1 1/2 oz) inverted sugar or neutral honey

1   Melt the two chocolates together
in a double-boiler (page 276).

2   Heat the cream and inverted sugar
or honey together until they begin to
boil, then mix using a whisk.

3   Pour the cream and sugar mixture over the
melted chocolate, away from the double-boiler, and
whisk well. Leave to cool for 1 1/2 to 2 hours and
use when it is between 35° (95°F) and 40°C (104°F).

WHITE CHOCOLATE GLAZE

Understand

WHAT IS IT?
A dramatic glaze made from white chocolate.

WHAT'S IT USED FOR?
Coating log cakes, tarts and desserts.

HOW LONG WILL IT TAKE?
Preparation: 15 minutes
Standing: 2 hours

SKILLS REQUIRED
Using a double-boiler (page 276)
Rehydrating gelatine (page 276)
Straining (page 276)

EQUIPMENT YOU WILL NEED
Hand blender
Thermometer

STORAGE
Store in an airtight container for up to 1 week in the refrigerator, 3 weeks in the freezer.

VARIATIONS
Add the seeds from one vanilla pod (bean) to the milk.
Colour the glaze with a food colouring of your choice.

ADVICE
Glaze should be used at around 40°C (104°F). The cake you are coating must be completely frozen for the glaze to adhere well to the surface. Always have more glaze to hand than required. If the glaze is too hot when it is poured, the coating will be too thin. If this happens, put the cake back into the freezer for 15 minutes, remove the glaze from the baking tray and mix with the remaining glaze. Take the cake out of the freezer and glaze again.

TO MAKE 500 G (1 LB 2 OZ) GLAZE

120 g (4 oz) milk
30 g (1 oz) water
50 g (2 oz) glucose syrup
6 g (3 sheets) gelatine
300 g (10 ½ oz) white chocolate

1 Rehydrate the gelatine in cold water (page 277). Melt the white chocolate in a double-boiler (page 276).

2 Heat the milk, water and glucose syrup in a pan and bring to the boil. When it boils, take off the heat. Drain the gelatine, add it to the mixture and whisk.

3 Pour this mixture onto the white chocolate and whisk. Remove the bowl from the double-boiler, then blend gently, taking care to add as little air as possible. Leave to stand for a few minutes, then blend again for another 2-3 minutes. Strain (page 276) then cover with film (plastic wrap). Allow to cool to room temperature (for use at around 40°C (104°F).

CHAPTER 2
CHOCOLATE DESSERTS AND PASTRIES

CHOCOLATES

SINGLE ORIGIN CHOCOLATE GANACHE
DIPPED CHOCOLATES 78
FLAVOURED CHOCOLATES DIPPED IN
DARK GANACHE VANILLA 82
MILK CHOCOLATE & CARAMEL
MOULDED CHOCOLATES 84
GANACHE DIPPED CHOCOLATES
HONEY 86
DIPPED CHOCOLATES VERBENA 88
MINT CHOCOLATE
MOULDED CHOCOLATES 90
RASPBERRY GANACHE
DIPPED CHOCOLATES 92
GRAND MARNIER
MOULDED CHOCOLATES 94
HAZELNUT AND SESAME
DIPPED CHOCOLATES 96
PRALINE FEUILLETINE
DIPPED CHOCOLATES 100
GIANDUJA MOULDED
CHOCOLATES 102
PRALINE ROCK CHOCOLATES 104
VANILLA AND COCONUT
ROCK CHOCOLATES 106
CARAMEL AND
CHOCOLATE FUDGE 108

MOULDED CHOCOLATES

CHOCOLATE EGG 110
CHOCOLATE HEN 114
CHOCOLATE BOX 118
CHOCOLATE FISH 122

BARS, SLABS AND SPECIAL CHOCOLATES

CHOCOLATE SLABS 124
MENDIANTS 126
ORANGETTES 128
MILLIONNAIRE'S SHORTBREAD 130
TRUFFLES 132
CHOCOLATE BARS 134

DESSERTS

MACARON DESSERT 138
SUCCESS CAKE 142
CHOCOLATE MACARONS 146
CHOCOLATE MOUSSE AND
MERINGUE CAKE 150
MARVELLOUS MERINGUES 154
RASPBERRY AND CHOCOLATE
FEUILLANTINE 156
GIANDUJA DESSERT 160
OPERA CAKE 164
PEAR AND CHOCOLATE
CHARLOTTE CAKE 168
PINEAPPLE CHOCOLATE AND
KAFFIR LIME DESSERT 172
COCONUT AND
CHOCOLATE DESSERT 176
BLACK FOREST GATEAU 180

CHOCOLATE LOGS

INTENSE CHOCOLATE LOG 184
PASSION FRUIT
MILK CHOCOLATE LOG 188

CHOUX PASTRIES

ÉCLAIRS 192
BLOND CHOCOLATE AND
CREAMY CHOCOLATE CHOUX 194
PARIS-BREST CAKE 198

TARTS

CHOCOLATE TART 202
MILK CHOCOLATE TART 206
SOUFFLÉ TARTLETS 210
CARAMEL TART 214
MILK CHOCOLATE PECAN PIE 218

CLASSICS

PAIN AU CHOCOLAT 222
BRIOCHE 226
BABA CAKES 230
GALETTE DES ROIS 234
MILLEFEUILLES 238

CAKES, COOKIES AND BISCUITS

MOELLEUX 242
CHOCOLATE CHIP COOKIES 244
BROWNIES 246
CHOCOLATE TRUFFLE CAKE 248
ROCK CAKE 250
MARBLE CAKE 254
TIGER CAKES 256
MADELEINES 258

MOUSSES AND ICE CREAM

CHOCOLATE MOUSSE 260
MARQUISE 262
ICE CREAM 264

SINGLE ORIGIN CHOCOLATE GANACHE DIPPED
CHOCOLATES

Understand

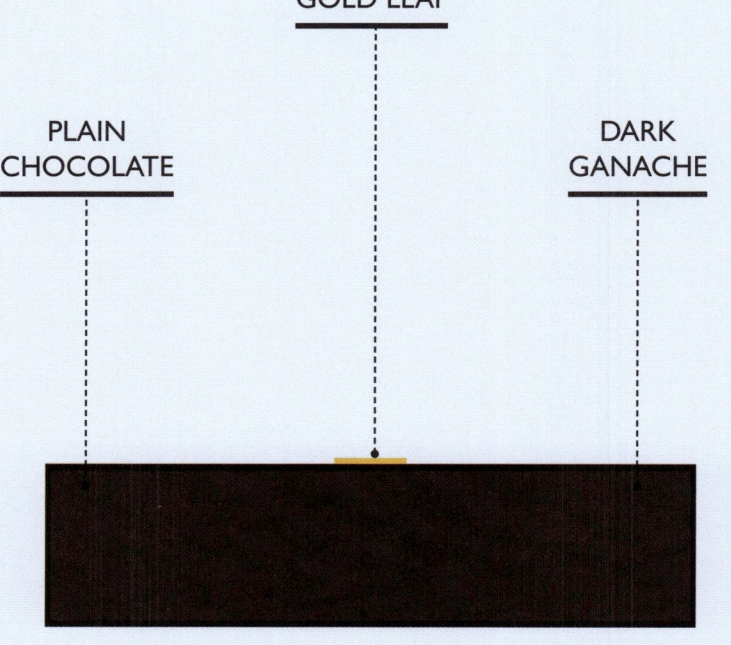

GOLD LEAF

PLAIN
CHOCOLATE

DARK
GANACHE

WHAT IS IT?

Dark chocolate ganache dipped in dark couverture chocolate.

HOW LONG WILL IT TAKE?

Preparation: 2 hours
Standing: 12 hours (ganache)
Setting: 48 hours

EQUIPMENT REQUIRED

Thermometer
Polyethylene sheet
Chocolate fork

VARIATION
Vary the origins of the chocolate, keeping the same percentage of cocoa.

TRICKY POINTS
Tempering the couverture chocolate
Coating the chocolates

SKILLS REQUIRED
Tempering chocolate (page 24)
Coating with a thin layer of chocolate (chabloning; page 273)
Coating with a dipping fork (page 32)
Decorating (page 36)

ADVICE
When the chocolates have been dipped, pour the remaining melted chocolate onto a baking sheet, leave to harden and keep in a dry place. Do not temper it again as it will lose its fluidity. Put butter in the boiling liquid to ensure pasteurisation. This will allow the ganache to be kept for longer. Chablon the top and bottom of the ganache to make it easier to handle when coating. If the ganache separates cut into solids and fat, add more milk.

PLANNING AND PREP
The day before
Ganache
On the day
Dipping

Learn

MAKES ABOUT 35 CHOCOLATES

FOR 350 G (12 OZ) GANACHE

190 g (6 ¹/₂ oz) dark couverture chocolate (70% cocoa)
180 g (6 ¹/₄ oz) whipping cream
15 g (¹/₂ oz) glucose syrup
10 g (¹/₂ oz) inverted sugar or neutral honey
15 g (¹/₂ oz) unsalted butter

COATING

800 g (1lb 12 oz) dark couverture chocolate (70% cocoa)
2 gold leaf fragments

Making chocolate sweets dipped in single origin ganache

1   Make a dark chocolate ganache: melt the chocolate in a double-boiler (page 276). Meanwhile, put the cream, glucose, inverted sugar/honey and butter in a saucepan and bring to the boil.

2   Strain half of the cream mixture into the chocolate using a conical strainer and mix with a whisk to start the emulsion.

3   Strain the rest of the mixture into the chocolate and finish the emulsion by stirring for about 1 minute without incorporating air. Cover with cling film (plastic wrap) and allow to cool at room temperature.

4   Cut a polyethylene sheet into 35 squares measuring 4 x 4 cm (1 $^1/_2$ x 1 $^1/_2$ in). Place them on another polyethylene sheet. When the ganache reaches 35°C (95°F), put it in a piping bag and pipe out 2 cm ($^3/_4$ in) diameter domes onto the squares.

5   Place a second polyethylene sheet on top then use a flat tray to press lightly, to give the sweets their final shape. Leave to set at a 15° to 17°C (59° to 63°F) for 12 hours.

6   Temper the coating chocolate (page 24). Coat (chablon) the tops and bottoms with a fine layer of chocolate (page 273).

7   Coat each one by dipping into the melted chocolate using a dipping fork (page 32). Scrape the fork over the rim to remove excess chocolate. Decorate with a gold leaf fragment (page 283) and immediately place a square of polyethylene sheet on top. Allow to set at room temperature, ideally between 15° and 17°C (59° to 63°F) for 48 hours.

80

FLAVOURED CHOCOLATES DIPPED IN DARK GANACHE
VANILLA

Understand

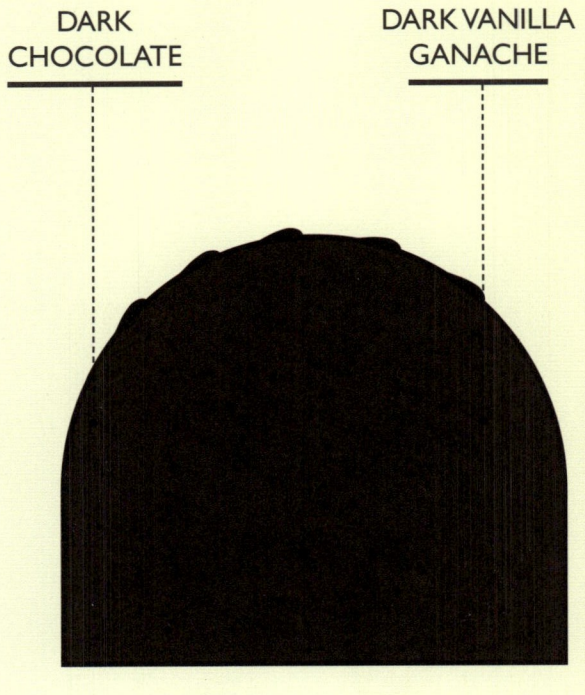

DARK
CHOCOLATE

DARK VANILLA
GANACHE

WHAT IS IT?

Dark vanilla flavoured ganache dipped
in dark couverture chocolate.

HOW LONG WILL IT TAKE?

Preparation: 2 hours
Standing: 12 hours (ganache), 48
hours (to set the sweets)

EQUIPMENT YOU WILL NEED

15 × 15 cm (6 × 6 in) baking frame
Thermometer
Polyethylene sheet
Dipping fork

VARIATION

Coffee ganache: instead of vanilla,
use 5 g ($^1/_4$ oz) instant coffee.

TRICKY POINTS

Tempering the couverture chocolate
Coating the chocolates

SKILLS REQUIRED

Tempering chocolate (page 24)
Coating with a thin layer of
chocolate (chabloning; page 273)
Coating with a dipping fork (page 32)
Decorating (page 36)
Coating with a thin layer of
chocolate (chabloning; page 273)

PLANNING AND PREP

The day before: Ganache
On the day: Coating

Learn

MAKES ABOUT 35 CHOCOLATES

VANILLA GANACHE

200 g dark couverture chocolate (66% cocoa)
180 g (6 ¼ oz) whipping cream
15 g (½ oz) butter
15 g (½ oz) glucose syrup
10 g (½ oz) inverted sugar or neutral honey
Vanilla pod (bean), split and scraped

COATING

800 g (1lb 12 oz) dark couverture chocolate (66% cocoa)

1 Make the vanilla ganache: melt the chocolate in a double-boiler (page 276). Meanwhile, put the cream, the split and scraped vanilla pod, the glucose, inverted sugar/honey and butter in a saucepan and bring to the boil.

2 Strain half of this mixture onto the chocolate and whisk to start the emulsion.

3 Strain the rest of the cream mixture into the chocolate mixture and finish the emulsion by mixing for about 1 minute without incorporating air (page 276).

4 When the ganache is at 35°C (95°F), put it in a piping bag and squeeze out lengths of chocolate. Leave to set at 15° to 17°C (59°F to 63°F) for 12 hours. For the coating, temper the rest of the couverture chocolate (page 24).

5 Cut the set ganache into 3 cm (1 ¼ in) lengths. Coat the undersides with a thin layer of chocolate (chablon) (page 273).

6 Coat each chocolate using the dipping fork (page 32). Scrape the fork over the rim to remove the excess chocolate. Allow to set at room temperature, ideally between 15° and 17°C (59°F to 63°F) for 48 hours.

MILK CHOCOLATE & CARAMEL MOULDED CHOCOLATES
CARAMEL

Understand

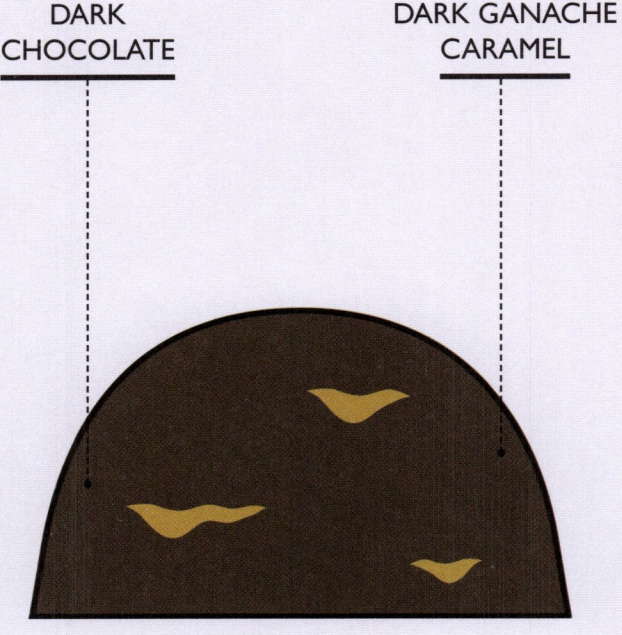

DARK
CHOCOLATE

DARK GANACHE
CARAMEL

WHAT IS IT?

Moulded dark chocolates filled with
caramel and milk chocolate ganache.

HOW LONG WILL IT TAKE?

Preparation: 2 hours
Standing: 12 hours after moulding the ganache,
then 36 hours when the chocolates are sealed.

EQUIPMENT YOU WILL NEED

Polycarbonate mould
Thermometrer
Polyethylene sheet

VARIATION

Instead of cream use passion
fruit or strawberry purée.

TRICKY POINT

Tempering the chocolate

SKILL REQUIRED

Making moulded chocolates (page 34)

ADVICE

Make the caramel in a large
saucepan to prevent burning when
adding the butter and cream.

TIP

When mixing, take care to add as little air
as possible: keep the blender blade on the
bottom of the bowl, stirring gently in order
to let the air escape, then mix for about
1 minute without lifting the blender

PLANNING AND PREP

The day before:
Moulding – ganache
On the day:
Sealing the sweets
Following day:
Unmoulding

Learn

MAKES ABOUT 35 CHOCOLATES

GANACHE

140 g (4 ½ oz) dark couverture chocolate (66% cocoa)
170 g (6 oz) couverture milk chocolate
200 g whipping cream
100 g (3 ½ oz) white caster (superfine) sugar
20 g unsalted butter
2 g (½ teaspoon) sea salt flakes

COATING

600 g (1 lb 5 oz) dark couverture (66% cocoa)

1 Temper 2/3 of the dark couverture and coat the bottoms of the moulds with it (page 24).

2 Make the ganache: boil the cream, set aside. To make a dry caramel: heat the sugar in a saucepan at a medium-high heat. When the sugar begins to dissolve into caramel, mix with a whisk. When the caramel turns a dark colour, take the pan off the heat and pour in a little cream. Once the cream is completely incorporated, add the butter, then add a little more cream. Add the cream in small quantities until it is completely blended in. Add the sea salt flakes, then cook for about 30 seconds, stirring all the time.

3 When the mixture boils, pour it into the chocolate, then blend, taking care not to incorporate air. Cover with cling film (plastic wrap).

4 When the ganache is at 27°C (80.6°F), pipe it out into the chocolate moulds using a piping bag. Leave to set at 15° to 17°C (59°F to 62°F) for 12 hours.

5 Temper the remaining dark couverture (page 24). Seal the chocolates (page 34). Allow to set at room temperature, ideally between 15° and 17°C (59°F to 62°F) for 48 hours.

GANACHE DIPPED CHOCOLATES
HONEY

Understand

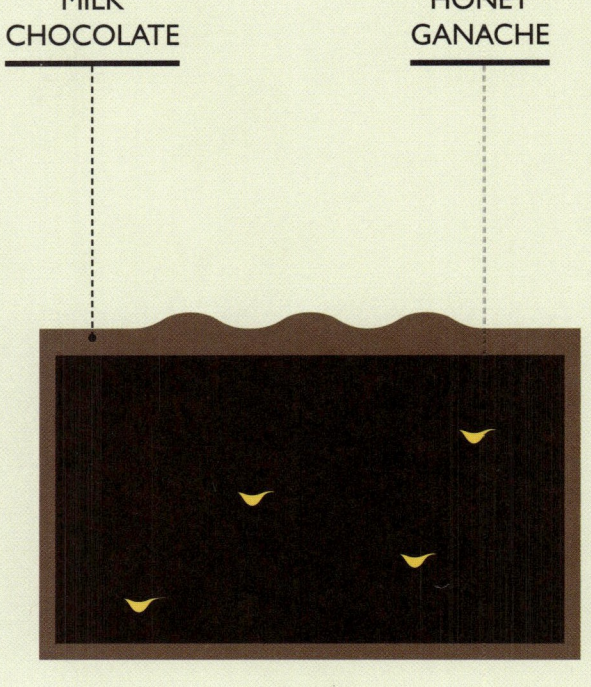

MILK
CHOCOLATE

HONEY
GANACHE

WHAT IS IT?

Chestnut honey ganache dipped in milk couverture chocolate.

HOW LONG WILL IT TAKE?

Preparation: 2 hours
Standing: 12 hours (ganache)
Setting: 48 hours

EQUIPMENT YOU WILL NEED

15 × 15 cm (6 × 6 in) baking frame
Thermometer
Polyethylene sheet
Dipping fork

VARIATION

Instead of chestnut honey, use mountain or lavender honey.

TRICKY POINTS

Tempering the couverture
Chocolate coating

SKILLS REQUIRED

Tempering chocolate (page 24)
Coating with a thin layer of chocolate (chabloning; page 273)
Tempering chocolate (page 24)
Coating chocolates using a dipping fork (page 32)
Decorating chocolates (page 36)

PLANNING AND PREP

The day before:
Ganache
On the day:
Dipping

Learn

MAKES ABOUT 35 CHOCOLATES

HONEY GANACHE

200 g (7 oz) couverture milk chocolate
200 g (7 oz) whipping cream
75 g (2 ½ oz) cocoa butter
75 g (2 ½ oz) chestnut honey

COATING

800 g (1lb 12 oz) milk couverture chocolate

1 Prepare 200 g (7 oz) chocolate coating and the baking frame (page 32). Make the honey ganache: melt the chocolate in a double-boiler (page 276). Bring the cream and cocoa butter to the boil and set aside.

2 Meanwhile, heat the honey to 130°C (266°F).

3 Remove from the heat and gradually mix in the cream/cocoa butter mixture.

4 Strain half of this mixture onto the chocolate and mix with a whisk to start the emulsion. Strain the rest onto the chocolate and finish the emulsion by mixing for about 1 minute without incorporating air (page 276).

5 When the ganache is at 32°C (89.6°F), pour it into the baking frame, smooth the top, then let it set (page 25) for 10 to 12 hours at 15° to 17°C (59°F to 62°F).

6 Temper the rest of the coating couverture. Remove the ganache from the frame by running the blade of a chef's knife along the edges. Coat the upper surface of the ganache with a thin layer of chocolate (see page 273). Before the thin layer cools completely, cut out 1 ½ × 3 cm (½ in × 1 ¼ in) chocolates.

7 Coat each one by dipping it into the tempered chocolate using a dipping fork (page 32). Scrape the fork on the rim to remove excess chocolate then decorate (page 36). Leave to set at room temperature, ideally between 15° and 17°C (59°F to 62°F) for 48 hours.

DIPPED CHOCOLATES
VERBENA

Understand

DARK
CHOCOLATE

VERBENA
GANACHE

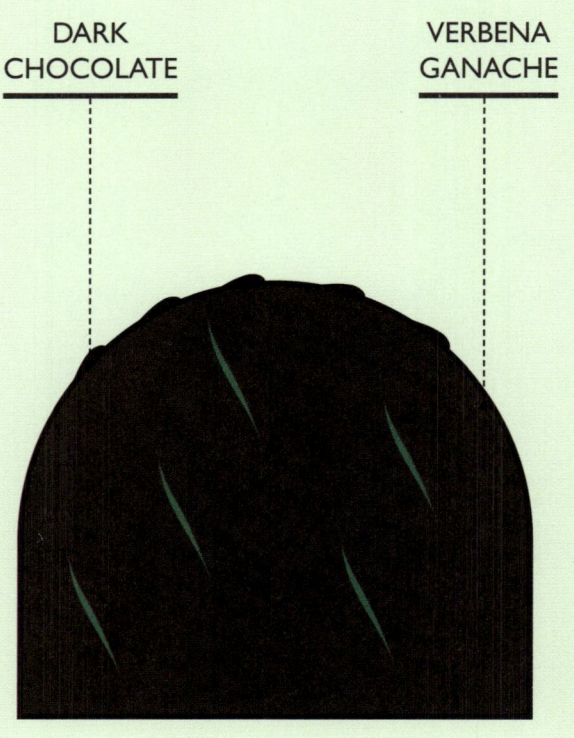

WHAT IS IT ?

Ganache flavoured with verbena, made with eggs and coated with dark chocolate.

HOW LONG WILL IT TAKE?

Preparation: 2 hours
Standing: 12 hours (ganache)
Setting: 48 hours

EQUIPMENT YOU WILL NEED

15 × 15 cm (6 × 6 in) baking frame
Thermometer
Polyethylene sheet
Dipping fork

VARIATION

Instead of verbena use the same amount of mint or a sprig of rosemary.

TRICKY POINTS

Tempering the couverture chocolate
Coating the chocolates

SKILLS REQUIRED

Coating with a fine layer of chocolate (chabloning; page 273)
Tempering chocolate (page 24)
Dipping chocolates (page 32)
Decorating chocolates (page 36)

ADVICE

For the best herbal flavour, let the verbena soak in the cream overnight in the refrigerator.

PLANNING, PREP AND STORAGE

The day before:
Ganache
On the day:
Dipping
Following day:
Ready to serve
Keep for:
1 week maximum

Learn

MAKES ABOUT 35 CHOCOLATES

VERBENA GANACHE

140 g (4 ½ oz) whipping cream
½ bunch of verbena
25 g (1 oz) inverted sugar or neutral honey
25 g (1 oz) egg yolks (2 yolks)
200 g (7 oz) dark couverture chocolate (66% cocoa)

COATING

800 g (1lb 12 oz) dark couverture chocolate (66% cocoa)

1 To make the verbena ganache: heat 140 g (4 ½ oz) cream with the verbena in a saucepan, bring to the boil then take off the heat, cover with cling film (plastic wrap) and leave to infuse for 30 minutes.

2 Strain the mixture into another saucepan and top up with cream to 140 g (4 ½ oz). Add the inverted sugar/honey and egg yolks and mix. Heat the mixture to 85°C (185°F), stirring with a whisk. Add the chocolate, mix then blend without incorporating air. Cover with cling film (plastic wrap) and set aside.

3 Cover a baking tray with a polyethylene sheet. When the ganache is at 27°C (80.6°F), put it in a piping bag and pipe out 1 ½ cm (½ in) diameter rolls the entire length of the tray. Leave to set for 10 to 12 hours at 15° to 17°C (59°F to 62°F).

4 Cut the rolls into short 2 ½ cm (1 in) lengths. Temper the remaining coating chocolate (page 24).

5 Coat the underside of the ganache with a fine layer of chocolate (page 273).

6 Dip each chocolate (page 32) into the coating chocolate, scrape the fork on the rim to remove excess and decorate using a cone (page 36). Allow to set at room temperature, ideally between 15° and 17°C (59°F to 62°F) for 48 hours.

CHOCOLATE MOULDED CHOCOLATES
MINT

Understand

COLOUR
DECORATION

WHITE
CHOCOLATE

MILK AND MINT
CHOCOLATE
GANACHE

WHAT IS IT?

Moulded chocolates made of white chocolate with a green decoration and filled with mint-flavoured milk chocolate ganache.

HOW LONG WILL IT TAKE?

Preparation: 2 hours
Standing: 12 hours after moulding the ganache, then 48 hours after sealing.

EQUIPMENT YOU WILL NEED

Polycarbonate mould
Thermometer
Polyethylene sheet

VARIATION
Instead of mint, use another flavouring.

TRICKY POINT
Tempering the chocolate

SKILLS REQUIRED
Tempering chocolate (page 24)
Making moulded chocolates (page 34)

CONSERVATION
Keep for up to 1 week

ADVICE
Leave the mint to soak in the cream overnight in the refrigerator.
It is important to use a fat-soluble colouring agent. Mix it in two stages, waiting 5 minutes between each addition to ensure even colouring.

TIP
Straining the cream results in a slight loss of quantity. Weigh the strained cream and top up if necessary

PLANNING AND PREP
The day before:
Moulding – ganache
On the day:
Sealing the chocolates
After 2 days:
Unmoulding

Learn

MAKES ABOUT 50 CHOCOLATES

115 g (4 oz) whipping cream
¼ bunch of mint
170 g (6 oz) couverture milk chocolate
25 g (1 oz) unsalted butter

COLOUR DECORATION

1 g cocoa butter
70 g (2 ½ oz) white couverture chocolate
1 drop of fat-soluble green colouring

COATING

600 g (1 1lb 5 oz) white couverture chocolate

1 Make the decoration mixture: melt the cocoa butter and white couverture chocolate in a double-boiler at 40°C (104°F). Add the colouring and mix in two stages waiting 5 minutes between each, then temper (page 24).

2 Using a dry brush, paint the bottom of the imprints of the mould with a broad stroke of green couverture chocolate. Temper two-thirds of the coating white chocolate and put it into the mould (page 36).

3 Make the mint ganache: heat the cream and mint in a saucepan and, when it boils, take off the heat, cover and leave to infuse for 30 minutes. Strain into another saucepan. Top up the cream to 115 g (4 oz), boil briefly, then pour over the milk couverture, blend, and cover with cling film (plastic wrap).

4 When the ganache is at 35°C (95°F), add the softened butter, mix. When at 32°C (89.6°F), pipe out into the moulds. Leave to set (page 25) for 10 to 12 hours.

5 Temper the remaining white coating couverture (page 24). Seal the chocolates (page 34) and leave to set (page 24) for 48 hours at room temperature, ideally between 15° and 17°C (59°F to 62°F).

GANACHE DIPPED CHOCOLATES
RASPBERRY

Understand

DARK
CHOCOLATE

GANACHE
RASPBERRY

WHAT IS IT?

Raspberry milk and dark couverture ganache
dipped in dark couverture chocolate.

HOW LONG WILL IT TAKE?

Preparation: 2 hours
Standing: 12 hours (ganache)
Setting: 48 hours

EQUIPMENT YOU WILL NEED

15 × 15 cm (6 × 6 in) baking frame
Thermometer
Polyethylene sheet
Dipping fork

VARIATION
Instead of raspberry, use passion fruit purée.

TRICKY POINTS
Tempering couverture chocolate
Coating the chocolates

SKILLS REQUIRED
Tempering chocolate (page 24)
Coating with a thin layer of
chocolate (chabloning; page 273)
Letting the chocolates set (page 24)
Coating with a dipping fork (page 32)
Decorating the chocolates (page 36)

ADVICE
To give a stronger raspberry taste, replace
the raspberry cream with raspberry brandy.
Decorate with dehydrated raspberry chips.

PLANNING AND PREP
The day before:
Ganache
On the day:
Dipping

Learn

MAKES ABOUT 35 CHOCOLATES

RASPBERRY GANACHE

150 g (5 oz) dark couverture (66% cocoa)
165 g (5 ½ oz) milk couverture
100 g (3 ½ oz) raspberry purée
20 g (¾ oz) white caster (superfine) sugar
2 g NH pectin (thermally reversible pectin, from specialist suppliers)
75 g (2 ½ oz) whipping cream
40 g (1 ½ oz) unsalted butter
10 g (½ oz) inverted sugar or neutral honey
20 g (¾ oz) raspberry cream

COATING

800 g (1lb 12 oz) dark couverture (66% cocoa)

1 To make the raspberry ganache: melt the two types of chocolate in a double-boiler (page 276). Boil the raspberry purée. Mix the sugar and pectin and add to the raspberry purée, then cook for 30 seconds and set aside.

2 Put the cream, butter and inverted sugar/honey in a saucepan and bring to the boil. Pour the hot mixture over the two types of chocolate, then add the sweet raspberry purée and the raspberry cream.

3 Mix with a whisk to start the emulsion. Mix for about 1 minute without incorporating air (page 276).

4 Place a polyethylene sheet on a baking tray. When the ganache is at 35°C (95°F), pipe out large drops (page 38) onto the polyethylene sheet. Leave to set for 10 to 12 hours at room temperature, ideally 15° to 17°C (59°F to 62°F).

5 Temper the coating couverture (page 24). Coat the underside of the ganache with a thin layer of chocolate (page 273). Coat by dipping each chocolate into the tempered chocolate with a fork (page 32). Scrape the fork over the rim to remove excess chocolate. Allow to set at room temperature, ideally between 15° and 17°C (59°F to 62°F) for 48 hours.

MOULDED CHOCOLATES
GRAND MARNIER

Understand

ORANGE PEEL
GANACHE

MILK CHOCOLATE,
ORANGE AND
LIQUEUR

MILK
CHOCOLATE

WHAT IS IT?

Milk chocolate moulded sweets filled
with Grand Marnier ganache.

HOW LONG WILL IT TAKE?

Preparation: 2 hours
Standing: 12 hours after moulding the ganache,
then 48 hours after sealing the chocolates.

EQUIPMENT YOU WILL NEED

Polycarbonate mould
Thermometer
Polyethylene sheet

VARIATION
Replace the Grand Marnier with another
spirit: whisky, rum or calvados.

TRICKY POINT
Tempering chocolate

SKILLS REQUIRED
Tempering chocolate (page 24)
Using a piping bag (page 278)
Making moulded chocolates (page 34)

TIP
When mixing, take care to incorporate as little
air as possible: push the stem of the mixer
down to the bottom of the bowl and stir gently
to allow air to escape from the blades. Mix
for about 1 minute without lifting the mixer.

PLANNING AND PREP
The day before:
Moulding – ganache
On the day:
Sealing
Two days later:
Unmoulding

Learn

MAKES ABOUT 35 CHOCOLATES

GANACHE

200 g (7 oz) milk couverture chocolate
100 g (3 ½ oz) whipping cream
30 g (1 oz) candied orange peel
35 g (1 oz) Grand Marnier

COATING

600 g (1 lb 5 oz) milk chocolate couverture

1 Temper two-thirds of the milk couverture chocolate and coat the moulds (page 24). Make the ganache: boil the cream and set aside.

2 Melt the chocolate in a double-boiler (page 276). Mix the chocolate with the cream and blend without incorporating air. Cover with cling film (plastic wrap). Finely chop the orange peel with a knife. When the cream-chocolate mixture is at 25°C (77°F), add the Grand Marnier.

3 Pipe out into the chocolate-coated moulds then scatter over the orange peel. Leave to set for 10 to 12 hours at room temperature, ideally at 15° to 17°C (59°F to 62°F). Temper the remaining milk couverture and seal the chocolates (page 34). Allow to set for 48 hours at room temperature, ideally 15° to 17°C (59°F to 62°F).

DIPPED CHOCOLATES
SESAME & HAZELNUT

Understand

MILK CHOCOLATE   SESAME SEEDS   HAZELNUT AND SESAME PRALINE

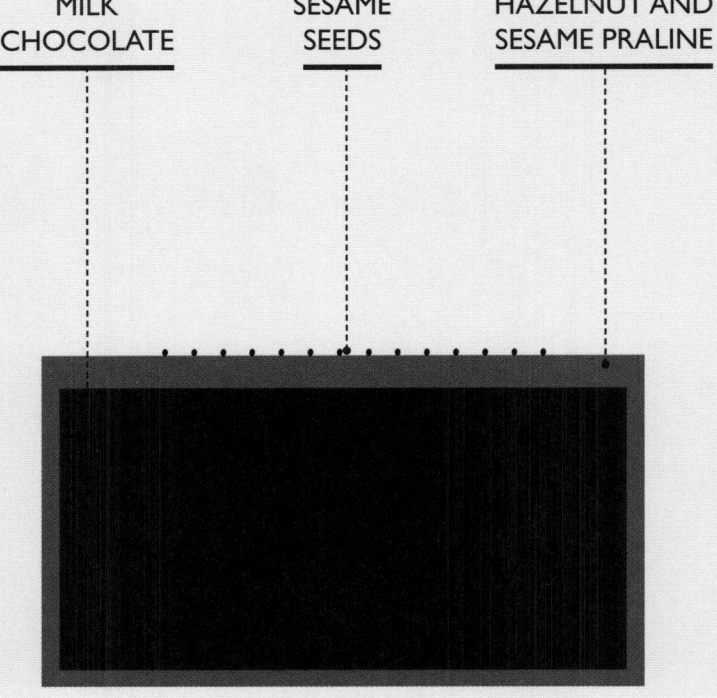

WHAT IS IT?

Hazelnut praline and sesame paste interior dipped in milk chocolate couverture.

HOW LONG WILL IT TAKE?

Preparation: 3 hours
Standing: 12 hours (hazelnut-sesame interior)
Setting: 48 hours

EQUIPMENT YOU WILL NEED

Blender
15 × 15 cm (6 × 6 in) baking frame
Thermometer
Polyethylene sheet
Dipping fork

TRICKY POINTS

Tempering the couverture chocolate
Coating the chocolates

SKILLS REQUIRED

Tempering chocolate (page 24)
Coating with a thin layer of chocolate (chabloning; page 273)
Letting chocolates set (page 24)
Coating with a dipping fork (page 32)
Decorating chocolates (page 36)

PLANNING AND PREP

2 days before:
Sesame paste – praline
The day before:
Hazelnut-sesame interior
On the day:
Dipping

Learn

MAKES ABOUT 35 CHOCOLATES

HAZELNUT PRALINE

100 g (3 ½ oz) shelled hazelnuts
100 g (3 ½ oz) white caster (superfine) sugar
35 g (1 oz) water

SESAME PASTE

200 g black sesame seeds

HAZELNUT – SESAME GIANDUJA

50 g (2 oz) couverture milk chocolate
150 g (5 oz) hazelnut praline
190 g (6 ½ oz) sesame paste
50 g (2 oz) cocoa butter

COATING

800 g (1lb 12 oz) milk couverture chocolate

Making the hazelnut-sesame dipped chocolates

1   Make the hazelnut praline (page 40).

2   Make the sesame paste: roast the sesame seeds in a pan over a low heat for 5 to 10 minutes, stirring regularly. Transfer to a baking tray and leave to cool. Process in a blender, scraping down the sides of the bowl 2 or 3 times using a spatula; a thin layer of oil will appear on the surface.

3   Temper 200 g (7 oz) of the coating chocolate and prepare the baking frame (page 24). To make the hazelnut-sesame gianduja: melt the chocolate in a double-boiler (page 276). Mix in the sesame paste and hazelnut praline, add the cocoa butter and the chocolate.

4   When the filling is at 30°C (86°F), pour it into the frame, smooth out and leave to set (page 25) for 10 to 12 hours at room temperature, ideally 15° to 17°C (59°F to 62°F).

5   Temper the rest of the coating chocolate. Remove the hazelnut-sesame gianduja from the frame by running the blade of a chef's knife along the edges. Coat the top with a fine layer of chocolate (page 273).

6   Before the fine chocolate topping layer has cooled completely, cut out individual chocolates measuring 2.5 × 2.5 cm (1 × 1 in).

7   Coat the chocolates using a dipping fork (page 32) and sprinkle immediately with sesame seeds (page 36). Allow to set at room temperature, ideally 15° to 17°C (59°F to 62°F) for 48 hours..

FEUILLETINE CHOCOLATES
PRALINE

Understand

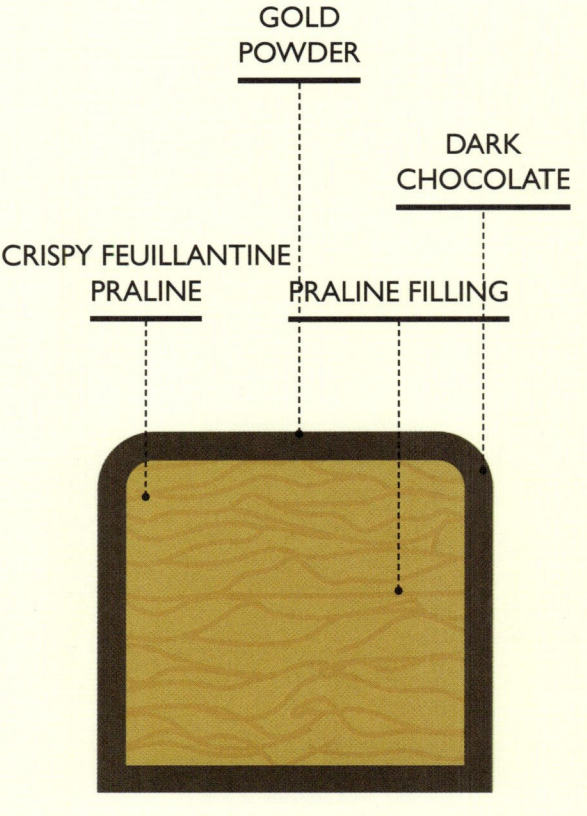

GOLD
POWDER

DARK
CHOCOLATE

CRISPY FEUILLANTINE
PRALINE

PRALINE FILLING

WHAT IS IT?

A crispy praline and feuilletine centre coated with dark chocolate.

HOW LONG WILL IT TAKE?

Preparation: 2 hours
Standing: 12 hours (ganache)
Setting: 48 hours

EQUIPMENT YOU WILL NEED

15 × 15 cm (6 × 6 in) baking frame
Stand mixer fitted with a flat beater
Thermometer
Polyethylene sheet
Chocolate fork

TRICKY POINTS

Tempering chocolate
Coating the chocolates

SKILLS REQUIRED

Coating with a thin layer of
chocolate (chabloning; page 273)
Tempering chocolate (page 24)
Dipping chocolates (page 32)

PLANNING AND PREP

Previous day:
Ganache
On the day:
Dipping
2 days later:
Ready to serve

MAKES ABOUT 35 CHOCOLATES

PRALINE

75 g (2 ¹/₂ oz) shelled almonds
75 g (2 ¹/₂ oz) shelled hazelnuts
150 g (5 oz) white caster (superfine) sugar
60 g (2 oz) water

CRISPY PRALINE FEUILLETINE

45 g (1 ³/₄ oz) dark couverture
chocolate (66% cocoa)
20 g (³/₄ oz) cocoa butter
250 g (9 oz) praline (from above)
125 g (4 oz) feuilletine flakes (crushed
crispy crêpes; from specialist suppliers)

Learn

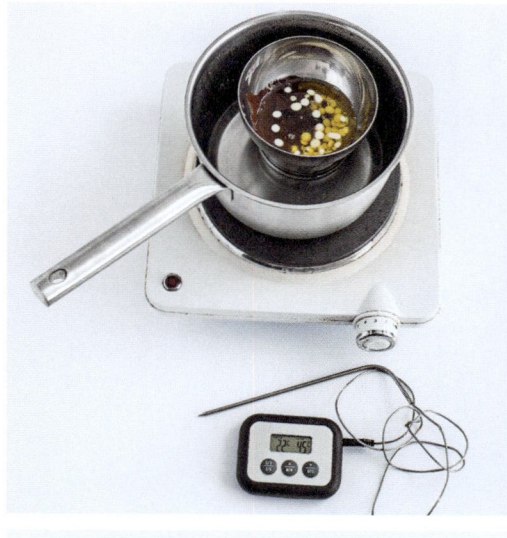  

COATING AND DECORATION

800 g (1lb 12 oz) dark couverture chocolate (66% cocoa)
10 g (½ oz) feuilletine
1 pinch of gold powder

1 Temper the coating chocolate and prepare the baking frame (page 24). Make the praline (page 40). To make the crispy praline feuilletine: melt the chocolate and cocoa butter in a double-boiler at 45°C (113°F) (page 276), then reduce the temperature to 29°C (84°F).

2 Put the praline in the bowl of the stand mixer and mix using the flat beater, pouring in the chocolate-cocoa butter preparation until well blended. The temperature should drop to around 24° to 25°C (75°F to 77°F).

3 Add the feuilletine and finish mixing gently using a spatula to prevent breaking the feuilletine as much as possible.

4 Pour the feuilletine into the baking frame 1 cm (½ in) deep, cover with the polyethylene sheet, then leave to set (page 25) for 10 to 12 hours at room temperature, ideally 15° to 17°C (59°F to 62°F).

5 Prepare the decoration: crush the feuilletine by hand in a bowl and add the gold powder. Remove the feuilletine from the frame by running the blade of a knife along the edges. Coat the top with a thin layer of chocolate (chablon; page 273), leave to set for a few minutes, then turn over. Before the chocolate coating has cooled completely, cut out 35-36 3 × 1.5 cm (1 ¼ × ½ in) chocolates using a chef's knife.

6 Dip the chocolates (page 32): scrape the fork on the rim to remove excess chocolate and decorate immediately with the feuilletine mixed with gold (page 283).

7 Allow to set at room temperature, ideally 15° to 17°C (59°F to 62°F), for 48 hours.

MOULDED CHOCOLATES
GIANDUJA

Understand

MILK
CHOCOLATE   GIANDUJA

WHAT IS IT?

Milk chocolate moulded chocolates filled
with milk chocolate and gianduja ganache.

HOW LONG WILL IT TAKE?

Preparation: 2 hours
Standing: 12 hours after moulding the ganache,
then 48 hours after the sweets are sealed.

EQUIPMENT YOU WILL NEED

Polycarbonate mould
Thermometer
Polyethylene sheet

TRICKY POINT
Tempering the chocolate

SKILL REQUIRED
Moulding chocolates (page 34)

ADVICE
Excess gianduja will keep in a sealed
container for up to 2 weeks at room
temperature for use in another recipe.

TIP
When mixing, take care to incorporate as little
air as possible: keep the stem of the blender at
the bottom of the bowl, stirring gently to allow
the air to escape from the blades, and mix for
about 1 minute without lifting the blender.

PLANNING AND PREP
The day before:
Moulding – ganache
On the day:
Sealing the sweets
2 days later:
Unmoulding

Learn

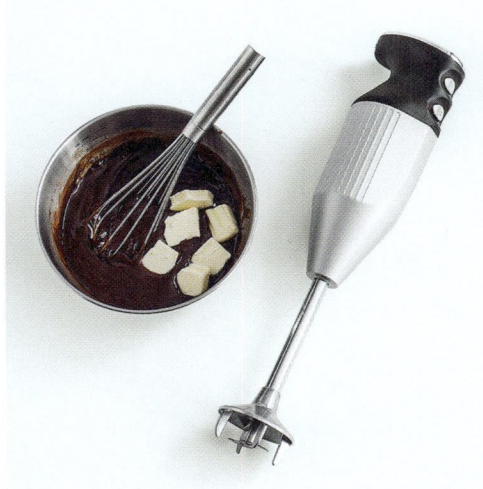

MAKES ABOUT 20

GIANDUJA

60 g (2 oz) dark chocolate (66% cocoa)

Praline

25 g (1 oz) shelled almonds
25 g (1 oz) shelled hazelnuts
50 g (2 oz) white caster (superfine) sugar
20 g (¾ oz) water

GIANDUJA GANACHE

150 g (5 oz) couverture milk chocolate
40 g (½ oz) gianduja (from above)
65 g (2 ½ oz) whipping cream
25 g (1 oz) inverted sugar (or neutral honey)
30 g (1 oz) unsalted butter

COATING

600 g (1 lb 5 oz) couverture milk chocolate

1. Temper two-thirds of the milk couverture chocolate and coat the moulds (page 24). Make the gianduja (page 40).

2. To make the ganache: melt the chocolate in a double-boiler (page 276) and add the gianduja away from the heat.

3. Put the cream and inverted sugar/honey in a saucepan and bring to the boil.

4. Pour over the ganache mixture. Mix together. Add the butter and blend. Cover with cling film (plastic wrap).

5. When the ganache is at 27°C (80.6°F), pipe it out into the chocolate moulds, then leave to set for 10 to 12 hours at room temperature, ideally 15° to 17°C (59°F to 62°F). Temper the remaining milk chocolate couverture. Seal the chocolates (page 34) and leave to set for 48 hours at room temperature, ideally 15° to 17°C (59°F to 62°F).

ROCK CHOCOLATES
PRALINE

Understand

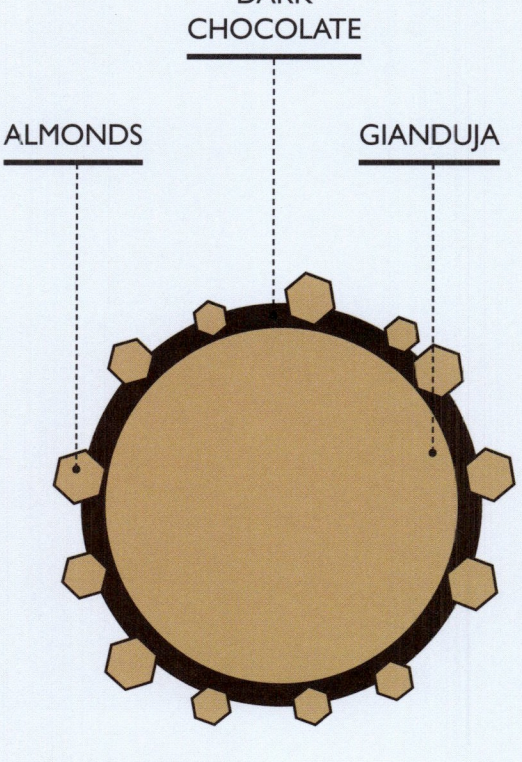

ALMONDS   DARK CHOCOLATE   GIANDUJA

WHAT IS IT?

Round gianduja rock chocolates covered with dark chocolate and chopped almonds.

HOW LONG WILL IT TAKE?

Preparation: 2 hours
Cooking: 20 minutes
Standing: 12 hours (ganache)
Setting: 48 hours

EQUIPMENT YOU WILL NEED

Thermometer
Piping bag
Kitchen gloves
Polyethylene sheet

VARIATIONS

Replace 10 g ($^{1}/_{2}$ oz) chopped shelled almonds with 10 g ($^{1}/_{2}$ oz) candied oranges, finely chopped.
Instead of dark chocolate, use milk chocolate; instead of almonds, use hazelnuts.

TRICKY POINTS

Tempering the chocolate
Coating the chocolates

SKILLS REQUIRED

Roasting (page 283)
Tempering chocolate (page 24)
Setting chocolate (page 24)
Dipping (page 32)

TIP

If you prefer the almonds to be visible, roll the rocks in the chopped almonds after dipping rather than mixing them into the couverture chocolate.

PLANNING AND PREP

The day before:
Praline (page 41) – gianduja
On the day:
Coating – Setting
2 days later:
Serve

Apprendre

MAKES ABOUT 30

GIANDUJA

120 g (4 oz) dark couverture chocolate (66% cocoa)
200 g (7 oz) praline (see page 41)
50 g (2 oz) shelled hazelnuts
50 g (2 oz) shelled almonds
100 g (3 ½ oz) white caster (superfine) sugar
35 g (1 oz) water

SHAPING

40 g (1 ½ oz) icing (confectioner's) sugar

COATING

500 g (1 lb 2 oz) dark couverture chocolate (66% cocoa)
40 g (1 ½ oz) chopped almonds

1 Make the gianduja (page 40). When the gianduja is at about 35°C (95°F), pipe out walnut-size domes. Leave to set (page 25) for 12 hours at room temperature.

2 Roast (page 283) the chopped almonds for 20 minutes at 160°C (320°F), then leave to cool. Wearing kitchen gloves, put a thin layer of icing sugar in the palm of your hand to prevent the gianduja from sticking. Roll the domes into balls, working quickly so that the gianduja does not melt.

3 Temper the coating couverture chocolate (page 24). Wearing kitchen gloves, put some of the chocolate in the palm of your hand. Roll into balls and put them on a baking sheet covered with baking paper (baking parchment).

4 Stir the chopped almonds into the rest of the coating chocolate and, wearing kitchen gloves, put some of the almond-couverture chocolate in the palm of your hand. Once again, roll into balls. Put each rock on the polyethylene sheet. Allow to set (page 25) at room temperature, ideally 15° to 17°C (59°F to 62°F) for 48 hours.

ROCK CHOCOLATES
VANILLA & COCONUT

Understand

VANILLA
FLAVOURED
WHIPPED GANACHE

WHITE
CHOCOLATE

COCONUT

WHAT IS IT?

Round chocolates made of white vanilla ganache, filled with a hazelnut and coated with white couverture chocolate and grated coconut.

HOW LONG WILL IT TAKE?

Preparation: 90 minutes
Baking: 20 minutes
Freezing: 6 hours
Standing: 6 to 24 hours

EQUIPMENT YOU WILL NEED

Piping bag with 8 mm (1/3 in) plain nozzle
Thermometer
Spherical mould
Kitchen gloves
Dipping fork
Stand mixer with flat beater attachment

VARIATION

Replace the vanilla with 15 g (1/2 oz) pistachio paste.

TRICKY POINT

Whipping up ganache

SKILL REQUIRED

Roasting (page 283)

TIP

Fill one half of the semi-spherical mould inserts to the top, then press a hazelnut into each. Put in the freezer for 4 hours. Unmould the chocolates and return to the freezer. Fill the other half moulds with chocolate, put the hazelnut chocolate halves on top to complete the spheres, and roll them so that they stick together well. Return to the freezer for 4 to 24 hours. Coat the chocolates.

PLANNING AND PREP

2 days before: Roasting – ganache
The day before: Moulding
On the day: Coating
Will keep for up to 1 week in a sealed container in the refrigerator

Learn

MAKES ABOUT 70

30 g whole shelled hazelnuts

VANILLA GANACHE

150 g (5 oz) white chocolate
250 g (9 oz) whipping cream
2 vanilla pods (beans)
2 g (1 sheet) sheet gelatine

COATING

3 g (^{1}/10 oz) cocoa butter
300 g (10 ^{1}/2 oz) white chocolate
80 g (3 oz) desiccated (dried shredded) coconut

1 Roast the hazelnuts (page 283) for about 20 minutes at 170°C (340°F/gas3). Leave to cool then set aside in a dry place.

2 Make the vanilla ganache (page 44), adding the split and scraped vanilla beans (pods) to the cream. Strain before pouring over the chocolate.

3 After leaving to stand, put the cold ganache in the bowl of the stand mixer fitted with the flat beater mix at low to medium power. Stop when it thickens. Transfer to a piping bag fitted with a 8 mm (^{1}/3 in) plain nozzle.

4 Place the mould on a baking tray. Fill the lower half of the spheres almost to the top, add a roasted hazelnut to each, pressing it in lightly, and cover with the top half of the mould. Fill up the spheres through the holes. Tap the tray lightly on the work surface to remove air bubbles. Re-fill if necessary. Put in the freezer for at least 6 hours.

5 Cover a sheet of baking paper (baking parchment) with the coconut. Temper the white couverture using the Mycryo butter method (page 30).

6 Unmould the spheres. Wearing kitchen gloves, put some couverture chocolate in the palm of your hand. Roll the spheres then, using a dipping fork, dip them in the chocolate and remove. Shake lightly to remove the excess, then roll them immediately in the grated coconut.

CARAMEL AND CHOCOLATE
FUDGE

CARAMEL CHOCOLATE
VANILLA

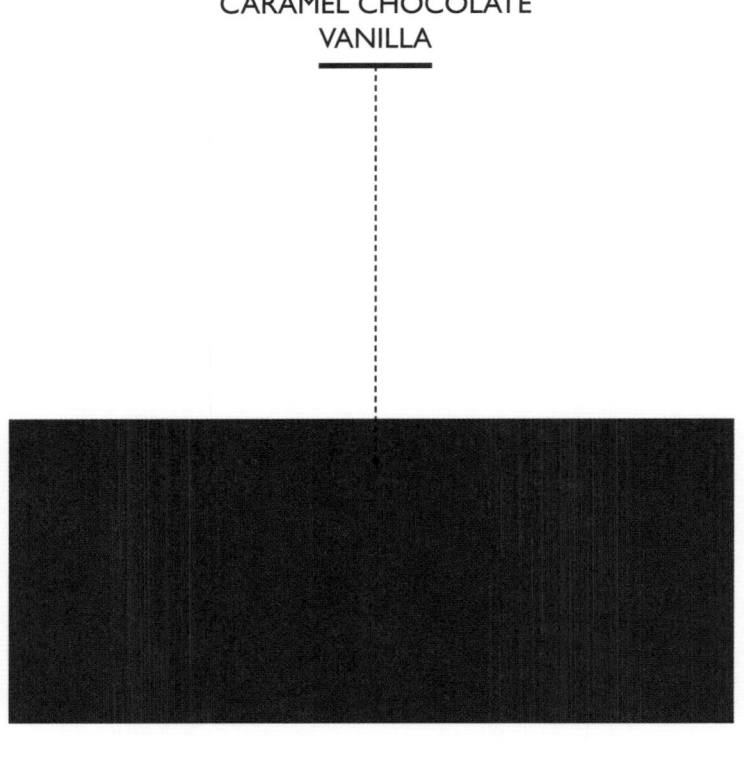

WHAT IS IT?

Soft caramel with chocolate and vanilla.

HOW LONG WILL IT TAKE?

Preparation: 1 hour
Standing: 12 hours

EQUIPMENT YOU WILL NEED

15 × 15 cm (6 × 6 in) baking frame
Thermometer
Silicone sheet

VARIATION
Add candied ginger cubes before
pouring into the frame.

TRICKY POINTS
Cooking
Pouring the thick mix

SKILL REQUIRED
Incorporating liquid into a caramel (page 282)

ADVICE
After cutting the sweets, wrap well
in cling film (plastic wrap) to prevent
any moisture from getting in.
When incorporating the cream into the
syrup, make sure that the temperature
does not fall below 110°C (230°F) so that
the mixture is smooth. To make a hard
caramel, cook the mixture at 121°C (250°F).

PLANNING AND PREP
The day before:
Caramel
On the day:
Cutting and wrapping

Learn

MAKES ABOUT 35 CHOCOLATES

50 g (2 oz) water
215 g (7 ½ oz) white caster (superfine) sugar
20 g (¾ oz) glucose syrup
135 g (4 ½ oz) whipping cream
1 vanilla pod (bean)
90 g (3 ¼ oz) unsalted butter
2 g (½ teaspoon) salt
70 g (2 ½ oz) pure cocoa paste

1 Put the silicone sheet on a baking tray and place the baking frame on it. Put the water then the sugar in a saucepan and bring to the boil, stirring. Remove the pan from the heat, then brush down the sides of the pan using using a wet brush. Add the glucose syrup and cook again. Cook at 145°C (293°F) without stirring.

2 Meanwhile, heat the cream with the scraped vanilla pod. When the cream boils, decrease the heat to a minimum, remove the vanilla bean and add the butter and salt.

3 Add the caramel cream in several stages, stirring.

4 Stir in the cocoa paste, increase the heat and cook to 118°C (244°F). Pour immediately into the frame, allow to cool and then cover with cling film (plastic wrap) to protect from moisture. Leave to stand for 12 hours.

5 Remove from the frame by running the blade of the knife along the edges. Mark off 2.5 × 2.5 cm (1 × 1 in) squares (page 273). Cut out the chocolates with a chef's knife.

CHOCOLATE
EGG

Understand

DARK
CHOCOLATE

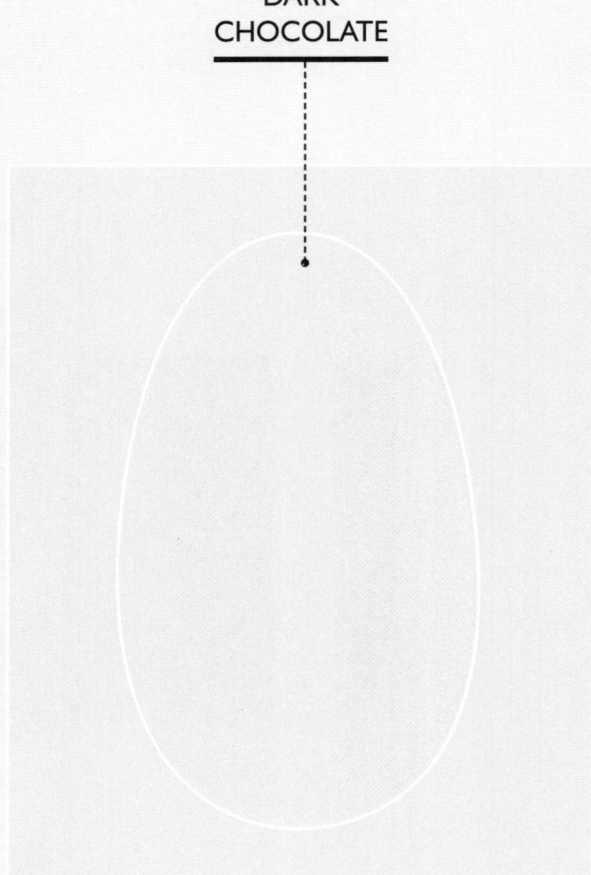

WHAT IS IT?

Chocolate made in an egg-shaped mould and filled with chocolate pieces.

HOW LONG WILL IT TAKE?

Preparation: 2 hours
Standing: 48 hours setting

EQUIPMENT YOU WILL NEED

Pastry ring [SIZE?]
Polycarbonate egg mould (20 cm/8 in)
Polyethylene sheet
Transparent acetate strip
Piping bag

VARIATION

Use milk or white couverture. If you use both, temper them separately.

SKILLS REQUIRED

Tempering chocolate (page 24)
Setting chocolate (page 24)

ADVICE

Do not hold the mould directly in your hands to prevent it form warming. Use kitchen gloves to prevent fingermarks.

PLANNING AND PREP

2 days before:
Moulding
On the day:
Decoration – Sealing the chocolate

Learn

TO MAKE ONE 20 CM (8 IN) EGG

1 kg (2 lb 4 oz) chocolate (minimum 60% cocoa)
150 g (5 oz) chocolate pieces (of your choice)

Making the chocolate egg

1   Clean the mould thoroughly with a clean cloth to remove any dust or finger marks. Place the pastry ring on a polyethylene sheet and secure with a strip of transparent acetate strip.

2   Temper 900 g (2 lb) couverture chocolate (page 24). Using a brush, apply a thin layer of couverture to each half of the mould to start making the two egg halves. Allow to set for a few minutes, then scrape off any excess (page 271). Fill the pastry ring with 1 cm ($^1/_2$ in) of couverture chocolate to make the stand for the egg.

3   Fill a half-egg mould with couverture chocolate, tap the mould to allow air bubbles to escape, turn over and run off most of the chocolate tapping continuously, then place on pastry rings to finish emptying the excess chocolate. Do the same with the second half-egg.

4   After a few minutes, scrape off the rough edges and pour another layer of chocolate into each egg half and place directly on a baking sheet to make a flat surface for sealing. Allow to set at room temperature, ideally 15° to 17°C (59°F to 62°F) for 48 hours.

5   To unmould the egg halves, slide them to one side touching only the inside of the chocolate, remove the ring and the acetate tape. Temper 100 g (3 $^1/_2$ oz) of couverture chocolate and, using a piping bag, decorate the egg halves with thin lines of chocolate.

6   Place a baking tray on a pan of boiling water. Wearing kitchen gloves, place en egg half on the warm tray for a few seconds to slightly melt the flat surface, then remove, and fill with chocolate pieces. Place the second egg half on the warm baking tray, then immediately put them together to form and seal the egg.

7   Wait a few minutes for the egg to seal properly, then warm the base of the egg and put it on the stand.

CHOCOLATE HEN

Understand

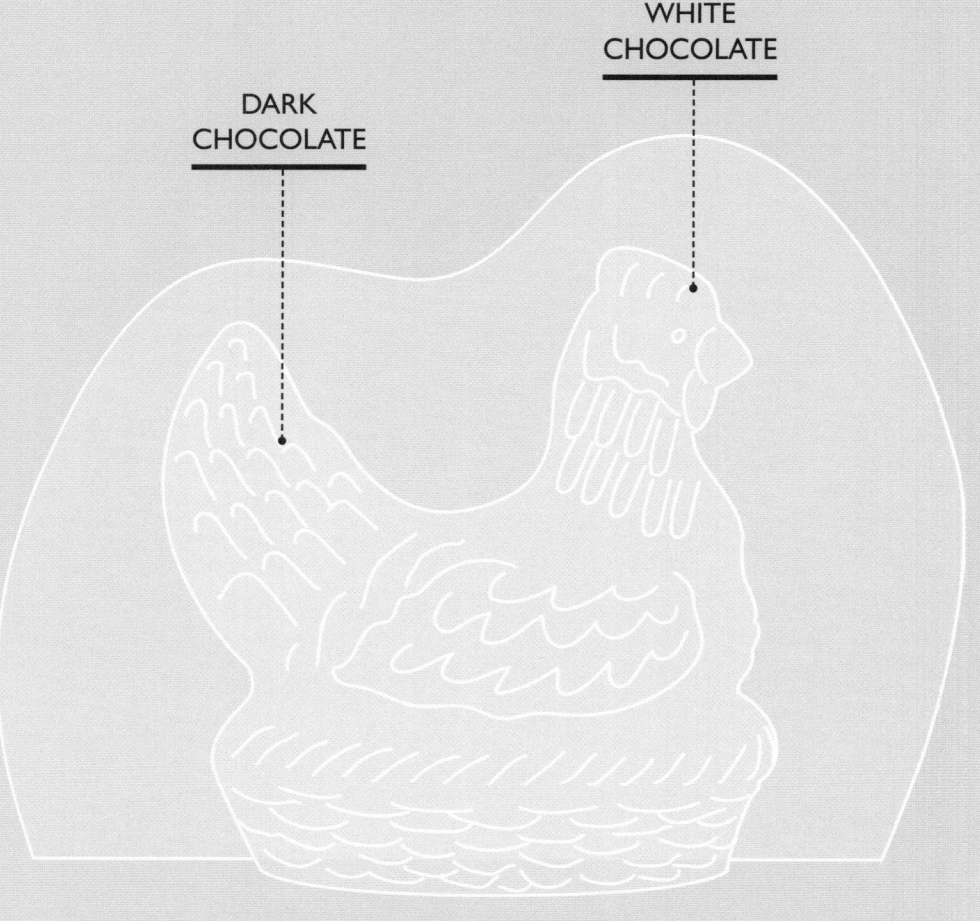

DARK
CHOCOLATE

WHITE
CHOCOLATE

WHAT IS IT?

Chocolate made in a hen-shaped mould.

HOW LONG WILL IT TAKE?

Preparation: 2 hours
Standing: 48 hours (setting)

EQUIPMENT YOU WILL NEED

15 cm (6 in) hen-shaped polycarbonate mould
(from specialist chocolate online retailers)
Cone
Fine paintbrush

SKILLS REQUIRED

Tempering chocolate (page 24)
Setting chocolate (page 24)

ADVICE

Do not hold the mould directly in
your hands, to prevent warming

PLANNING AND PREP

2 days before:
Moulding
On the day:
Unmoulding

114

Learn

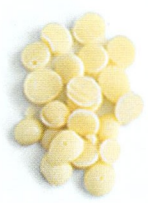

TO MAKE ONE 15CM HEN

100 g (3 ½ oz) white couverture chocolate
1 g cocoa butter
600 g (1 1lb 5 oz) dark couverture
chocolate (minimum 60% cocoa)

Making the chocolate hen

1   Clean the mould well with a clean cloth.

2   Temper the white couverture chocolate using the Mycryo butter technique (page 30). Apply to the eyes, beak and comb using the cone. Apply a thin layer to the wings and tail using the brush.

3   Temper the dark couverture chocolate, then apply a thin layer with a brush on both sides of the mould, then close the two halves together and seal.

4   Wait a few minutes, then fill the mould with the melted chocolate, tapping lightly to allow the air bubbles to escape. Turn the mould over to let any extra chocolate run off, wait a few minutes, then repeat with a second coat of chocolate.

5   Leave to set at room temperature, ideally 15° to 17°C (59°F to 62°F) for 48 hours.

6   Unmould by very carefully separating the two moulds.

116

CHOCOLATE BOX

Understand

DARK
CHOCOLATE

WHAT IS IT?

Chocolate moulded in the shape
of a cylindrical box.

HOW LONG WILL IT TAKE?

Preparation: 2 hours
Standing: 48 hours (setting)

EQUIPMENT YOU WILL NEED

8 cm (3 in) pastry ring
6 cm (2 ¹/₂ in) pastry ring
22 (8 ¹/₂ in) cm pastry ring
24 (9 ¹/₂ in) cm pastry ring

Wire brush
Paintbrush
Triangular spatula
Transparent acetate strip

TRICKY POINT
Brushing

SKILLS REQUIRED
Tempering chocolate (page 24)
Setting chocolate (page 24)

PLANNING AND PREP
2 days before:
Moulding
On the day:
Brushing – Finishing

ADVICE
Be sure to brush on several coats of
chocolate to make the base of the box: the
cling film (plastic wrap) used to support
the base is much less rigid than the metal
ring around the circumference. If you plan
to fill the finished box with chocolates,
the base needs to be quite strong.
Take care not to damage the chocolate
box when using the wire brush.
Remove the chocolate dust using a dry brush.

Learn

TO MAKE A 22 CM (8 ½ IN) BOX

1.2 kg (2 lb 4 oz) dark couverture chocolate (minimum 60% cocoa)

PREPARE THE EQUIPMENT

For the box and the lid: cover the bottom of the two larger rings with cling film, holding it in place on the sides with an elastic (rubber) band. For the handle: cover the base of the 8 cm (3 in) pastry ring with cling film and line the inside of the rim with a strip of transparent acetate strip. Line the outer rim of the 6 cm (2 ½ in) ring with a strip of transparent acetate strip and place it inside the 8 cm (3 in) ring.

Making the chocolate box

1 Temper the couverture chocolate (page 24). To make the lid: cover the bottom of the lined 24 cm (9 ¹/₂ in) ring with a layer of chocolate 5 mm (¹/₄ in) thick. To make the handle: fill the outer ring formed by the two small lined rings of different diameters to a depth of 1 cm (¹/₂ in).

2 For the box: brush a thin layer of chocolate onto the rim and the base of the 22 cm (8 ¹/₂ in) ring. Leave to set for a few minutes, then scrape the sides clean (page 271). Repeat this operation 3 to 4 times until a strong base has been formed.

3 For the sides: fill the ring, tilting it all over on its sides to cover the outer edges with chocolate. Turn over to run off the excess chocolate. Leave to set for a few minutes, then repeat until the chololate is 3 cm (1 ¹/₄ in) thick.

4 Turn over onto a baking sheet and smooth the edges. Turn the box over and after a few minutes, trim the edges using a triangular spatula. Leave the three parts of the box to set at room temperature, ideally 15° to 17°C (59°F to 62°F) for 48 hours.

5 Unmould the base of the box, the lid and the handle.

6 Using a knife with a warm blade, cut the chocolate ring for the handle into 2 semi-circles.

7 Roughen the top of the lid and the handle carefully using the wire brush.

8 Gently brush the whole of the outside of the box using the wire brush.

9 Heat a baking tray on a double-boiler (page 276). Place the base of the semi-circular handle on the warmed tray for a few seconds to melt it slightly, then immediately fix it in place on the lid. Fill with chocolates of your choice.

CHOCOLATE
FISH

Understand

DARK, WHITE OR
MILK CHOCOLATE

WHAT IS IT?

Dark, white or milk chocolate
moulded shapes traditionally
representing small fish or shellfish.

HOW LONG WILL IT TAKE?

Preparation: 1 hour
Setting: 48 hours

EQUIPMENT YOU WILL NEED

Polycarbonate mould
Thermometer
Polyethylene sheet
Paintbrush

TRICKY POINT
Tempering the chocolate

SKILLS REQUIRED
Tempering chocolate (page 24)
Setting chocolate (page 24)

ADVICE
For a speckled effect, separately temper (page
25) 100 g (3 ¹/₂ oz) white couverture and 300 g
(10 ¹/₂ oz) dark couverture. Using a dry brush,
tap spots of white couverture into the mould,
wait a few minutes, then scrape off any excess
(page 271). Fill with black couverture chocolate.

PLANNING AND PREP
2 days before:
Tempering – Moulding
On the day:
Unmoulding

Learn

TO MAKE 300 G (10 ½ OZ) SMALL FISH

300 g (10 ½ oz) dark, milk or white couverture chocolate

1. Temper (page 24) the couverture chocolate of your choice.

2. Using a dry brush, tap some couverture into the bottom of the mould inserts, wait a few minutes, then scrape off any excess.

3. Fill up the mould with the couverture chocolate, tapping the side of the mould with the handle of a spatula to remove any air bubbles.

4. Scrape off excess chocolate using a spatula. Place a polyethylene sheet on top and use the spatula to smooth the top.

5. Leave to set (page 25) at room temperature, ideally 15° to 17°C (59°F to 62°F) for 48 hours. After setting, remove from the mould.

CHOCOLATE
SLABS

Understand

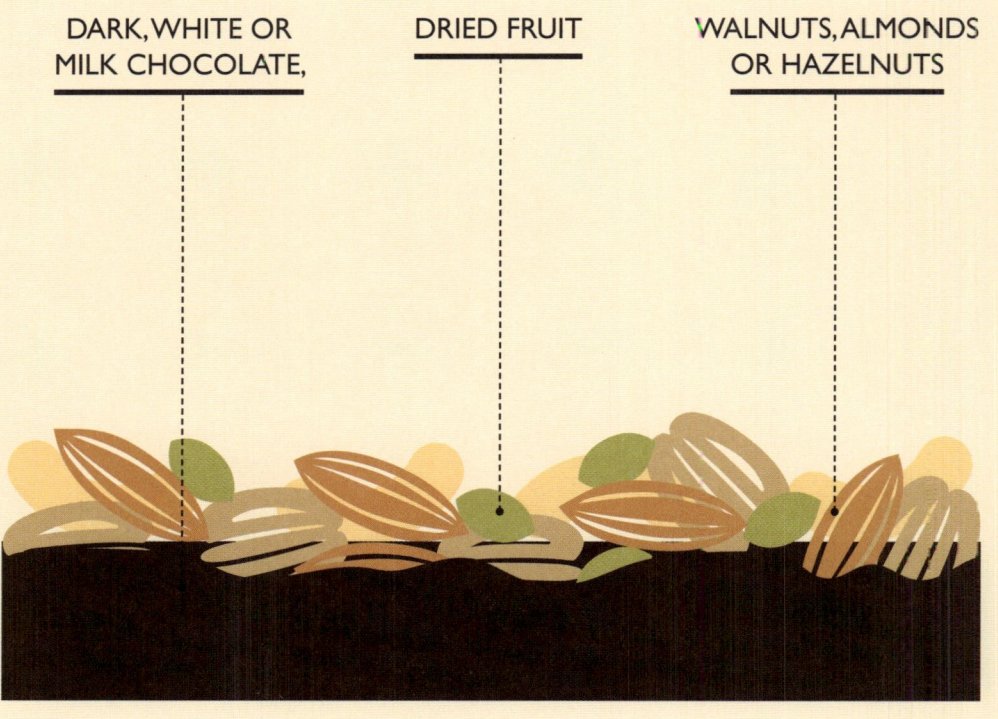

DARK, WHITE OR
MILK CHOCOLATE,

DRIED FRUIT

WALNUTS, ALMONDS
OR HAZELNUTS

WHAT IS IT?

Slabs of dark, white or milk chocolate, covered
with dried and crystallised (candied) fruit.

HOW LONG WILL IT TAKE?

Preparation: 1 hour
Cooking: 20 minutes
Setting: 48 hours

EQUIPMENT YOU WILL NEED

15 × 15 cm (6 $^1/_2$ × 6 $^1/_2$ in) baking frame
Thermometer
Polyethylene sheet

TRICKY POINT
Tempering chocolate

SKILLS REQUIRED
Roasting (page 283)
Tempering chocolate (page 24)
Setting chocolate (page 24)

TIP
If you don't have a polyethylene sheet,
use baking paper (baking parchment)

PLANNING AND PREP
On the day:
Tempering – making – setting
2 days later:
Ready to enjoy

Learn

TO MAKE 1 SLAB OF DARK, WHITE OR MILK CHOCOLATE

MILK CHOCOLATE

300 g (10 ½ oz) couverture milk chocolate
30 g (1 oz) whole blanched hazelnuts
30 g (1 oz) whole blanched almonds
30 g (1 oz) shelled walnut halves
30 g (1 oz) whole shelled pistachios

DARK CHOCOLATE

300 g (10 ½ oz) dark couverture chocolate (66% cocoa)
30 g (1 oz) puffed rice
30 g (1 oz) crystallised (candied) lemon
40 g (1 ½ oz) cranberries
20 g (½ oz) dried bananas

WHITE CHOCOLATE

300 g (10 ½ oz) white couverture chocolate
10 g (½ oz) dried strawberries
15 g (½ oz) dried blueberries
30 g (1 oz) roasted cashews
10 g (½ oz) goji berries
15 g (½ oz) cranberries

1 Roast the dried fruit for 20 minutes at 160°C (320°F), then leave to cool (page 283). Cut the crystallised fruit into 1 cm (½ in) wide sticks. Temper your chosen chocolate (page 24).

2 For the slab of dark chocolate, stir the puffed rice into the chocolate couverture before pouring.

3 Place the baking frame on the polyethylene sheet and pour the chocolate in a uniform layer. Add the dried and candied fruit immediately, pushing it into the surface slightly. Leave to set (page 25) at room temperature, ideally 15° to 17°C (59°F to 62°F) for 48 hours.

4 After setting, break into pieces by dropping the slab onto the worktop, or by using a knife or mallet. It's ready for you to enjoy.

MENDIANTS

Understand

DARK CHOCOLATE   DRIED FRUIT

WHAT IS IT?

Dark chocolate discs covered with
dried and candied fruit.

HOW LONG WILL IT TAKE?

Preparation: 1 hour Cooking: 20 min
Standing: 48 hours to crystallize

EQUIPMENT YOU WILL NEED

Thermometer
Polyethylene sheet
Piping bag

VARIATION

Replace some of the dried fruit with
pecans, goji berries or dried bananas.

TRICKY POINT

Tempering chocolate (page 24)

SKILLS REQUIRED

Roasting (page 283)
Tempering chocolate (page 24)
Setting chocolate (page 24)

ADVICE

Avoid holding the piping bag in your hands
for too long as you work: body temperature
is higher than the temperature at which the
chocolate is used, and the warming may cause
the chocolate to develop a white 'bloom'.

TIP

If you don't have a polyethylene sheet,
use baking paper (baking parchment).

PLANNING AND PREP

On the day:
Tempering – making – setting
2 days later:
Ready to enjoy

Learn

MAKES 40 MENDIANTS

300 g (10 ½ oz) dark couverture chocolate (66% cocoa)
30 g (1 oz) whole shelled hazelnuts
30 g (1 oz) whole shelled almonds
30 g (1 oz) cranberries
30 g (1 oz) pistachios
40 g (1 oz) crystallised (candied) orange and lemon

1 Roast the almonds and hazelnuts for 20 minutes in a 160°C (320°F/gas 4) oven, then leave to cool (page 283).

2 Cut the crystallised oranges into 1 cm (½ in) sticks.

3 Temper the couverture (page 24). Transfer it to a piping bag and cut a small hole in a corner of the bag. Pipe out a row of discs on the polyethylene sheet: hold the piping bag upright, squeeze the end between thumb and forefinger to stop the flow, then without moving the bag let the chocolate run out to form a 2 cm (¾ in) diameter disc. Squeeze the bag again to stop the flow, move the piping bag along and repeat the process. At the end of the row, put the bag down and tap the tray to enlarge the discs to a diameter of 3 to 4 cm (1 ¼ to 1 ½ in). Arrange the dried and crystallised fruit neatly on top of the chocolate discs, pressing it lightly into the surface.

4 Leave to set (page 25) at room temperature, ideally 15° to 17°C (59°F to 62°F), for 48 hours.

ORANGETTES

Understand

CRYSTALLISED (CANDIED) ORANGE

DARK CHOCOLATE

WHAT IS IT?

Candied orange sticks coated with dark chocolate.

HOW LONG WILL IT TAKE?

Preparation: 90 minutes
Setting: 48 hours

EQUIPMENT YOU WILL NEED

Thermometer
Dipping fork

VARIATION

Instead of crystallised orange use crystallised ginger, lemon or grapefruit. Crystallised lemon and grapefruit go well with milk chocolate couverture.

TRICKY POINTS

Tempering
Coating

SKILLS REQUIRED

Tempering chocolate (page 24)
Setting chocolate (page 24)

ADVICE

To prevent any residual moisture from coming out of the dried fruit, sprinkle it with a mixture of icing (confectioner's) sugar and potato starch.

PLANNING AND PREP

On the day:
Coating – Setting
2 days later:
Ready to enjoy

Learn

MAKES ABOUT 50

150 g (5 oz) crystallised orange sticks
30 g (1 oz) icing (confectioner's) sugar
30 g (1 oz) potato starch

COATING

300 g (10 ½ oz) dark couverture chocolate (66% cocoa)

1. Mix the potato starch and icing sugar in a bowl. Add the crystallised orange sticks and coat well. Sieve to remove the excess.

2. Temper the coating couverture (page 24).

3. Dip the sticks into the chocolate one by one, making up-and-down movements with each stick to coat thoroughly. The chocolate should cling to the fruit and not run off the stick when you transfer it to the sheet. Scrape the fork over the rim to remove the excess chocolate.

4. Leave to set (page 25) at a temperature of 15° to 17°C (59°F to 62°F) for 48 hours.

MILLIONAIRE'S
SHORTBREAD

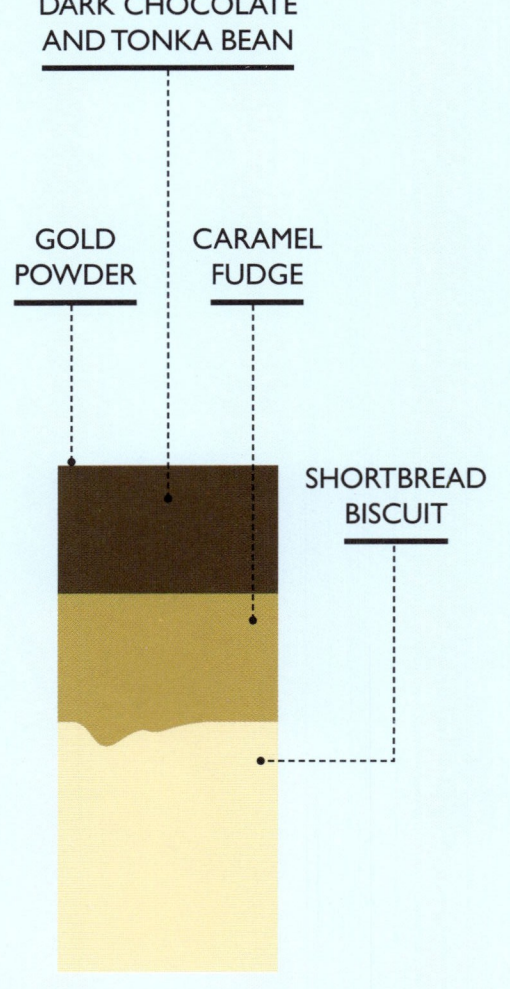

DARK CHOCOLATE
AND TONKA BEAN

GOLD
POWDER

CARAMEL
FUDGE

SHORTBREAD
BISCUIT

WHAT IS IT?

Shortbread biscuit covered with a rich caramel
of butter, sugar and sweetened condensed milk,
topped with tonka bean-flavoured chocolate.

HOW LONG WILL IT TAKE?

Preparation: 90 minutes
Cooking: 45 minutes
Standing: 24 hours
Freezing: 30 minutes

EQUIPMENT YOU WILL NEED

16 × 16 cm (6 $^1/_2$ × 6 $^1/_2$ in) baking frame
Thermometer
Spatula
Paintbrush

VARIATION

Add 40 g (1 $^1/_2$ oz) pure cocoa paste to
the fudge as it finishes cooking.

TRICKY POINTS

Tempering
Cooking the fudge

SKILLS REQUIRED

Making buttercream (page 281)
Tempering chocolate (page 24)

ADVICE

If the caramel starts to stick to the bottom of
the pan, change to a clean pan immediately.

PLANNING, PREP
AND STORAGE

2 days before: Shortbread – fudge
The day before: Couverture – tempering
On the day: Ready to enjoy
Store at room temperature for up to
three days. Do not refrigerate.

Learn

MAKES ABOUT 50 RECTANGLES (3 × 1 ½ CM)

1 SHORTBREAD BISCUIT

110 g (3 ½ oz) unsalted butter
50 g (2 oz) white caster (superfine) sugar
135 g (4 ½ oz) flour

2 CARAMEL FUDGE

125 g (4 oz) unsalted butter
125 g (4 oz) brown sugar
25 g (¾) honey
200 g (7 oz) sweetened condensed milk

3 DECORATION

200 g (7 oz) dark couverture chocolate (66% cocoa)
½ tonka bean (from online suppliers) or 1 cm (½ in) vanilla pod (bean)
1 pinch of gold powder

1 Preheat the oven to 160°C (320°F/gas 4). To make the shortbread biscuit: cream the butter with the sugar in a bowl (page 281). Add the flour, mix until evenly blended, then gather into a ball of dough and gently knead with the palm of your hand (page 284).

2 Spread the dough 3 mm thick on a sheet of baking paper (baking parchment), then prick holes in it with a fork. Place the baking frame on top of the dough and press to remove the excess. Freeze for 30 minutes. Transfer to the oven and cook for 20 to 30 minutes. Leave to cool.

3 To make the caramel fudge: put all the ingredients in a saucepan, cook and stir continuously until it reaches 112°C (234°F).

4 Immediately pour the fudge over the shortbread, level the surface with a spatula and leave to cool at room temperature.

5 Temper the couverture chocolate (page 24) and pour immediately over the caramel fudge layer. Grate the tonka/vanilla bean onto the chocolate.

6 As soon as the couverture begins to set, score the surface with the size of cakes you want using a chef's knife. Add gold powder using a paintbrush.

7 Cut out the cakes using a chef's knife.

TRUFFLES

Understand

COCOA

DARK CHOCOLATE

DARK CHOCOLATE GANACHE

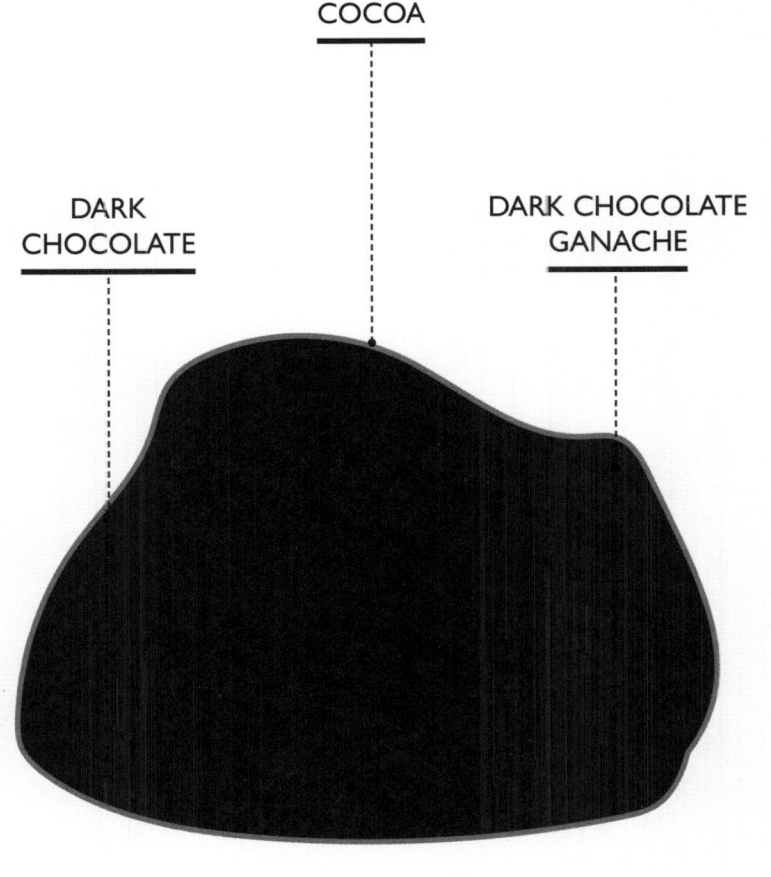

WHAT IS IT?

Dark chocolate-coated ganache rolled in cocoa (unsweetened chocolate) powder.

HOW LONG WILL IT TAKE?

Preparation: 2 hours
Standing: 12 hours (ganache)
Setting: 48 hours

EQUIPMENT YOU WILL NEED

Thermometer
Piping bag with a 10 mm (¹/₂ in) nozzle
Kitchen gloves
Dipping spoon

VARIATIONS

Flavour the ganache with any spice you like, such as sichuan or espelette pepper.

TRICKY POINTS

Tempering the chocolate
Dipping

SKILLS REQUIRED

Tempering chocolate (page 24)
Setting chocolate (page 24)
Dipping chocolates (page 32)

PLANNING AND PREP

The day before:
Ganache
On the day:
Coating – setting
2 days later:
Ready to enjoy

132

Learn

MAKES ABOUT 35 CHOCOLATES

FOR 350 G (12 OZ) GANACHE

190 g (6 ½ oz) dark couverture chocolate (66% cocoa)
130 g (4 oz) whipping cream
30 g (1 oz) milk
15 g (½ oz) unsalted butter
15 g (½ oz) glucose syrup
10 g (½ oz) inverted sugar or neutral honey

SHAPING

40 g (1 ½ oz) icing (confectioner's) sugar

COATING

600 g (1 1lb 5 oz) dark couverture chocolate (66% cocoa)
60 g (2 oz) cocoa (unsweetened chocolate) powder

1 To make the dark ganache: melt the chocolate in a double-boiler (page 276).

2 Meanwhile, put the cream, milk, butter, glucose syrup and inverted sugar/honey in a saucepan and bring to the boil. Strain half of this mixture onto the chocolate and whisk to start the emulsion. Strain the rest onto the chocolate and finish the emulsion by stirring for about 1 minute without letting any air in. Cover with cling film (plastic wrap) and allow the temperature to drop to about 35°C (95°F).

3 Put the mixture in a piping bag with a 10 mm (½ in) nozzle, press out 2 cm (¾ in) dome shapes (page 278) and leave to set (page 25) for 12 hours at room temperature, ideally 15 to 17°C (59°F to 62°F). Put on kitchen gloves and sprinkle a thin layer of icing sugar in the palms of your hand to prevent the ganache from sticking. Roll the domes into balls.

4 Temper the coating couverture (page 25). Wearing kitchen gloves, put a little couverture chocolate in the palms of your hand and roll the balls in it. Dip the balls into the coating couverture with a dipping fork (page 32). Roll them in cocoa powder, transfer to a sieve and roll to remove excess cocoa. Leave to set at a temperature of 15° to 17°C (59°F to 62°F) for 48 hours.

CHOCOLATE BARS

Understand

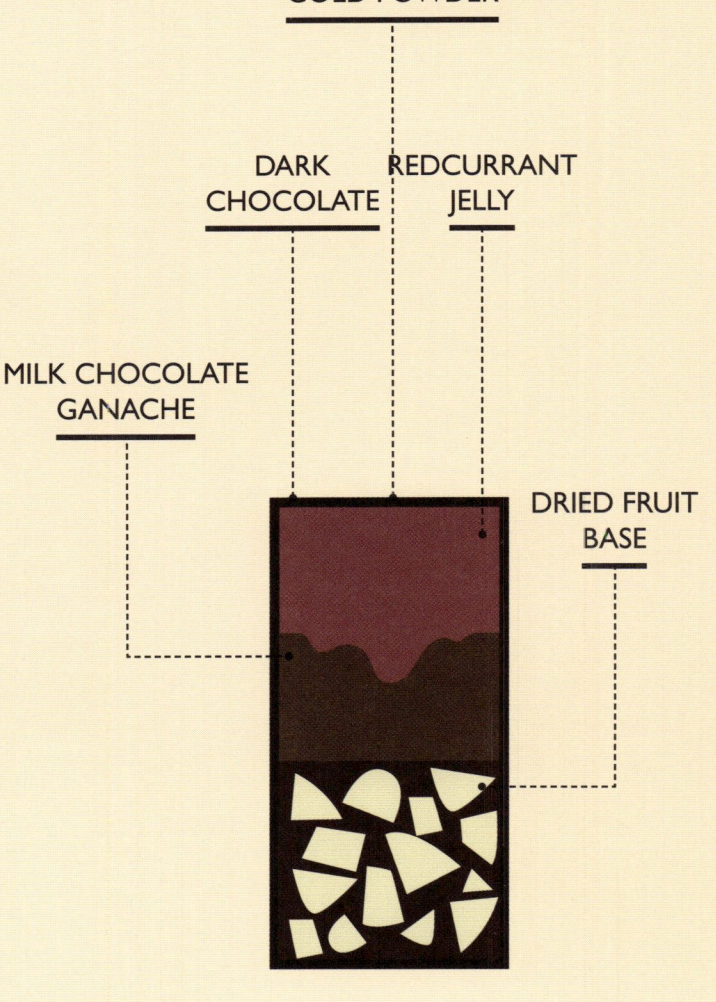

GOLD POWDER

DARK CHOCOLATE

REDCURRANT JELLY

MILK CHOCOLATE GANACHE

DRIED FRUIT BASE

WHAT IS IT?

Crispy bar covered with milk ganache and redcurrant jelly and coated with dark chocolate.

HOW LONG WILL IT TAKE?

Preparation: 3 hours
Cooking: 20 minutes
Setting: ganache, 12 hours
jelly, 4 hours
bar, 48 hours

EQUIPMENT YOU WILL NEED

16 × 16 cm (6 ¹/₂ × 6 ¹/₂ in) baking frame
Thermometer
Polyethylene sheet
Paint brush
Pastry bag

VARIATIONS

Vary the fruit according to taste by replacing redcurrant with raspberry or passion fruit.

SKILLS REQUIRED

Roasting (page 283)
Using a double-boiler (page 276)
Tempering (page 25)
Rehydrating gelatine (page 277)
Setting (page 25)

Coating with a thin layer of chocolate (chabloning; page 273)
Decorating with gold (page 283)

PLANNING, PREP AND STORAGE

4 days before
Crispy base – ganache
3 days before
Jelly
The day before:
Coating – setting
The bars will keep for 1 week in an airtight box at room temperature.

Learn

MAKES 10 BARS

1 CRISPY BASE

25 g (1 oz) macadamia nuts, crushed
40 g (1 ½ oz) almonds, chopped
100 g (3 ½ oz) dark chocolate (66% cocoa)
8 g (¼ oz) cocoa butter
15 g (½ oz) pumpkin seeds
15 g (½ oz) dried blueberries

2 MILK GANACHE

75 g (2 ½ oz) whipping cream
20 g (¾ oz) unsalted butter
25 g (1 oz) inverted sugar or neutral honey
100 g (3 ½ oz) milk chocolate

3 REDCURRANT JELLY

250 g (9 oz) redcurrant purée
20 g (¾ oz) inverted sugar or neutral honey
25 g (1 oz) white caster (superfine) sugar
6 g (¼ oz) powdered pectin
4 g (2 sheets) sheet gelatine

4 COATING AND FINISHING

600 g (1 lb 5 oz) dark couverture chocolate (66% cocoa)
Gold powder

Making chocolate bars

1   To make the crispy base: roast the almonds and crushed macadamia nuts for 20 minutes at 160°C (320°F). Melt the chocolate and cocoa butter in a double-boiler (page 276), then, away from the double-boiler, add the pumpkin seeds, dried blueberries, almonds and macadamia nuts. Mix and spread on the polyethylene sheet. Level the surface using a spatula.

2   To make the milk ganache: boil the cream, butter and inverted sugar/honey. Pour over the chocolate, wait 1 minute, then stir. Mix, taking care to incorporate as little air as possible (page 276), cover with cling film (plastic wrap) and leave to cool to 32°C (89.6°F).

3   When that temperature is reached, spread the ganache over the crispy base using a spatula. Leave to set (page 25) for 12 hours.

4   To make the redcurrant jelly: rehydrate the gelatine in cold water (page 277). Mix the sugar and pectin. Bring the gooseberry purée and inverted sugar/honey to the boil in a saucepan. Add the sugar-pectin mixture and cook for 1 minute, whisking all the time. Add the gelatine, stir, then transfer to a bowl and cover with cling film (plastic wrap).

5   When the jelly is at around 28°C (82°F), whisk it well to make it smooth, then spread it over the ganache layer using a palette knife. Transfer to the refrigerator to set for at least 4 hours. Remove any traces of condensation using paper towels.

6   Temper the couverture (page 24), then use a paintbrush to coat the jelly layer with a thin layer of chocolate. Before the chocolate layer hardens, mark out 8 × 3 cm (3 × 1 in) rectangles. Cut the rectangles immediately using a chef's knife.

7   Put the rectangles on a rack set over a baking tray, spacing them out. Make a small hole in a piping bag and pipe the remaining chocolate out onto each bar. Gently shake the rack to allow excess chocolate to run off.

8   Place the chocolate bars on a tray covered with the polyethylene sheet. Using a dry paintbrush, decorate with gold powder (page 283). Leave to set at room temperature, ideally 15° to 17°C (59°F to 62°F), for 48 hours.

MACARON
DESSERT

Understand

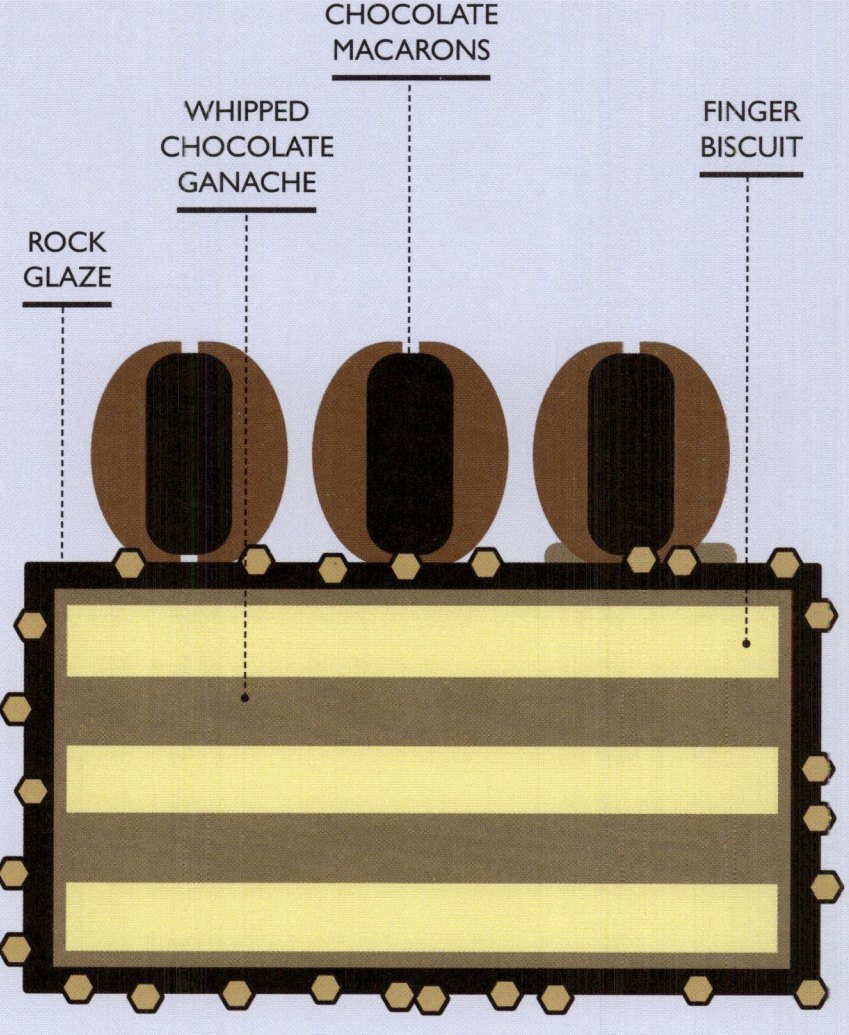

CHOCOLATE
MACARONS

WHIPPED
CHOCOLATE
GANACHE

FINGER
BISCUIT

ROCK
GLAZE

WHAT IS IT?

Dessert made of a finger biscuit base soaked
in syrup and ganache, covered with rock glaze
and decorated with chocolate and macarons.

HOW LONG WILL IT TAKE?

Preparation: 3 hours Cooking: 15 minutes
Refrigeration: base, 2 hours
macarons, 12 hours
glazed dessert, 12 hours

EQUIPMENT YOU WILL NEED

Piping bag with No 8 plain nozzle
Piping bag with a basket-weave nozzle
Piping bag with an open star nozzle
Angled palette knife

PLANNING AND PREP

2 days before:
Ganache – finger biscuits
The day before:
Macaron shells – syrup – filling –
making dessert base (biscuit plus
ganache) – making macarons – glaze
On the day:
Decoration – finishing

Learn

SERVES 12

1 FINGER BISCUIT

Base
150 g (5 oz) egg yolks (10 yolks)
65 g (2 ½ oz) white caster (superfine) sugar
65 g (2 ½ oz) flour
65 g (2 ½ oz) potato starch

French meringue
165 g (5 ½ oz) egg whites (5 or 6 whites)
65 g (2 ½ oz) white caster (superfine) sugar

2 CHOCOLATE COATING

60 g (2 oz) dark chocolate (66% cocoa)

3 SOAKING SYRUP

150 g (5 oz) water
75 g (2 ½ oz) white caster (superfine) sugar
1 vanilla pod (bean)

4 WHIPPED GANACHE

600 g (1 lb 5 oz) whipping cream
300 g (10 ½ oz) dark chocolate (66% cocoa)
4 g (2 sheets) sheet gelatine

5 ROCK GLAZE

150 g (5 oz) dark chocolate (66% cocoa)
130 g (4 oz) milk chocolate
25 g (¾ oz) grapeseed oil
80 g (3 oz) blanched chopped almonds

6 MACARON SHELLS

Base
250 g (9 oz) ground (powdered) almonds
220 g (8 oz) icing (confectioner's) sugar
30 g (1 oz) cocoa (unsweetened chocolate) powder
1 pinch red food colouring
100 g (3 ½ oz) egg white (3 or 4 whites)

Italian meringue
80 g (3 oz) water
250 g (9 oz) white caster (superfine) sugar
100 g (3 ½ oz) egg whites (3 or 4 whites)

7 DECORATION

300 g (10 ½ oz) dark couverture chocolate (66% cocoa)
3 g Mycryo powdered cocoa butter

Making the chocolate macaron dessert

1 Make the whipped ganache (page 44) and separate into three containers: 50 g (2 oz) for the decoration, 300 g (10 ½ oz) to decorate the macarons and the rest for the dessert base.

2 Make a finger biscuit base on a lined 40 × 30 cm (16 × 12 in) baking tray (page 60). Make mini macarons (page 146). To make the soaking syrup: heat the water, sugar and scraped vanilla bean in a saucepan, stirring until it boils to dissolve the sugar. Take off the heat and leave to cool at room temperature.

3 To make the dessert base: coat the finger biscuit base with the melted dark chocolate using a paintbrush. When the chocolate has hardened, turn the base out onto baking paper (baking parchment) and remove the baking sheet. Soak in syrup using the cleaned paintbrush and cut into three 6 × 24 cm (2 ½ × 9 ½ in) rectangles.

4 Make the ganache for the base of the dessert (page 44). Using a piping bag with a plain No 8 nozzle, pipe out lengths of ganache tightly packed together onto the first biscuit (page 278). Put the second biscuit on top of the ganache, then pipe out another layer of ganache and put the last biscuit on top.

5 Put the rest of this ganache in a piping bag and, using a basket-weave nozzle, cover the whole dessert except for the underside, and smooth using a palette knife. Leave to harden for 2 hours in the refrigerator.

6 Prepare the ganache for the macarons (page 44) and fill them (page 285). Store in the refrigerator overnight.

7 Make the rock glaze (page 72). When it is warm, glaze the dessert base: put it on a baking rack on a rimmed baking tray to collect the excess as the glaze is poured over. Set aside in the refrigerator overnight.

8 Put the ganache for the decoration in a piping bag with an open star nozzle. Put the dessert on a serving dish, then pipe rosettes of ganache along the length of the dessert. To finish, push two rows of macarons into the top of the dessert, to stand on their edges.

SUCCESS CAKE

Understand

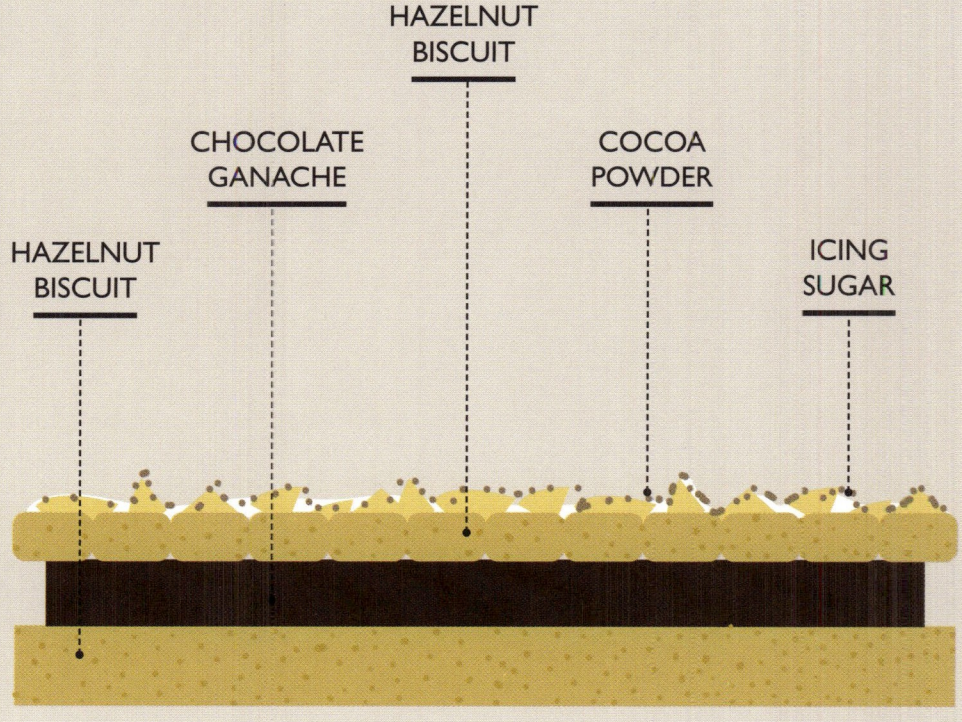

HAZELNUT BISCUIT

CHOCOLATE GANACHE

HAZELNUT BISCUIT

COCOA POWDER

ICING SUGAR

HAZELNUT BISCUIT

WHAT IS IT?

A sandwich cake made of two large hazelnut meringue biscuits with a layer of chocolate ganache in between.

HOW LONG WILL IT TAKE?

Preparation: 40 minutes
Cooking: 20 to 30 minutes
Refrigeration: 6 hours

EQUIPMENT YOU WILL NEED

Three 22 cm (8 ¹/₂ in) pastry rings
Piping bag with No 12 plain nozzle
Hand-held blender
Transparent acetate strip

VARIATION

Replace the ground (powdered) hazelnuts with ground almonds, pistachios or walnuts.

TRICKY POINT

Emulsifying the ganache

SKILLS REQUIRED

Using a double-boiler (page 276)
Using a piping bag (page 278)

ADVICE

Use the ring to draw a template for the biscuits on a baking sheet

TIP

If you do not have invert sugar, use multifloral or acacia honey.

PLANNING AND PREP

The day before:
Ganache
On the day:
Biscuit – assembly

Learn

SERVE 8-10

1 BISCUIT BASE

40 g (1 1/2 oz) flour
120 g (4 oz) ground (powdered) hazelnuts
120 g (4 oz) white caster (superfine) sugar

2 MERINGUE

180 g (6 1/4 oz) egg whites (6 whites)
60 g (2 oz) white caster (superfine) sugar

3 CHOCOLATE GANACHE

330 g (11 oz) dark chocolate (66% cocoa)
360 g (12 oz) whipping cream
60 g (2 oz) inverted sugar or honey

4 DECORATION

30 g (1 oz) icing (confectioner's) sugar
10 g (1/2 oz) cocoa (unsweetened chocolate) powder

Making the success cake

1 To make the ganache: melt the chocolate in a double-boiler (page 276). Bring the cream and inverted sugar/honey to the boil in a saucepan. Remove the chocolate from the double-boiler and pour a third of the cream-inverted sugar/ honey mixture onto the chocolate. Mix in the centre using a spatula to start the emulsion.

2 Add another third of the cream-inverted sugar to the chocolate, mix. Add the remaining third, then mix thoroughly to make a perfect emulsion. Cover the bottom and sides of one pastry ring with cling film (plastic wrap) and place on a lined baking tray. Place a strip of transparent acetate on the inside edges of the pastry ring. Pour the mixture into the ring and refrigerate for at least 6 hours.

3 Preheat the oven to 180°C (350°F/gas 6). Make the biscuit base: sieve the flour into a bowl, add the ground hazelnuts and 120 g (4 oz) sugar and mix well. Make the French meringue (page 69). Add the ingredients and mix with a spatula.

4 Using a No 12 nozzle, pipe the biscuit dough into the second pastry ring, spiralling outwards from the centre (page 278). Pipe out tightly packed domes into the third pastry ring.

5 Bake in the oven for 20 minutes. The biscuits should be golden brown. Remove from the oven and take the biscuits off the baking trays so that they do not dry out.

6 When the biscuits have cooled, turn the spiralled biscuit out onto a serving dish, remove the baking sheet and put the ganache on top. Remove the baking sheet from the second biscuit and place it on top.

7 To serve, sprinkle with plenty of icing (confectioner's) sugar and dust with a little cocoa powder.

CHOCOLATE
MACARONS

Understand

MACARON SHELLS

DARK CHOCOLATE
GANACHE

WHAT IS IT?

A biscuit made with meringue, icing (confectioner's) sugar and ground (powdered) almonds, filled with dark chocolate ganache.

HOW LONG WILL IT TAKE?

Preparation: 2 hours Cooking: 12 to 15 minutes
Standing: 24 hours for the ganache and 24 hours for the filled macarons to mature.

EQUIPMENT YOU WILL NEED

3 cm (1 1/4 in) cutter
Stand mixer fitted with whisk attachment
Flexible kitchen scraper
Thermometer
Piping bag with No 8 nozzle

VARIATION

Spicy chocolate macarons: infuse 1/2 cinnamon stick, 1 star anise and/or 10 cardamom seeds for 30 minutes in the ganache milk.

TRICKY POINTS

Italian meringue
Cooking the macaron shells

SKILLS REQUIRED

Piping (page 278)
Ribbon technique (page 281)

PLANNING, PREP AND STORAGE

Two days before:
Ganache
Previous day:
Shells – filling – maturing
On the day:
Serve
Filled macarons can be kept for 2 weeks well wrapped in a box in the freezer.
Macaron tops can be kept for 1 month in a container in the freezer.

Learn

MAKES 40 TO 50

1 MIX FOR THE SHELLS

250 g (9 oz) ground (powdered) almonds
220 g (8 oz) icing (confectioner's) sugar
30 g (1 oz) cocoa (unsweetened chocolate) powder
1 pinch of red food colouring
100 g (3 １/２ oz) egg whites (3 to 4 whites)

2 ITALIAN MERINGUE

80 g (3 oz) water 250 g (9 oz) white caster (superfine) sugar
100 g (3 １/２ oz) egg whites (3 to 4 whites)

3 DARK WHIPPED GANACHE

300 g (10 １/２ oz) whipping cream
150 g (5 oz) dark chocolate (66% cocoa)
2 g (1 sheet) sheet gelatine

Making chocolate macarons

1   Make the whipped ganache (page 44). To make templates: use the 3 cm (1 ¼ in) cutter to draw 40 to 50 circles on a sheet of baking paper (baking parchment).

2   Preheat the oven to 140°C (280°F/gas 3). To make the Italian meringue: heat the water and sugar in a saucepan and whisk to dissolve the sugar. When the mixture boils, clean the edges of the pan with a wet paintbrush, then stop whisking. Cook at 121°C (250°F). Remove the pan from the heat. In the bowl of the stand mixer, whisk the egg whites at medium speed. When there are no more bubbles in the syrup, pour it in a thin stream into the whites, continuing to whisk until cool.

3   To make the mixture for the meringue shells: put the ground almonds, icing sugar and cocoa powder in a bowl, add the food colouring and egg whites then mix with the scraper until well blended.

4   Incorporate one third of the Italian meringue into the previous mixture using the scraper.

5   Add the remaining meringue and continue to stir, pressing down with the scraper. Take a large amount of the mixture and check how well it 'ribbons' (page 281): it should run off the scraper in a continuous, folding ribbon. If not, mix again. The mixture should spread out evenly in the bowl.

6   Fill the piping bag. Cover a baking tray with the baking paper with the templates drawn on it, with the drawn circle templates underneath so that they can be seen through the paper. Using a piping bag with a No 8 nozzle, pipe out 3 cm (1 ¼ in) diameter discs (page 285) to make the macaron shells. Bake for 12 to 15 minutes. The surface of the shells should not move when touched. Take out of the oven and carefully remove the sheet from the baking tray. Leave to cool.

7   Whip the ganache (page 44). Put the ganache in a piping bag then pipe out onto a macaron shell, stopping 3 mm from the edge (page 285), then place the second shell on top twisting slightly to push the ganache out to the edge. Repeat until all the shells are filled. Leave to stand for 24 hours in an airtight box in the refrigerator.

CHOCOLATE MOUSSE AND MERINGUE
CAKE

Understand

SWISS
MERINGUE

WOLF
FANGS

CHOCOLATE
MOUSSE

DARK CHOCOLATE
SURROUND

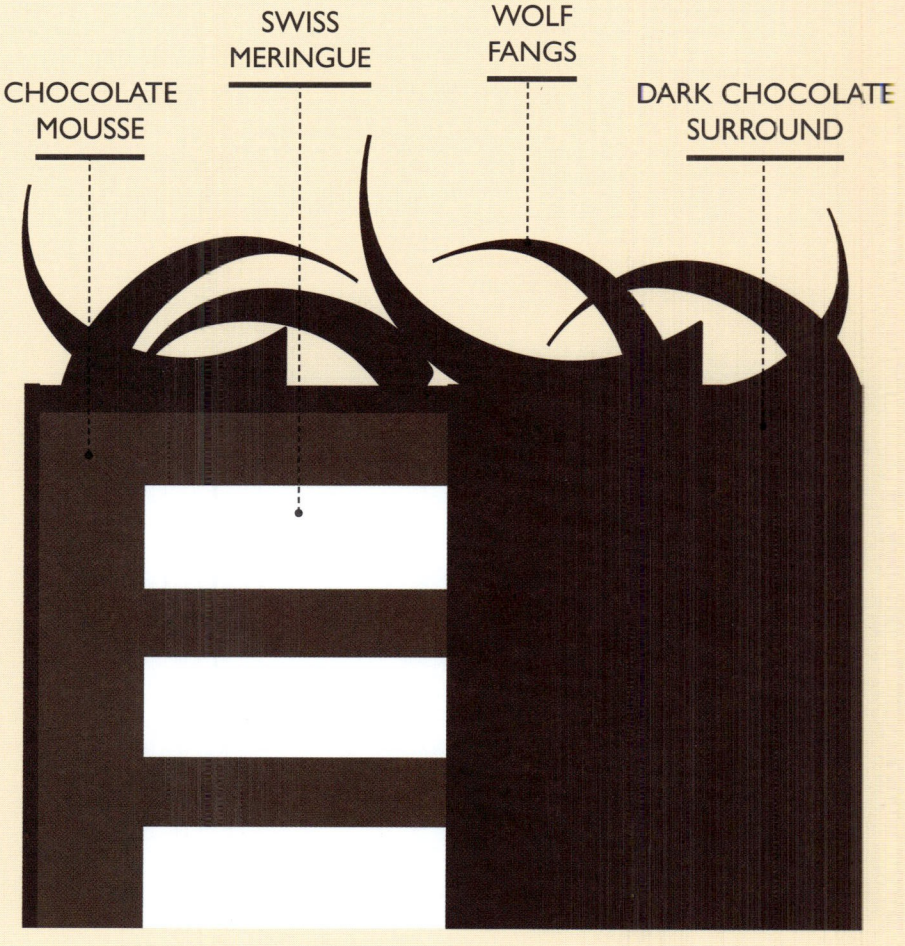

WHAT IS IT?

A dessert made of meringue discs and chocolate mousse, decorated with dark chocolate.

HOW LONG WILL IT TAKE?

Preparation: 2 $^{1}/_{2}$ hours
Cooking: 90 minutes
Standing: 3 hours

EQUIPMENT YOU WILL NEED

22 cm (8 $^{1}/_{2}$ in) pastry ring
24 cm (10 in) 10 cm (4 in) deep pastry ring
Piping bag fitted with No 12 plain nozzle
Transparent acetate strip
Polyethylene sheet
Paintbrush

SKILLS REQUIRED

Coating with a thin layer of chocolate (chabloning; page 273)
Piping (page 278)
Using a double-boiler (page 276)

PLANNING AND PREP

The day before:
Meringue
On the day:
Chocolate mousse – assemble – decorate

ADVICE

If you do not have a pastry ring deep enough for assembling the dessert, double the height of the transparent acetate strip, overlapping the ends and holding them together with adhesive tape, and use a standard-depth ring.

Learn

SERVES 10

1 SWISS MERINGUE

150 g (5 oz) egg whites (5 whites)
150 g (5 oz) white caster (superfine) sugar
150 g (5 oz) icing (confectioner's) sugar

2 CHOCOLATE COATING LAYER

100 g (3 ½ oz) dark chocolate (66% cocoa)
20 g (¾ oz) cocoa butter

3 CHOCOLATE MOUSSE

300 g (10 ½ oz) dark chocolate
(minimum 60% cocoa)
60 g (2 oz) water
150 g (5 oz) white caster (superfine) sugar
120 g (4 oz) egg yolks (8 yolks)
500 g (1 lb 2 oz) whipping cream

4 DECORATION

600 g (1 lb 5 oz) dark chocolate (66% cocoa)

Making the cake

1   Preheat the oven to 90°C (200°F/gas ¼). Draw 3 x 22 cm (8 ½ in) circles on a sheet of baking paper using the pastry ring as a template. Make the Swiss meringue (page 68). Put in a piping bag fitted with the No 12 nozzle, then pipe out 3 discs. Cook for 90 minutes, then cool completely.

2   To make the chocolate coating layer: melt the cocoa butter and chocolate in a double-boiler (page 276) and coat the meringues completely using a paintbrush. Leave to harden for 15 minutes in the refrigerator. Make the chocolate mousse (page 48). Place the 24 cm (10 in) pastry ring on a polyethylene sheet and put a double layer of transparent acetate strips on the sides if necessary. Pipe out the mousse 2 cm (¾ in) thick (page 278), making it thicker along the outer edge, then use a spatula to bring the mousse up along the inside of the pastry ring.

3   Place the first disc of meringue inside and press down gently, pipe out another 2 cm (¾ in) chocolate mousse and add the second meringue disc.

4   Repeat until the last disc of meringue is level with the top of the pastry ring. Leave to set for 3 hours in the refrigerator.

5   Take the dessert out of the refrigerator, turn it out onto a serving dish, remove the pastry ring, the transparent acetate strips and the polyethylene sheet.

6   Make the chocolate decorations (page 38): cover the sides of the dessert with a wide strip of chocolate and decorate the top with wolf fangs.

MARVELLOUS
MERINGUES

Understand

CHOCOLATE
SHAVINGS

BUTTERCREAM

SWISS
MERINGUE

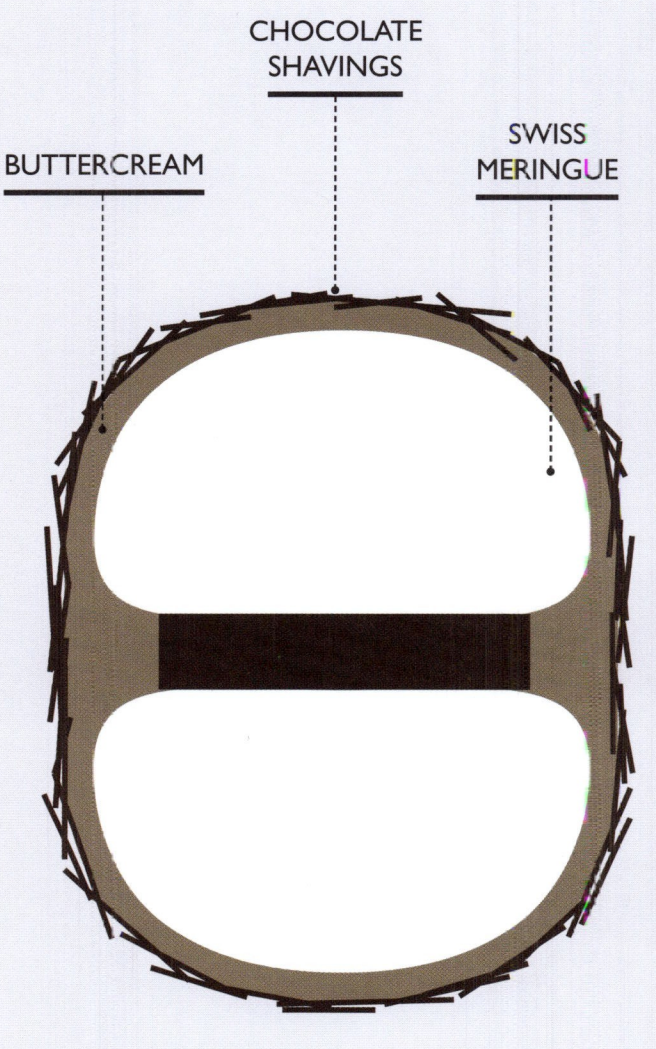

WHAT IS IT?

Individual Swiss meringues coated
with chocolate buttercream and
decorated with chocolate shavings.

HOW LONG WILL IT TAKE?

Preparation: 90 minutes
Cooking: 2 hours

EQUIPMENT YOU WILL NEED

Piping bag
Plain No 12 nozzle
Basket-weave nozzle

VARIATIONS
Fill with whipped cream

SKILL REQUIRED
Piping (page 278)

ADVICE
When incorporating the melted pure
cocoa paste, make sure that it is not
too hot, ideally around 25°C (77°F).

PLANNING AND PREP
The day before: Meringue – shavings
On the day: Buttercream – assemble

MAKES 30

SWISS MERINGUE

150 g (5 oz) egg whites (3 or 4 whites)
150 g (5 oz) white caster (superfine) sugar
150 g (5 oz) icing (confectioner's) sugar

BUTTERCREAM

400 g (14 oz) unsalted butter
150 g (5 oz) pure cocoa paste
200 g (7 oz) eggs (4 eggs)
100 g (3 1/2 oz) water
260 g (9 oz) white caster (superfine) sugar

Learn

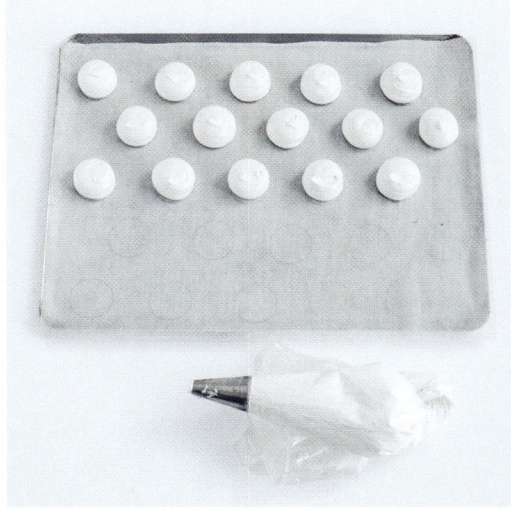

CHOCOLATE COATING LAYER

50 g (2 oz) dark chocolate shavings (66% cocoa), melted

DECORATION

300 g (10 ½ oz) dark chocolate shavings (66% cocoa) (page 38)

1 Preheat the oven to 90°C (200°F/gas ¼). Make the Swiss meringue (page 68). Make 60 dome shapes 3 cm (1 ½ in) wide and 3 cm (1 ½ in) high using the piping bag fitted with a plain No 12 nozzle (page 278). Bake for about 2 hours then leave to cool.

2 To make the buttercream: take the butter out of the fridge 30 minutes in advance so that it has a soft, creamy consistency. Melt the pure cocoa paste in a double-boiler (page 276).

3 In a bowl, combine the water, sugar and eggs (page 46). When cool, gradually add the softened butter, whisking continuously, followed by the melted cocoa paste.

4 Put a small amount of buttercream on the base of a meringue and stick a second meringue on top to form a ball. Dip the base in the melted chocolate. Put a toothpick through each meringue. Fill a piping bag (page 278) with buttercream and cover the ball completely with the buttercream.

5 Roll in the shavings immediately. Repeat the operation with the other meringues. Remove the toothpicks.

RASPBERRY & CHOCOLATE
FEUILLANTINE

DARK CHOCOLATE
DECORATION

RASPBERRY

DARK CHOCOLATE
MOUSSE

FEUILLANTINE

RASPBERRY
JELLY

CHOCOLATE
BISCUIT

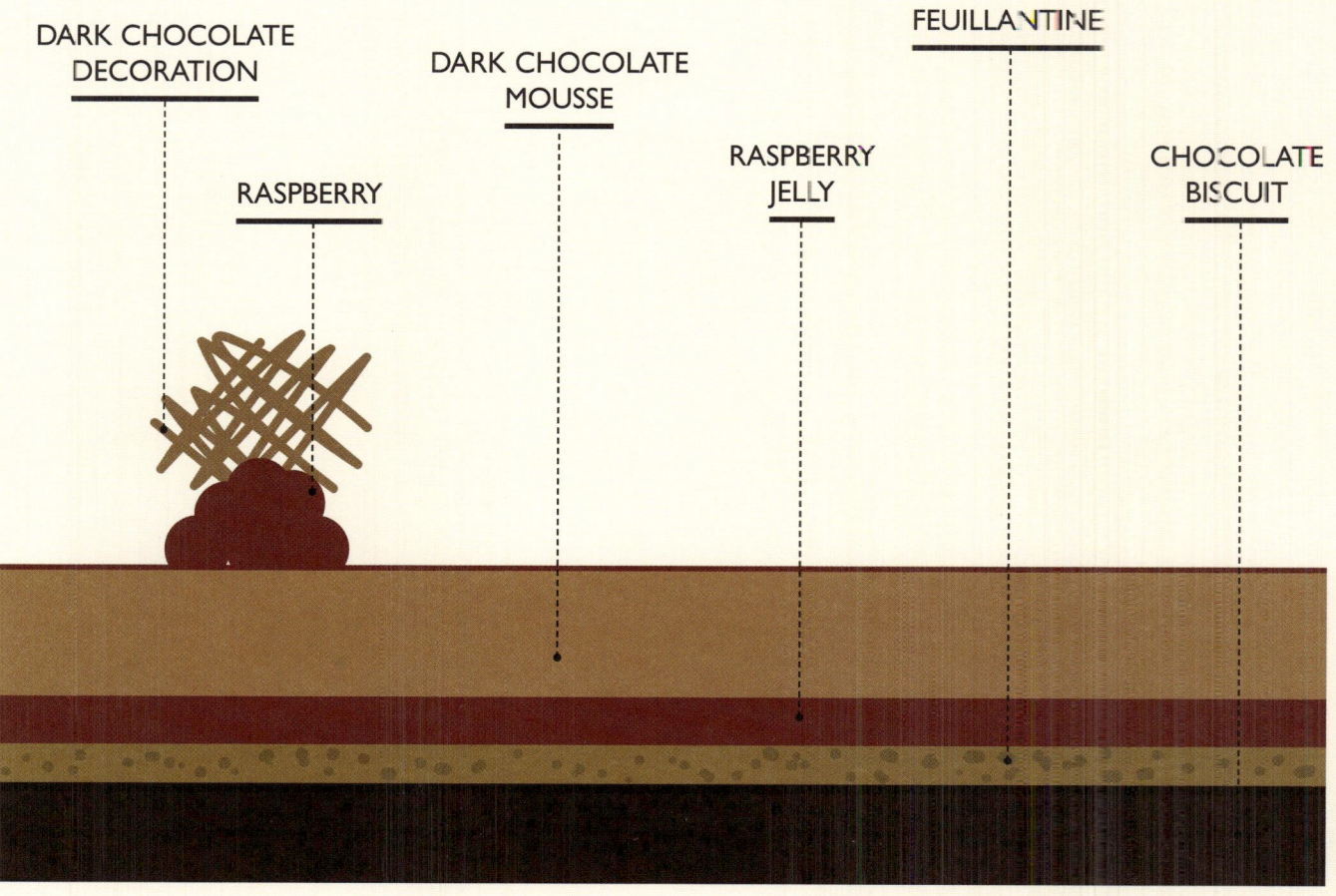

WHAT IS IT?

A dessert with a crunchy centre, on a
flourless chocolate biscuit base coated with
raspberry jelly and chocolate mousse.

HOW LONG WILL IT TAKE?

Preparation: 3 hours
Cooking: 2 ¹/₂ hours
Freezing: 2 hours 20 min
Refrigeration: 4 hours

EQUIPMENT YOU WILL NEED

16 × 16 cm (6 ¹/₂ × 6 ¹/₂ in) baking frame
Angled palette knife
Stand mixer fitted with flat beater attachment

VARIATIONS

For a chocolate-passion fruit dessert, replace
the raspberry purée with passion fruit purée
For a pure chocolate version,
leave out the raspberry jelly.

SKILLS REQUIRED

Rehydrating gelatine (page 277)
Using a double-boiler (page 276)

TIP

This dessert can be made and kept
for up to 3 months in the freezer, well
wrapped in cling film (plastic wrap).
Decorate it just before serving.

PLANNING, PREP AND STORAGE

2 days before
Chocolate decorations
The day before:
Preparation – assemble
On the day:
Decorate

Learn

SERVES 10

1 FLOURLESS CHOCOLATE BISCUIT

Meringue
65 g (2 ½ oz) egg whites (4 whites)
35 g (1 oz) white caster (superfine) sugar

Biscuit base
45 g (1 ¾ oz) egg yolks (3 yolks)
35 g (1 oz) white caster (superfine) sugar
20 g cocoa (unsweetened chocolate) powder

2 CHOCOLATE COATING

50 g (2 oz) dark chocolate (60% cocoa), melted

3 CRUNCHY FEUILLANTINE CENTRE

30 g (1 oz) white chocolate
70 g (2 ½ oz) feuilletine flakes (crushed crispy crêpes; from specialist suppliers)
120 g (4 oz) praline (50%; see page 40)
20 g (¾ oz) softened unsalted butter

4 RASPBERRY JELLY

200 g (7 oz) raspberry purée
55 g (2 oz) white caster (superfine) sugar
6 g (3 sheets) sheet gelatine

5 CHOCOLATE MOUSSE

150 g (5 oz) dark chocolate (minimum 60% cocoa)
25 g (1 oz) water
60 g (2 oz) white caster (superfine) sugar
50 g (2 oz) egg yolks (3 or 4 yolks)
250 g (9 oz) whipping cream

6 DECORATION

Velvet effect spray colouring (from specialist suppliers)
125 g (4 oz) raspberries

Chocolate decorations
150 (5 oz) g dark chocolate (66% cocoa)

To make the raspberry and chocolate feuillantine

1   Make the chocolate decorations (page 38). Make the flourless chocolate biscuit (page 62) in the baking frame. When cool, coat with a thin layer of the melted chocolate (chablon; page 273). Place the chocolate-coated side down on a baking tray covered with a baking sheet, place the frame on top and trim off the excess using a chef's knife.

2   To make the crunchy feuillantine centre: melt the white chocolate in a double-boiler (page 276). Put the praline and the feuilletine in the bowl of the stand mixer bowl fitted with the flat beater and mix at low speed for 3 minutes.

3   Add the white chocolate and softened butter. Mix at low speed. When the mixture is blended, spread evenly on the biscuit using an angled palette knife.

4   To make the raspberry jelly: rehydrate the gelatine (page 277). Boil 100 g (3 $^1\!/_2$ oz) raspberry purée with the sugar in a saucepan. Remove from the heat, add the gelatine and mix. When the gelatine has melted, add the rest of the fruit purée, away from the heat, and mix well.

5   Pour onto the feuillantine layer and transfer to the freezer for 20 minutes for the jelly to set.

6   Make the chocolate mousse (follow the instructions on page 48), spread the mousse immediately on top of the fruit jelly, smooth the top and return to the freezer for at least 2 hours.

7   Put the velvet spray in hot water for 15 minutes, take the dessert out of the freezer and spray at a distance of 30 cm (12 in) to produce the velvet finish. Remove from the frame, smooth the edges with a knife and put in the fridge for at least 4 hours before serving.

8   Decorate with raspberries and chocolate.

GIANDUJA
DESSERT

Understand

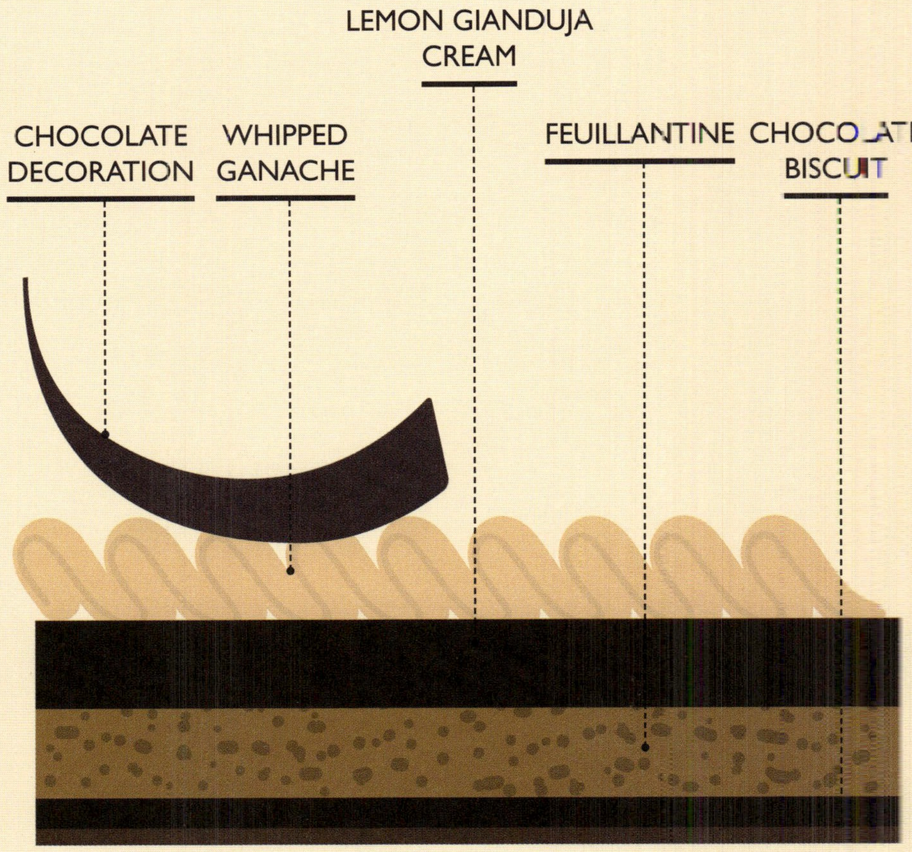

LEMON GIANDUJA
CREAM

CHOCOLATE   WHIPPED   FEUILLANTINE CHOCOLATE
DECORATION   GANACHE   BISCUIT

WHAT IS IT?

Gianduja and lemon cream dessert on a
crunchy chocolate biscuit base, topped
with milk chocolate whipped ganache.

HOW LONG WILL IT TAKE?

Preparation: 2 $^1/_2$ hours
Refrigeration: 1 hour

EQUIPMENT YOU WILL NEED

16 × 16 cm (6 $^1/_2$ × 6 $^1/_2$ in) baking frame
Stand mixer bowl with flat beater attachment
Angled palette knife
Piping bag with basket-weave nozzle

VARIATION

For a passion fruit cream, replace the
lemon juice with passion fruit purée.

SKILLS REQUIRED

Coating with a thin layer of
chocolate (enrobing; page 273)
Piping bag (page 278)
Using a double-boiler (page 276)
Making a caramel (page 282)

PLANNING AND PREP

Previous day:
Ganache – Flourless chocolate biscuit
On the day:
Feuillantine – gianduja cream
– assemble – decorate

Learn

SERVES 10

1 FLOURLESS CHOCOLATE BISCUIT

Meringue
65 g (2 ½ oz) egg whites (4 whites)
35 g (1 oz) white caster (superfine) sugar

Biscuit base
45 g (1 ¾ oz) egg yolks (3 yolks)
35 g (1 oz) white caster (superfine) sugar
20 g (¾ oz) cocoa (unsweetened chocolate) powder

2 CHOCOLATE COATING
50 g (2 oz) dark chocolate (60% cocoa), melted

3 FEUILLANTINE
70 g (2 ½ oz) feuilletine flakes (crushed crispy crêpes; from specialist suppliers)
120 g (4 oz) 50% praline (see page 40)
30 g (1 oz) white chocolate
20 g (¾ oz) softened unsalted butter

4 GIANDUJA-LEMON CREAM
120 g (4 oz) 50% praline (see page 40)
120 g (4 oz) dark chocolate (66% cocoa)
100 g (3 ½ oz) lemon juice (around 6 lemons)
50 g (2 oz) whipping cream

5 WHIPPED MILK GANACHE
300 g (10 ½ oz) whipping cream
150 g (5 oz) milk chocolate
2 g (1 sheet) sheet gelatine

6 DECORATION
150 g (5 oz) couverture chocolate (66% cocoa)

Making the gianduja dessert

1 Make wolf fangs (page 38). Make the whipped ganache (page 44). Make the flourless chocolate biscuit (page 62) directly in the baking frame. When cooled, coat it with dark chocolate (page 273).

2 To make the feuillantine base: melt the white chocolate in a double-boiler (page 276). Put the praline and the feuilletine in the bowl of the stand mixer bowl, using the flat beater, mix on slow speed for 3 minutes. Add the white chocolate and the softened butter. Mix on slow speed.

3 When the mixture is smoothly blended, spread evenly on the biscuit using an angled palette knife.

4 To make the lemon-gianduja cream: melt the dark chocolate in a double-boiler (page 276). Roll the lemons firmly with your hands on the tabletop, then squeeze out the juice with a juice extractor (page 276). Put the praline in a bowl, add the melted chocolate and mix in with a spatula. Heat the cream to around 50°C (122°F) and pour over the chocolate mixture. Add the lemon juice and mix.

5 Pour out onto the feuillantine base. Leave to set for 1 hour in the refrigerator.

6 Remove the dessert from the frame. Using a chef's knife cut into two 8 cm (3 in) halves, then into 3 cm (1 ¹/₂ in) pieces.

7 Make the ganache (page 44), put it in the piping bag with a basket weave nozzle and pipe onto each portion. Decorate with wolf fangs.

162

OPERA CAKE

OPERA GLAZE

ALMOND BISCUIT

COFFEE SYRUP

CHOCOLATE GANACHE

DARK CHOCOLATE

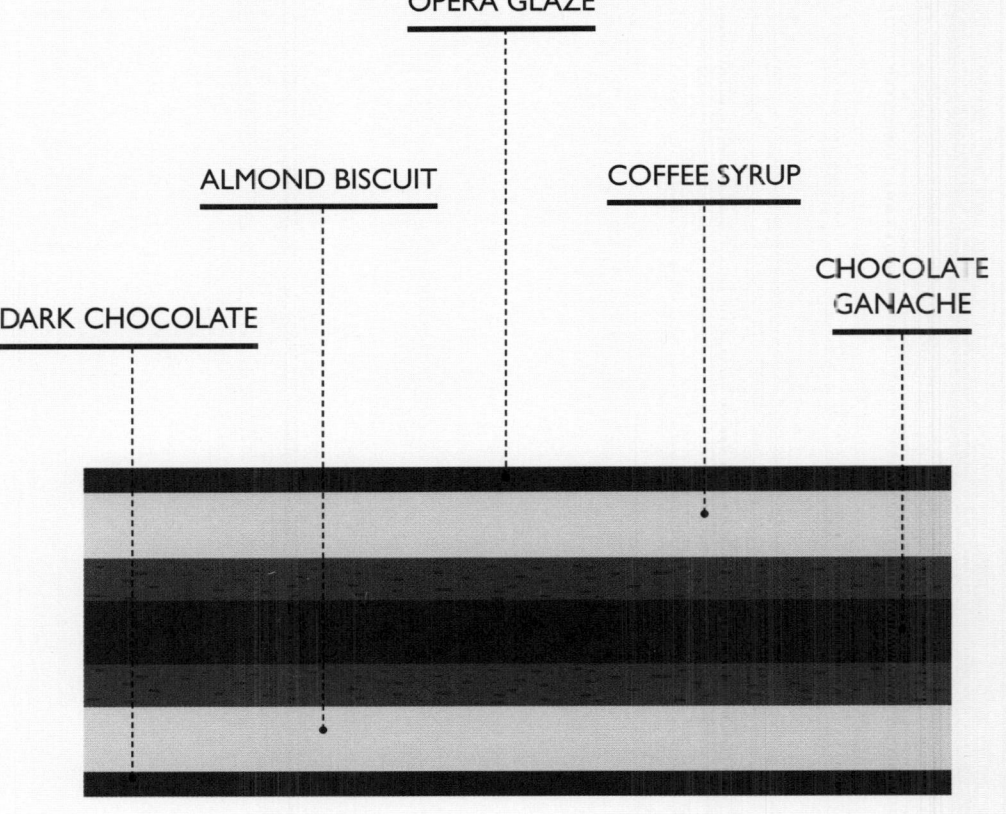

WHAT IS IT?

A dessert made of almond biscuit, ganache and coffee buttercream, covered with an opera glaze.

HOW LONG WILL IT TAKE?

Preparation: 2 hours
Cooking: 8 to 15 minutes
Refrigeration: 4 hours 30 minutes

EQUIPMENT YOU WILL NEED

Square 28 cm (12 in) baking frame
Stand mixer fitted with whisk attachment

TRICKY POINT
Assembling

SKILLS REQUIRED
Coating with a thin layer of chocolate (chabloning; page 273)
Using a double-boiler (page 276)
Piping bag (page 278)

ADVICE
When assembling, the cake parts should be at room temperature so that they are easy to work.

PLANNING AND PREP
The day before:
Biscuit – ganache – buttercream
– punch – assembling
On the day:
Glazing – cutting
Opera cake can be kept, well-wrapped, for 1 month in the freezer before glazing

Learn

SERVES 16

1 ALMOND BISCUIT

Base
200 g (7 oz) ground (powdered) almonds
150 g (5 oz) icing (confectioner's) sugar
300 g (10 1/2 oz) eggs (6 eggs)
170 g (6 oz) egg yolks (10 to 12 yolks)
30 g (1 oz) flour

Meringue
200 g (7 oz) egg whites (6 to 7 whites)
80 g (3 oz) white caster (superfine) sugar

2 COFFEE SYRUP

230 g (8 oz) water
175 g (6 oz) white caster (superfine) sugar
15 g (1/2 oz) instant coffee

3 GANACHE

200 g (7 oz) whipping cream
250 g (9 oz) dark chocolate (60% cocoa)
35 g (1 oz) unsalted butter

4 BUTTERCREAM

600 g (1 lb 5 oz) softened unsalted butter
300 g (10 1/2 oz) eggs (6 eggs)
150 g (5 oz) water
390 g (14 oz) white caster (superfine) sugar
30 g (1 oz) coffee extract

5 CHOCOLATE COATING

60 g (2 oz) dark chocolate (66% cocoa), melted

6 OPERA GLAZE

250 g (9 oz) dark chocolate (66% cocoa)
40 g (1 1/2 oz) sunflower oil

Making the opera cake

1   Make the almond biscuit (page 64). Divide the mixture between three 30 × 40 cm (12 × 16) baking paper (baking parchment)-lined baking trays, putting 300 g (10 ½ oz) on each tray. Bake for 10 minutes at 190°C (375°F). The biscuit should peel away easily from the sheet when you run your finger underneath. Transfer to a cooling rack.

2   To make the coffee syrup: bring the water and sugar to the boil in a saucepan. Turn off the heat and add the instant coffee. Leave to cool. Make the ganache: bring the cream to the boil, then pour onto the chocolate. Wait a few moments, stir, add the butter and blend without incorporating air (page 276).

3   Make the buttercream. Combine the ingredients in a mixing bowl (page 46) and allow to cool. Gradually add the butter, whisking continuously, and then add the coffee extract.

4   To remove the sheet of biscuit from the baking sheets: sprinkle some icing (confectioner's) sugar on a sheet of baking paper then turn the biscuit over onto it. Place another baking tray on top and, holding the tray with one hand, pull the baking paper off the biscuit with the other.

5   Chocolate-coat a sheet of biscuit (page 273). Put the biscuit in the baking frame with the layer of chocolate underneath. Soak generously with the coffee syrup: when you press with your finger the syrup should come to the surface.

6   Spread half of the buttercream over using a palette knife. Add a second sheet of biscuit, then soak again.

7   Spread the ganache over, using a palette knife. Place the last sheet of biscuit on top, soak with the syrup and spread over the remaining buttercream. Chill in the refrigerator for 4 hours.

8   To make the opera glaze: melt the chocolate in the double-boiler (page 276), add the oil and blend. Pour the glaze over the cake in a 2 mm thick layer. Chill in the fridge for 30 minutes.

9   Remove the baking frame. Trim the sides using a chef's knife and cut into 9 x 3.5 cm (3 ½ x 1 ½ in) portions.

PEAR & CHOCOLATE CHARLOTTE
CAKE

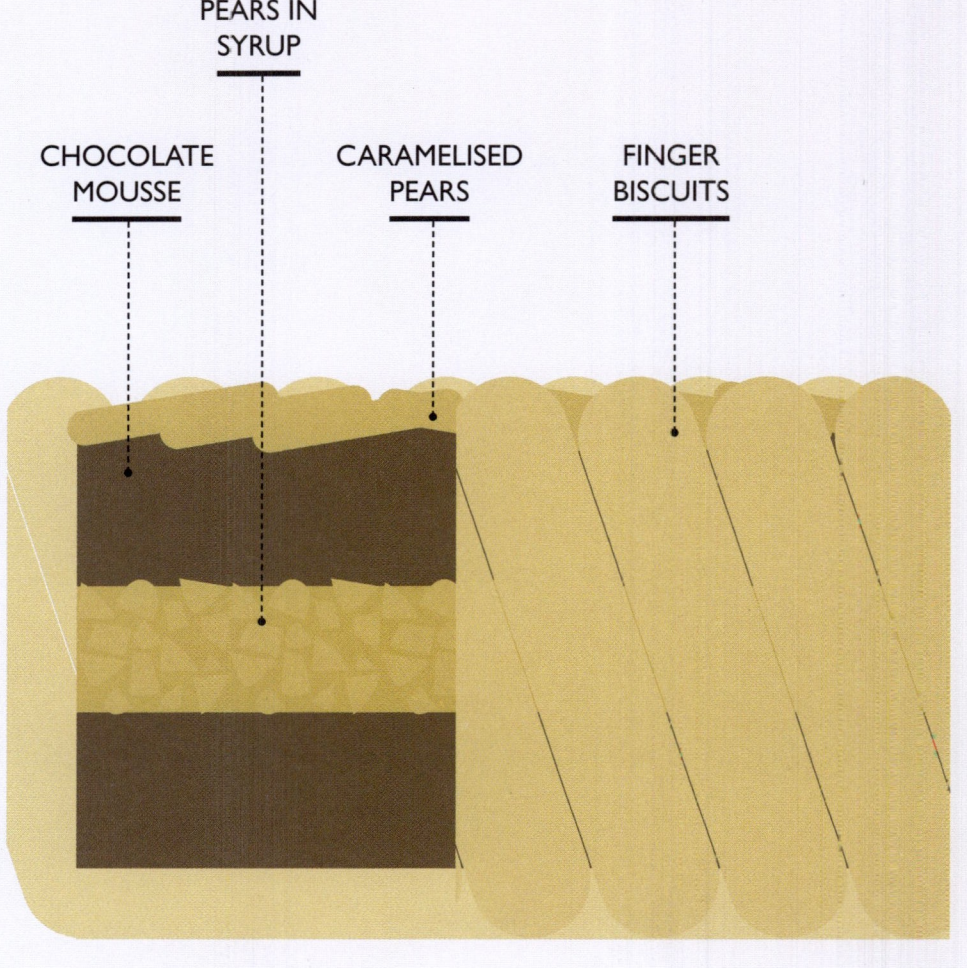

PEARS IN
SYRUP

CHOCOLATE
MOUSSE

CARAMELISED
PEARS

FINGER
BISCUITS

WHAT IS IT?

A dessert cake made of finger biscuits,
chocolate mousse and syrup-soaked pears.

HOW LONG WILL IT TAKE?

Preparation: 2 hours
Cooking: 30 minutes
Refrigeration: 2 hours

EQUIPMENT YOU WILL NEED

24 cm (9 ¹/₂ in) pastry ring
Piping bag fitted with plain No 10 nozzle
Transparent acetate strip

TRICKY POINT
Piping out the biscuit

SKILL REQUIRED
Piping bag (page 278)

TIP
For a spongier version (or if the finger
biscuit is too dry and tends to break when
assembling), using a paintbrush, soak it
in the syrup from the cooked pears.

PLANNING AND PREP
Previous day:
Biscuit – cook the pears – caramelise pears
On the day:
Chocolate mousse – assembling – decorating

Learn

SERVES 8 TO 10

1 FINGER BISCUIT

Biscuit base
200 g (7 oz) egg yolks (14 to 15 yolks)
90 g (3 ¼ oz) white caster (superfine) sugar
90 g (3 ¼ oz) flour
90 g (3 ¼ oz) potato starch

French meringue
220 g (8 oz) egg whites (7 or 8 whites)
90 g (3 ¼ oz) white caster (superfine) sugar

2 CHOCOLATE MOUSSE

90 g (3 ¼ oz) whipping cream
90 g (3 ¼ oz) milk
35 g (1 oz) egg yolks (2 yolks)
15 g (½ oz) white caster (superfine) sugar
260 g (9 oz) dark chocolate (66% cocoa)
340 g (11 oz) whipping cream

3 PEARS IN SYRUP

1 litre (34 fl oz/4 cups/2 lb 4 oz) water
400 g (14 oz) white caster (superfine) sugar
1 vanilla pod (bean)
3 firm conference pears

4 CARAMELISED PEARS

5 firm conference pears
400 g white caster (superfine) sugar

To make the pear and chocolate charlotte cake

1   To make the pear syrup: peel the pears, cut in half and remove and discard the pips. Bring the water, sugar and scraped vanilla to the boil in a saucepan, reduce to a simmer and add the pear halves. Cook for about 15 minutes: they should be tender. Drain. Once cooled, cut into small cubes.

2   To make the caramelised pears: peel, cut in half and remove and discard the pips. In a frying pan, make a dry caramel (page 282), add the pears away from the heat, mix gently with a spatula, reduce the heat to medium, and cook, stirring from time to time, until the edges of the pears are translucent. Drain and leave to cool.

3   Make the finger biscuit mixture (page 60). Preheat the oven to 200°C (400°F/gas 7). Put the mixture in the piping bag. Draw 2 circles, 22 cm (8 1/2 in) in diameter, on a sheet of baking paper (baking

parchment). Put on a baking sheet then pipe out spirals of the biscuit mixture on the paper, working evenly from the centre outwards (page 278). To make the outside of the charlotte, pipe two rows of tightly packed, 6 cm (2 1/2 in) cylindrical finger biscuits evenly onto a lined baking sheet the full length of the tray. Bake for 8 to 15 minutes. Leave to cool.

4   Place the pastry ring, lined with transparent acetate strip, on a baking tray covered with baking paper (baking parchment). Cut off the edges of one of the finger biscuit rows, and stand it vertically on the inside of the pastry ring. Cut off the edges of the second row of finger biscuits and join it to the first one inside the ring.

5   Carefully slice a finger biscuit disc into the bottom. Make the crème anglaise chocolate mousse (page 60). Pour out the mousse 2 cm (1 in) thick onto the biscuit disc.

6   Add half of the pear cubes. Pour out another 2 cm (1 in) of mousse, place the second biscuit disc on top and repeat the above steps.

7   Finish with a layer of mousse. Refrigerate for 2 hours.

8   Cut the caramelised pears into thin slices and arrange in a rosette on the top of the charlotte cake.

PINEAPPLE CHOCOLATE & KAFFIR LIME
DESSERT

DRIED
PINEAPPLE

PINEAPPLE AND
KAFFIR LIME INSERT

CHOCOLATE
MOUSSE

DARK
GLAZE

ALMOND
CHOCOLATE DISC

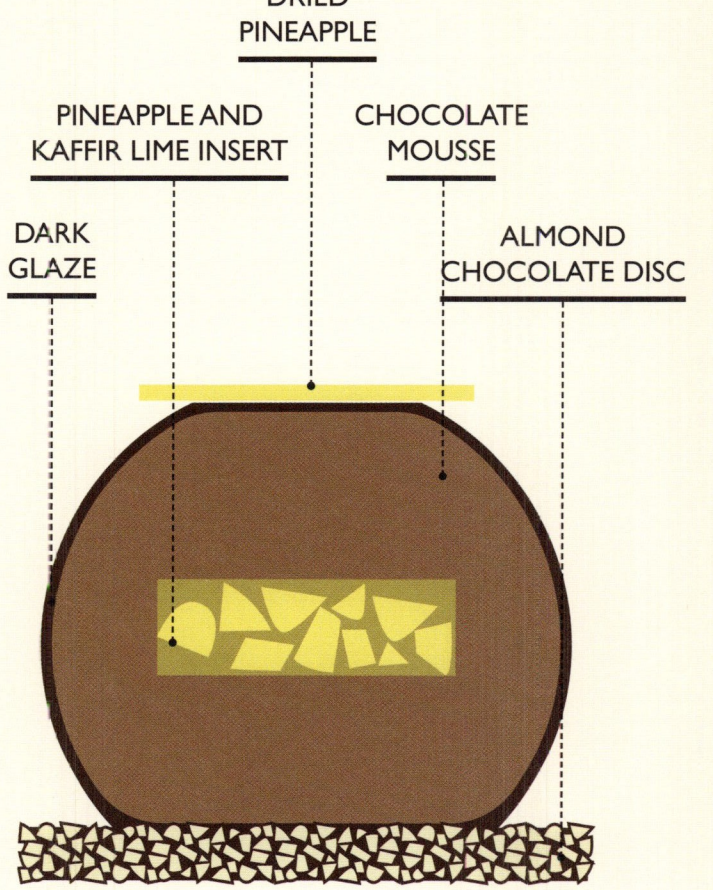

WHAT IS IT?

Dark chocolate mousse sphere with a
pineapple and kaffir lime jelly centre,
set on an almond chocolate disc.

HOW LONG WILL IT TAKE?

Preparation: 3 hours Cooking:
2 hours Freezing: 2 × 6 hours
Defrosting: 4 hours

EQUIPMENT YOU WILL NEED

6 to 8 cm (2 ¹/₂ in to 3 in)
diameter spherical mould

3 × 2 cm (1 in) silicone imprints
6 cm (2 ¹/₂ in) round biscuit cutter
Silicone sheet
Piping bag
Spatula
Toothpick

VARIATION
Replace the kaffir lime with ordinary lime.

SKILLS REQUIRED
Rehydrating gelatine (page 277)
Using a double-boiler (page 276)
Dipping (page 32)

ADVICE
To cut out regular pineapple slices, use a
6 cm (2 ¹/₂ in) round cutter. Keep the discs
and the dried pineapple slices in a dry place.

TIP
If a Victoria pineapple is not available,
use an ordinary pineapple.

PLANNING AND PREP
2 days before:
Pineapple - kaffir lime insert – dried pineapple
The day before:
Discs – mousse sphere
On the day:
Glaze – Decorate

Learn

MAKES 8

1 PINEAPPLE AND KAFFIR LIME CENTRE WITH DRIED PINEAPPLE

2 ripe Victoria pineapples
150 g (5 oz) water
200 g (7 oz) white caster (superfine) sugar
6 g (3 sheets) sheet gelatine
1 kaffir lime

2 ALMOND CHOCOLATE DISCS

150 g (5 oz) chopped blanched almonds
50 g (2 oz) syrup (from the pineapple preparation)
10 g (½ oz) cocoa butter
100 g (3 ½ oz) dark chocolate (66% cocoa)

3 CHOCOLATE MOUSSE

60 g (2 oz) whipping cream
60 g (2 oz) milk
25 g (1 oz) egg yolks (2 yolks)
10 g (½ oz) white caster (superfine) sugar
175 g (6 oz) dark chocolate (66% cocoa)
25 g (1 oz) whipping cream

4 DARK GLAZE

120 g (4 oz) water
100 g (3 ½ oz) whipping cream
220 g (8 oz) white caster (superfine) sugar
80 g (3 oz) cocoa (unsweetened chocolate) powder
10 g (5 sheets) sheet gelatine

To make the pineapple chocolate and kaffir lime dessert

1 To make the centres: peel the pineapples, cut off about ten 2 mm thin slices and cut the rest of the pineapple into 5 mm (¹/₄ in) cubes (discard the cores). Bring the water and sugar to the boil to make a syrup. Set aside 50 g (2 oz) of this syrup to caramelise the almonds. Add the pineapple cubes and slices to the remaining syrup, reduce heat to a simmer and cook for 15 minutes. Take off the heat and drain the pineapple, collecting the syrup in a separate bowl.

2 Place the pineapple slices on a silicone sheet and dry in a low oven 90°C (200°F/gas ¹/₄) for about 90 minutes, turning them over halfway through.

3 Rehydrate the gelatine (page 277), reheat 150 g (5 oz) of the pineapple syrup, remove from the heat and add the drained gelatine and lime peel. Put a few pineapple cubes in each of the silicone moulds, then fill with the jellied syrup, spread the syrup evenly with the back of a spoon and freeze for at least 6 hours (ideally overnight).

4 Preheat the oven to 160°C (320°F/gas 4). To make the discs: mix together the almonds and the syrup you set aside earlier. Spread out on a baking tray lined with baking paper (baking parchment) and bake in the oven for about 20 minutes, stirring occasionally with a spatula. Leave to cool. Melt the cocoa butter and chocolate in a double-boiler (page 276). Remove from the double-boiler and add the caramelised almonds. Using the biscuit cutter as a guide, form eight 1 cm (¹/₂ in) thick discs. Press down gently then leave to harden.

5 Make the chocolate mousse (page 50). Using the piping bag, pipe out the mousse into the base of the spherical mould in a 3 cm (1 ¹/₄ in) thick layer (page 278). Using a spatula, push the mousse up the sides of the imprints. Unmould the pineapple inserts and place one in the centre of each sphere. Close the moulds and fill with mousse through the holes. Freeze for at least 6 hours (ideally overnight).

6 Make the dark glaze (page 70). Remove the spheres from the mould, place them on toothpicks and dip in the glaze, scraping the bases against the side of the bowl to remove the excess then place directly on the discs. Leave to defrost for at least 4 hours in the refrigerator.

7 Top with a slice of dried pineapple just before serving

174

COCONUT CHOCOLATE
DESSERT

Understand

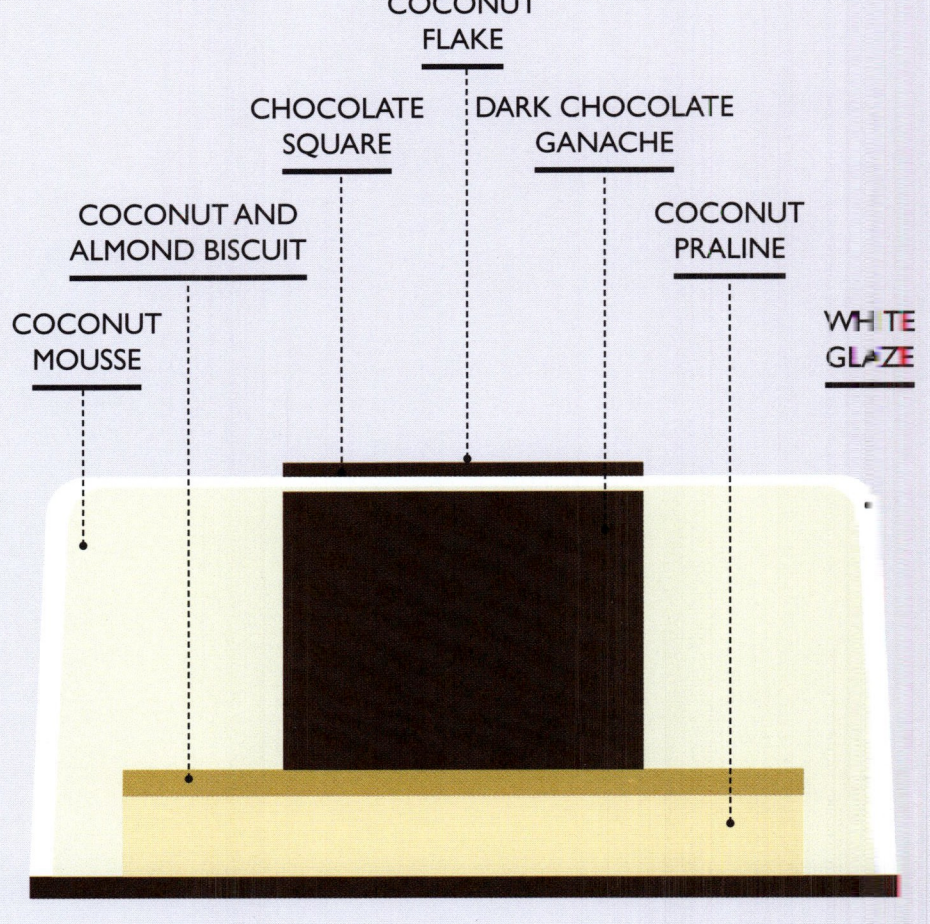

COCONUT
FLAKE

CHOCOLATE
SQUARE

DARK CHOCOLATE
GANACHE

COCONUT AND
ALMOND BISCUIT

COCONUT
PRALINE

COCONUT
MOUSSE

WHITE
GLAZE

WHAT IS IT?

A dessert made of almond and coconut biscuit, coconut praline, creamy ganache and a coconut mousse, decorated with white icing sugar and grated coconut.

HOW LONG WILL IT TAKE?

Preparation: 3 hours
Cooking: 1 hour
Freezing: 2 × 6 hours
Defrosting: 4 hours

EQUIPMENT YOU WILL NEED

six 7 cm (3 in) dessert rings
6 cm (2 ¹/₂ in) round pastry cutter
Silicone mould with 3 cm (1 ¹/₄ in) diameter 2 cm (³/₄ in) deep disc imprints
Polythene sheet
Transparent acetate strip

SKILLS REQUIRED

Coating with a thin layer of chocolate (chabloning; page 273)
Whipping cream (page 280)

PLANNING AND PREP

2 days before: Coconut decoration – almond-coconut biscuit – coconut praline – creamy ganache – assemble insert – freezing
The day before: Coconut mousse – assemble dessert
On the day: Icing – Decorate

MAKES 6

1 ALMOND COCONUT BISCUIT

Base

25 g (1 oz) ground (powdered) almonds
50 g (2 oz) grated OR desiccated (dried shredded) coconut
75 g (2 ¹/₂ oz) icing (confectioner's) sugar
40 g (1 ¹/₂ oz) egg yolks (2 yolks)
70 g (2 ¹/₂ oz) whole eggs (1 or 2 eggs)
65 g (2 ¹/₂ oz) flour

Meringue française

115 g (3 ³/₄ oz) egg whites (4 whites)
50 g (2 oz) white caster (superfine) sugar

Learn

2 CHOCOLATE COATING

60 g (2 oz) white chocolate, melted

3 COCONUT PRALINE

200 g (7 oz) grated or desiccated (dried shredded) coconut
200 g (7 oz) white caster (superfine) sugar
1 g (¼ teaspoon) flaky fleur de sel

4 CREAMY GANACHE

125 g (4 oz) milk
25 g (1 oz) egg yolks (2 yolks)
25 g (1 oz) white caster (superfine) sugar
75 g (2 ½ oz) dark chocolate (66% cocoa)

5 COCONUT MOUSSE

Base
160 g (5 oz) whipping cream
6 g (3 sheets) sheet gelatine
200 g (7 oz) coconut purée

Egg yolk syrup mixture
15 g (½ oz) water
35 g (1 oz) white caster (superfine) sugar
50 g (2 oz) egg yolks (3 or 4 yolks)

6 WHITE CHOCOLATE GLAZE

120 g (4 oz) milk
30 g (1 oz) water
50 g (2 oz) glucose syrup
6 g (3 sheets) sheet gelatine
300 g (10 ½ oz) white chocolate

7 COCONUT DECORATION

150 g (5 oz) couverture chocolate (66% cocoa)
1 coconut

To make the coconut and chocolate dessert

1   Make the chocolate squares for the decoration (page 38). Make the finger biscuit base (page 60).

2   To make the coconut praline: roast the grated or desiccated coconut for 15 minutes in the oven at 160°C (320°F/gas 4). Make a dry caramel with the sugar and the fleur de sel (page 282). When it is a light caramel colour, remove from the heat, add the roasted coconut and mix. Spread out on a baking sheet and leave to cool, then grind in a blender to make a smooth paste. Spread the paste between two sheets of baking paper then roll out using a rolling pin. Peel off one of the sheets and place the finger biscuit base on top. Turn the whole cake over and leave to cool.

3   Make the creamy ganache (page 42) and fill six moulds up to the top. Using the biscuit cutter, stamp out out 4 cm (1 ½ in) discs of biscuit and place on top of the ganache. Apply

a thin layer of the melted white chocolate (you will use the rest later). Freeze for 6 hours.

4   To make the coconut mousse: whip the cream (page 280) and set aside in the fridge. Rehydrate the gelatine (page 277). Bring to a boil 50 g (2 oz) of the coconut purée then, away from the heat, add the drained gelatine into it. Transfer to a heatproof bowl, add the remaining coconut purée and mix well. Make an egg yolk syrup mixture (page 46). Put one-third of the whipped cream into the coconut-gelatine mixture and whisk briskly. Add the egg yolk syrup mixture and whisk gently, then add the remaining cream and mix gently using a spatula.

5   Unmould the frozen ganache inserts and return them to the freezer. Put the pastry rings on the polyethylene sheet and line each with transparent acetate strip. Pipe out a 3 cm (1 ¼ in) thick layer

of coconut mousse (page 278) onto each. Remove the inserts from the freezer. One by one, insert them with the ganache underneath and the chablon on top, making a quarter turn so that the mousse rises properly up the side, removing any excess. If necessary add more mousse so that the biscuit is level with the top of the ring. Freeze for 6 hours.

6   Make the white chocolate glaze (page 75). Unmould the rings onto a rack, with the biscuit underneath, remove the transparent acetate strip, then glaze each dessert and leave to defrost on the sheet in the refrigerator for at least 4 hours.

7   Serve with a square of chocolate and a coconut flake on top.

BLACK FOREST GATEAU

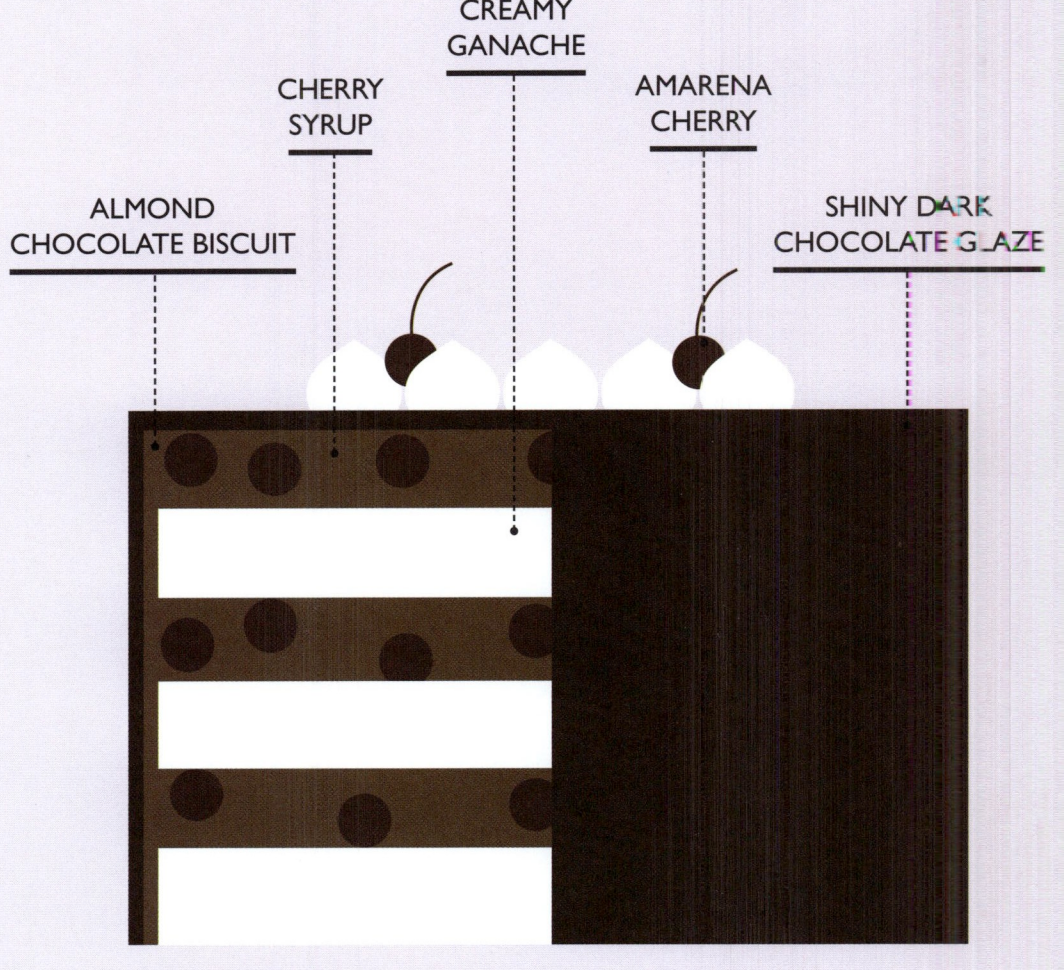

CREAMY GANACHE

CHERRY SYRUP

AMARENA CHERRY

ALMOND CHOCOLATE BISCUIT

SHINY DARK CHOCOLATE GLAZE

WHAT IS IT?

A syrup-soaked chocolate biscuit cake filled with creamy ganache, covered with amarena cherries and white ganache, coated with glossy dark chocolate glaze.

HOW LONG WILL IT TAKE?

Preparation: 3 hours
Cooking: 25 minutes
Freezing: 4 hours

EQUIPMENT YOU WILL NEED

22 cm (8 ¹/₂ in) pastry ring
24 cm (9 ¹/₂ in) pastry ring
12 cm (4 ¹/₂ in) pastry ring
Transparent acetate tape
Polyethylene sheet
Piping bag with grooved nozzle

TRICKY POINT

Glazing

SKILLS REQUIRED

Coating with a thin layer of chocolate (chabloning; page 273)
Piping (page 278)

ADVICE

If you assemble the cake upside-down, the result is much neater and it also prevents the top of the cake from sinking when kept in the freezer.

TIP

To make cutting and soaking easier, leave the biscuit to stand in a cloth for 2 to 3 days at room temperature.

ORGANIZATION

2 days before: White ganache – creamy ganache – biscuit – chocolate decorations
1 day before: Syrup – assembling
On the day: Glazing – Decorate

Learn

SERVES 10

1 ALMOND-CHOCOLATE BISCUIT

75 g (2 ½ oz) ground (powdered) almonds
75 g (2 ½ oz) icing (confectioner's) sugar
40 g (1 ½ oz) egg yolks (3 yolks)
70 g (2 ½ oz) eggs (1 or 2 eggs)
115 g (3 ¾ oz) egg whites (4 whites)
50 g (2 oz) white caster (superfine) sugar
35 g (1 oz) flour
30 g (1 oz) cocoa (unsweetened chocolate) powder

2 CHOCOLATE COATING

50 g (2 oz) dark chocolate (66% cocoa), melted

3 WHIPPED WHITE GANACHE

600 g (1 1lb 5 oz) whipping cream
2 vanilla pods (beans)
150 g (5 oz) white chocolate
6 g (3 sheets) sheet gelatine

4 CREAMY GANACHE

250 g (9 oz) milk
50 g (2 oz) egg yolks (3 or 4 yolks)
50 g (2 oz) white caster (superfine) sugar
200 g (7 oz) dark chocolate (60% cocoa)

5 SOAKING SYRUP

200 g (7 oz) amarena cherry syrup
30 g (1 oz) white caster (superfine) sugar
70 g (2 ½ oz) water

6 TOPPING

250 g (9 oz) amarena cherries

7 SHINY DARK CHOCOLATE GLAZE

180 g (6 ¼ oz) water
150 g (5 oz) whipping cream
330 g (11 oz) white caster (superfine) sugar
120 g (4 oz) cocoa (unsweetened chocolate) powder
14 g (7 sheets) sheet gelatine

8 CHOCOLATE DECORATION

200 g (7 oz) dark chocolate (66% cocoa)
50 g (2 oz) cherries

To make the Black Forest gateau

1   Make the chocolate discs for the decoration (page 38). Make the whipped ganache (page 44) and the creamy ganache (page 42). Make the almond-chocolate biscuit (page 64) incorporating the cocoa powder and the flour at the same time. Bake in the 22 cm (8 ½ in) pastry ring lined with baking paper (baking parchment) for about 25 minutes at 180°C (350°F/gas 6), then leave to cool on a rack.

2   Prepare the soaking syrup: put the water, sugar and cherry syrup in a saucepan, bring to the boil and leave to cool. Using a serrated knife, cut a very thin slice off the top of the biscuit and cut the rest of the cake into three discs of equal thickness. Lightly coat the bottom disc with a thin layer of chocolate (page 273) and leave to harden in the refrigerator for 5 minutes.

3   Make the white ganache (reserving 200 g (7 oz) for the decoration) and put in a piping bag. Line the 24 cm (9 ½ in) pastry ring with the transparent acetate tape and place on a baking tray lined with the polyethylene sheet. Put the ganache in a piping bag then pipe out a 5 mm (¼ in) thick base of white ganache, spiralling from the centre outwards. When you reach the edge of the ring, pipe out 3 thicknesses around the circumference, then work the ganache up to the top of the ring using a palette knife.

4   Add one of the plain biscuit discs, press down gently, and soak with syrup using a paintbrush; when you press down with your finger, the syrup should rise to the surface. Working from the centre outwards, pipe out a 5 mm (¼ in) thick layer of ganache, then add 250 g (9 oz) of creamy ganache and place half of the cherries on top. Place the second biscuit disc on top, soak with syrup, then add the rest of the white ganache, the creamy ganache and the cherries. Soak the chocolate-coated biscuit with syrup and place it on the ganache with the coated layer uppermost. Put in the freezer for at least 4 hours.

5   Make the glossy dark glaze (page 70). Turn the dessert over on a rack, remove the pastry ring and the acetate strip. Glaze starting at the edges and moving towards the centre. Remove excess glaze using a palette knife then transfer to a serving dish. Leave to defrost for at least 4 hours in the refrigerator.

6   Mark out a circle on the glaze using a 12 cm (4 ½ in) pastry ring. Whisk the white ganache again if necessary then put in a clean piping bag fitted with a grooved nozzle and pipe out dome shapes onto the circle. Top with the cherries and the chocolate disc decorations.

INTENSE CHOCOLATE
LOG

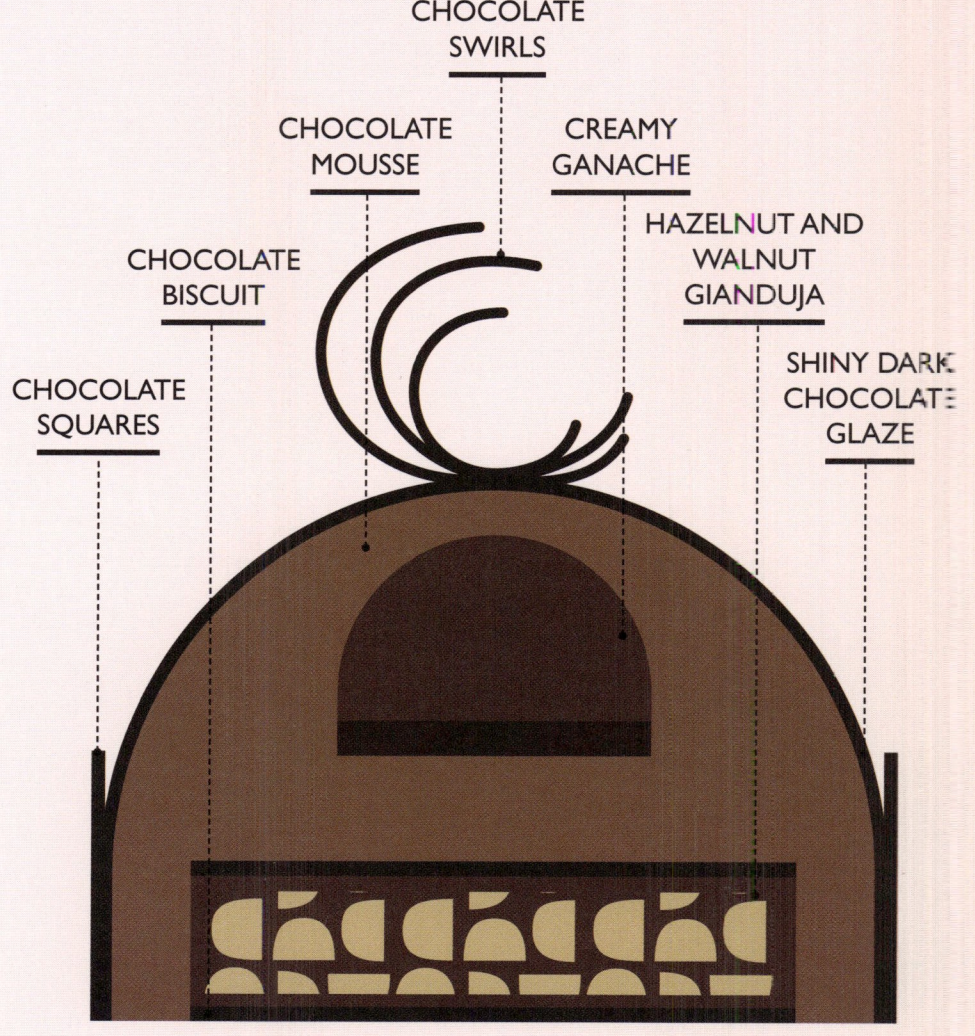

CHOCOLATE SWIRLS

CHOCOLATE MOUSSE

CREAMY GANACHE

HAZELNUT AND WALNUT GIANDUJA

CHOCOLATE BISCUIT

SHINY DARK CHOCOLATE GLAZE

CHOCOLATE SQUARES

WHAT IS IT?

A log made on a flourless chocolate biscuit base, with hazelnut and walnut gianduja, a creamy ganache centre and dark chocolate mousse, coated with a dark chocolate glaze and topped with chocolate decorations.

HOW LONG WILL IT TAKE?

Preparation: 2 $^1/_2$ hours
Cooking: 30 minutes
Freezing: 12 hours
Standing: 2 hours

EQUIPMENT YOU WILL NEED

30 × 4.5 × 3.5 cm (12 × 1 $^3/_4$ × 1 $^1/_2$ in) stainless steel insert mould
30 × 9 × 6 cm (12 × 3 $^1/_2$ × 2 $^1/_2$ in) stainless steel log cake mould
30 × 8 × 8 cm (12 × 3 × 3 in) cake tin
Log cake presentation board

TRICKY POINTS

Unmoulding
Glazing

SKILLS REQUIRED

Making chocolate decorations (page 38)
Coating with a thin layer of chocolate (chablonin; page 273)
Making glaze (page 279)

ADVICE

To remove the ganache insert from its mould, quickly run hot water over the mould, then twist the mould slightly to let air in. Return the chocolate insert to the freezer for 30 minutes before handling.

PLANNING, PREP AND STORAGE

2 days before: Decorations – biscuit – ganache insert
1 day before: Mousse – assembling
On the day: Glazing – Decorate – Defrost
Make the log up to 3 weeks in advance and keep wrapped in cling film (plastic wrap) in the freezer. Make the glaze before serving.

Learn

SERVES 8 TO 10

1 HAZELNUT AND WALNUT GIANDUJA

45 g roasted chopped hazelnuts
45 g roasted chopped walnuts
80 g (3 oz) chocolate
135 g 50% praline (see page 40)
35 g (1 oz) blanched almonds
35 g (1 oz) blanched hazelnuts
70 g (2½ oz) white caster (superfine) sugar
30 g (1 oz) water

2 FLOURLESS CHOCOLATE BISCUIT BASE

40 g (1½ oz) cocoa (unsweetened chocolate) powder
90 g (3¼ oz) egg yolks (5 or 6)
125 g (4 oz) egg whites (4 whites)
70 g (2½ oz) + 70 g (2½ oz + 2½ oz) white caster (superfine) sugar

3 CHOCOLATE COATING LAYER

40 g (1½ oz) dark chocolate, melted

4 CREAMY GANACHE

150 g (5 oz) dark chocolate (60% cocoa)
50 g (2 oz) egg yolks (3 or 4 yolks depending on the size of the eggs)
50 g (2 oz) white caster (superfine) sugar
250 g (9 oz) milk

5 CHOCOLATE MOUSSE

200 g (7 oz) dark chocolate (60% cocoa)
40 g (1½ oz) water
100 g (3½ oz) white caster (superfine) sugar
80 g (3 oz) egg yolks (5 or 6 yolks)
350 g whipping cream

6 GLOSSY DARK CHOCOLATE GLAZE

180 g (6¼ oz) water
150 g (5 oz) whipping cream
330 g (11 oz) white caster (superfine) sugar
120 g (4 oz) cocoa (unsweetened chocolate) powder
14 g (7 sheets) sheet gelatine

7 CHOCOLATE DECORATIONS

300 g (10½ oz) dark chocolate (60% cocoa)

To make the intense chocolate log

1   Make the chocolate decorations (page 38). Make the flourless chocolate biscuit base (page 62). Make the creamy ganache centre (page 42) and pour it into the insert mould. Cut the biscuit to the size of the insert using a chef's knife, place it on the base of the insert and put it in the freezer for 6 hours.

2   Make the gianduja (page 40). Coat the rest of the biscuit with a thin layer of chocolate (page 273), and put it, chocolate-coated side down, in the base of the baking paper (baking parchment)-lined cake tin (so that it can be easily removed after setting in the refrigerator). Pour the gianduja over the biscuit on the side without the chocolate layer and spread evenly using a spatula. Leave to set in the refrigerator for 1 $^{1}/_{2}$ hours.

3   Make the chocolate mousse (page 50). Pour 3 cm (1 $^{1}/_{4}$ in) of it into the log mould. Using a spatula, work the mousse up to cover the sides. Unmould the creamy chocolate insert and place it in the log mould with the rounded side downwards.

4   Pour in the remaining mousse up to 1 cm ($^{1}/_{2}$ in) from the top edge. Trim the gianduja/biscuit base so that it is smaller than the log mould, place it on the mousse with the chocolate-coated layer uppermost, press down gently so that the mousse rises on the sides until it is on a level with the mould. Put in the freezer for at least 6 hours.

5   Make the glossy dark chocolate glaze (page 70). Glaze the log (page 79). Place it on a log cake presentation board and put in the freezer for 1 minute to allow the glaze to set, then transfer to the refrigerator.

6   Trim off the ends off the log. Before serving, decorate the sides with chocolate squares and the top with chocolate swirls.

PASSION FRUIT MILK CHOCOLATE
LOG

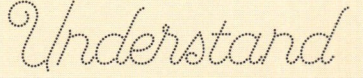

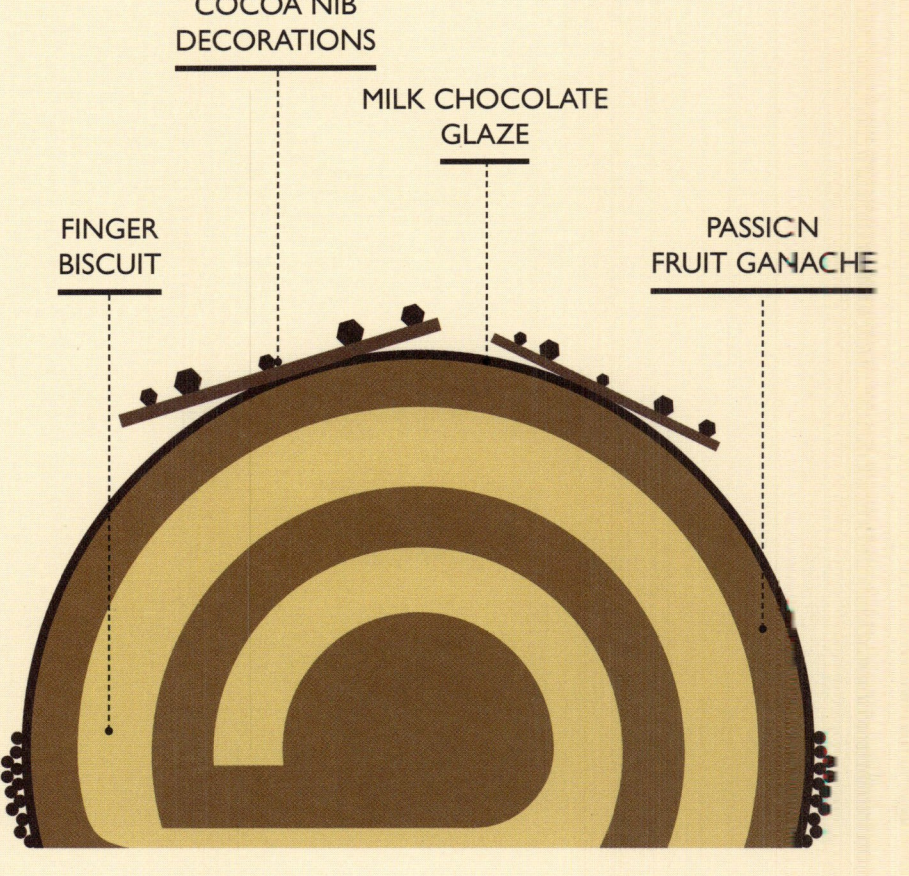

COCOA NIB
DECORATIONS

MILK CHOCOLATE
GLAZE

FINGER
BISCUIT

PASSION
FRUIT GANACHE

WHAT IS IT?

A log roll made of finger biscuit soaked in passion fruit syrup, filled with milk chocolate and passion fruit ganache, glazed with milk chocolate and decorated with cocoa nibs.

HOW LONG WILL IT TAKE?

Preparation: 2 ½ hours
Cooking: 30 minutes
Freezing: 4 ¼ hours
Standing: 6 hours

EQUIPMENT YOU WILL NEED

Angled palette knife
Decorative presentation board
Paintbrush

VARIATION

Replace the passion fruit with raspberry and the cocoa nibs with chopped almonds.

TRICKY POINTS

Glazing
Rolling

SKILLS REQUIRED

Using a double-boiler (page 276)
Making a syrup (page 282)

Making chocolate decorations (page 38)
Coating a log cake (page 279)
Glazing (page 279)

TIP

To make the passion fruit purée, cut the fruit in half, put it into a fine sieve over a bowl and scrape with a spatula to extract the juice.

PLANNING AND PREP

2 days before:
Finger biscuit – ganache –
chocolate decorations
The day before
Assembling – coating
On the day:
Glaze – decorate

188

Learn

SERVES 8 TO 10

1 PASSION FRUIT GANACHE

450 g (1 lb) milk chocolate
240 g (9 oz) passion fruit purée
(juice from 15 fruits)
90 g (3 ¼ oz) softenend butter

2 FINGER BISCUIT

200 g (7 oz) egg yolks (14 or 15 yolks)
90 g (3 ¼ oz) white caster (superfine) sugar
90 g (3 ¼ oz) flour
90 g (3 ¼ oz) potato starch
220 g (8 oz) egg whites (7 or 8 whites)
90 g (3 ¼ oz) white caster (superfine) sugar

3 PASSION FRUIT SOAKING SYRUP

75 g (2 ½ oz) passion fruit purée
(juice from 5 fruits)
75 g (2 ½ oz) water
75 g (2 ½ oz) white caster (superfine) sugar

4 MILK GLAZE

250 g (9 oz) milk chocolate
90 g (3 ¼ oz) dark chocolate
225 g whipping cream
40 g (1 ½ oz) inverted sugar or neutral honey

5 CHOCOLATE DECORATIONS

300 g (10 ½ oz) milk couverture chocolate
50 g (2 oz) cocoa nibs

To make the passion fruit milk chocolate log

1 Make the cocoa nib discs (page 38). To make the ganache: melt the chocolate in a double-boiler (page 276), bring the fruit purée to the boil (page 276), then pour over the chocolate, away from the double-boiler. Mix with a whisk, add the butter and stir until smooth. Pour into a container, cover with cling film (plastic wrap) and set aside in the fridge for at least 6 hours. Make the finger biscuit (page 60). Make the passion fruit soaking syrup (page 282). Remove the biscuit from the baking sheet, then put on a sheet of baking paper (baking parchment) and soak the non-crusted side with the syrup using a paintbrush.

2 Stir the ganache gently using a spatula and set 250 g (9 oz) aside in the fridge for coating the log. Spread the remaining ganache on the biscuit using an angled palette knife.

3 Roll up into a cylindrical shape, keeping it tight to avoid trapping any air inside. Leave in the baking paper to keep the shape. Put in the freezer for at least 2 hours.

4 Take the log out of the freezer and coat it (page 279) completely with the ganache from the refrigerator. Return to the freezer for at least 2 hours.

5 Make the milk chocolate glaze (page 74). Glaze the log (page 279). Place it on a log cake presentation board. Freeze for 15 minutes to set the glaze then transfer to the refrigerator.

6 Trim off the ends of the log. Make the chocolate decorations (page 38). To serve, sprinkle cocoa nibs on the sides of the log and top with the decorations.

ÉCLAIRS

Understand

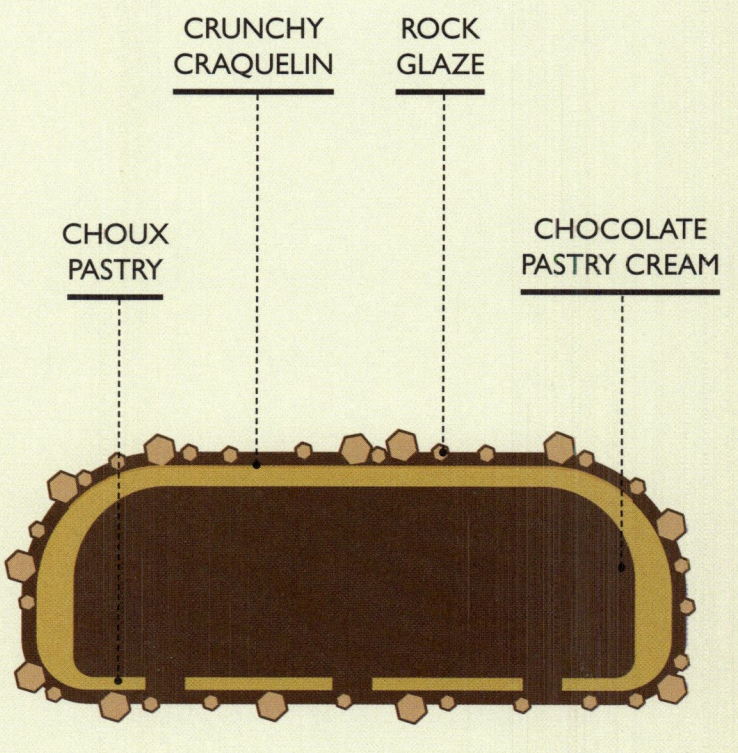

CRUNCHY
CRAQUELIN

ROCK
GLAZE

CHOUX
PASTRY

CHOCOLATE
PASTRY CREAM

WHAT IS IT?

Choux pastry filled with chocolate
pastry cream and coated with crunchy
craquelin and rock glaze.

HOW LONG WILL IT TAKE?

Preparation: 2 hours
Cooking: 40 minutes
Freezing: 30 minutes
Standing: 1 hour

EQUIPMENT YOU WILL NEED

Piping bag with PF 12 nozzle
Piping bag with a plain No 8 nozzle
Wooden skewer

SKILL REQUIRED

Piping bag (page 278)

TIP

Replace the pure cocoa paste with 120 g
(4 oz) dark chocolate (66% cocoa).

PLANNING AND PREP

The day before:
Craquelin – custard cream
On the day:
Choux dough– filling – glaze

MAKES 12 TO 15

CHOUX PASTRY

100 g (3 ½ oz) water
100 g (3 ½ oz) milk
90 g (3 ¼ oz) unsalted butter
2 g (½ teaspoon) salt
120 g (4 oz) flour
200 g (7 oz) eggs (4 eggs)

CRUNCHY CRAQUELIN

75 g (2 ½ oz) unsalted butter
100 g (3 ½ oz) brown sugar
100 g (3 ½ oz) flour

Learn

CHOCOLATE PASTRY CREAM

500 g (1 lb 2 oz/17 fl oz/2 cups) milk
100 g (3 1/2 oz) egg yolks (6 or 7 yolks)
120 g (4 oz) white caster (superfine) sugar
50 g (2 oz) cornflour (cornstarch)
80 g (3 oz) pure cocoa paste

ROCK GLAZE

150 g (5 oz) dark chocolate (66% cocoa)
130 g (4 oz) milk chocolate
25 g (1 oz) grapeseed oil
80 g (3 oz) chopped almonds

1 Make the craquelin (page 66). Make the pastry cream (page 52) using pure cocoa paste instead of butter.

2 Make the choux dough (page 66). Preheat the oven to 230°C (450°F/gas 8). Put the dough in a piping bag with a PF 12 nozzle and pipe out 12 cm (5 in) long eclairs (page 278) onto a baking tray.

3 Cut the craquelin into 12 × 2 cm (5 in × 1 in) rectangles using a chef's knife. Place a rectangle of craquelin on top of each eclair.

4 Turn down the heat to 170°C (340°F/gas 5) and put the pastry in the oven. After baking for 20 minutes, open the oven door briefly to allow steam to escape. Bake until evenly coloured (about 10-20 minutes more) then remove and cool.

5 When the éclairs have cooled, make 3 holes in the underside of each using the tip of a knife. Whisk the pastry cream briskly to make it smooth, put in a piping bag fitted with a plain No 8 nozzle and fill each éclair through the 3 holes. The cream should ooze out and the weight should feel evenly distributed. Place in the freezer for 30 minutes.

6 Make the rock glaze (page 72). Push a wooden skewer through each éclair. Transfer the rock glaze to a tall, thin measuring glass. Dip the whole eclair into it, take it out and scrape the base on the edge of a bowl to remove the excess, then place the éclair on a baking sheet and remove the skewer. Put in the refrigerator for at least 1 hour before serving.

BLOND CHOCOLATE & CREAMY CHOCOLATE
CHOUX

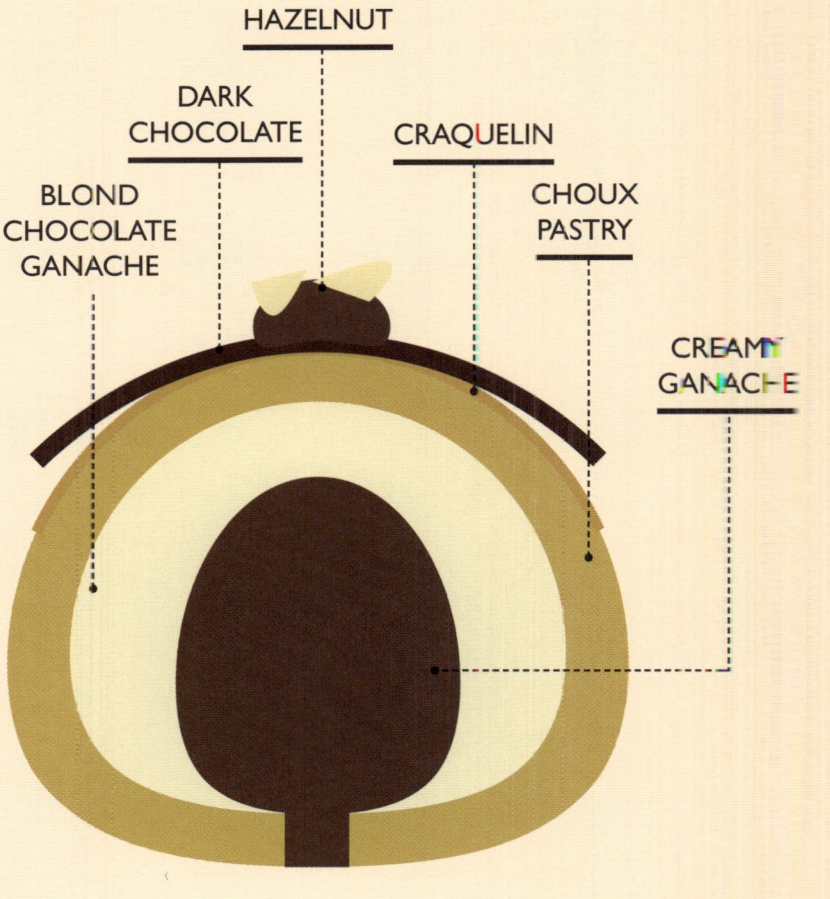

BLOND
CHOCOLATE
GANACHE

DARK
CHOCOLATE

HAZELNUT

CRAQUELIN

CHOUX
PASTRY

CREAMY
GANACHE

WHAT IS IT?

Crispy choux pastry filled with blond chocolate ganache with a dark ganache centre, topped with crunchy craquelin covered with chocolate and scattered with hazelnut.

HOW LONG WILL IT TAKE?

Preparation: 2 hours
Cooking: 30 to 45 minutes
Freezing: 20 minutes
Refrigeration: 12 + 4 hours

EQUIPMENT YOU WILL NEED
Piping bag with a plain No 8 nozzle
Piping bag with a plain No 6 nozzle
Thermometer
Semi-spherical mould
3 cm (1 ¼) round biscuit cutter

VARIATION
Replace the blond chocolate with white chocolate.

SKILLS REQUIRED
Rehydrating gelatine (page 277)
Using a double-boiler (page 276)
Mixing without incorporating air (page 276)
Using a piping bag (page 278)

PLANNING AND PREP
The day before:
Blond chocolate ganache – creamy ganache – craquelin
On the day:
Choux pastry – filling – decoration

Learn

MAKES 20 TO 25

1 BLOND CHOCOLATE GANACHE

150 g (5 oz) milk
3 g (1 1/2 sheets) gelatine
280 g blond chocolate, such as Valrhona Dulcey chocolate
300 g (10 1/2 oz) whipping cream

2 CREAMY GANACHE

125 g (4 oz) milk
25 g (1 oz) egg yolks (2 yolks)
25 g (1 oz) white caster (superfine) sugar
50 g (2 oz) dark chocolate (60% cocoa)

3 CRUNCHY CRAQUELIN

75 g (2 1/2 oz) unsalted butter
100 g (3 1/2 oz) brown sugar
100 g (3 1/2 oz) flour

4 CHOUX PASTRY

100 g (3 1/2 oz) water
100 g (3 1/2 oz) milk
90 g (3 1/4 oz) unsalted butter
2 g (1/2 teaspoon) salt
120 g (4 oz) flour
200 g (7 oz) eggs (4 eggs)

5 CHOCOLATE COVERING

200 g (7 oz) dark chocolate (66% cocoa)
5 g (1 teaspoon) cocoa butter

6 DECORATION

30 g (1 oz) roasted chopped hazelnuts

To make the blond chocolate and creamy chocolate choux pastries

1   Make the blond chocolate ganache: rehydrate the gelatine in cold water (page 276), melt the chocolate in a double-boiler (page 276), bring the milk to the boil, then remove from the heat and melt the gelatine into it. Pour one-third of the milk-gelatine mixture over the blond chocolate, whisking to start the emulsion. Pour in another third, whisk, then pour the rest to complete the emulsion. Add the cream while mixing without incorporating air (page 276), set aside in a container covered with cling film (plastic wrap) and leave to cool overnight in the refrigerator.

2   Make the creamy ganache (page 42) and crunchy craquelin (page 66). Set aside in the refrigerator overnight.

3   Preheat the oven to 230°C (450°F/gas 8). Make the choux dough (page 66). Put the dough in a piping bag and pipe out 20 to 25 3 cm (1 1/4 in)

round choux buns (page 278) onto a baking tray lined with baking paper (baking parchment). Cut out 3 cm (1 1/4 in) discs of craquelin using a pastry cutter. Place a craquelin disc on top of each choux.

4   Reduce the oven temperature to 170°C (340°F gas 5) and transfer the choux buns to the oven. Open the oven door briefly after 20 minutes of cooking to let the steam escape. Bake until evenly coloured (about 10-20 minutes more).

5   Set aside 50 g (2 oz) of the blond chocolate cream for decoration. Make a small hole in the bottom of each choux using the tip of a knife, then fill with the blond chocolate cream using a piping bag fitted with a No 8 nozzle. Put the creamy ganache into a piping bag fitted with a No 6 nozzle then fill the buns again, pushing the nozzle a little further into the centre of each choux.

6   Make the chocolate covering: melt the chocolate and cocoa butter in a double-boiler. Transfer to a piping bag (page 278) then pipe out a layer about 1 cm (1/2 in) thick into the bottom of the semi-spherical moulds and put the choux on top. Put in the freezer for 20 minutes. Remove the choux and unmould. Put the reserved blond chocolate cream in a clean piping bag. Pipe out blond chocolate cream rose shapes on top of each, then sprinkle with crushed hazelnut.

PARIS-BREST
CAKE

Understand

PRALINE
CREAM

CREAMY
GANACHE

COCOA
NIBS

ICING
SUGAR

CHOUX
PASTRY

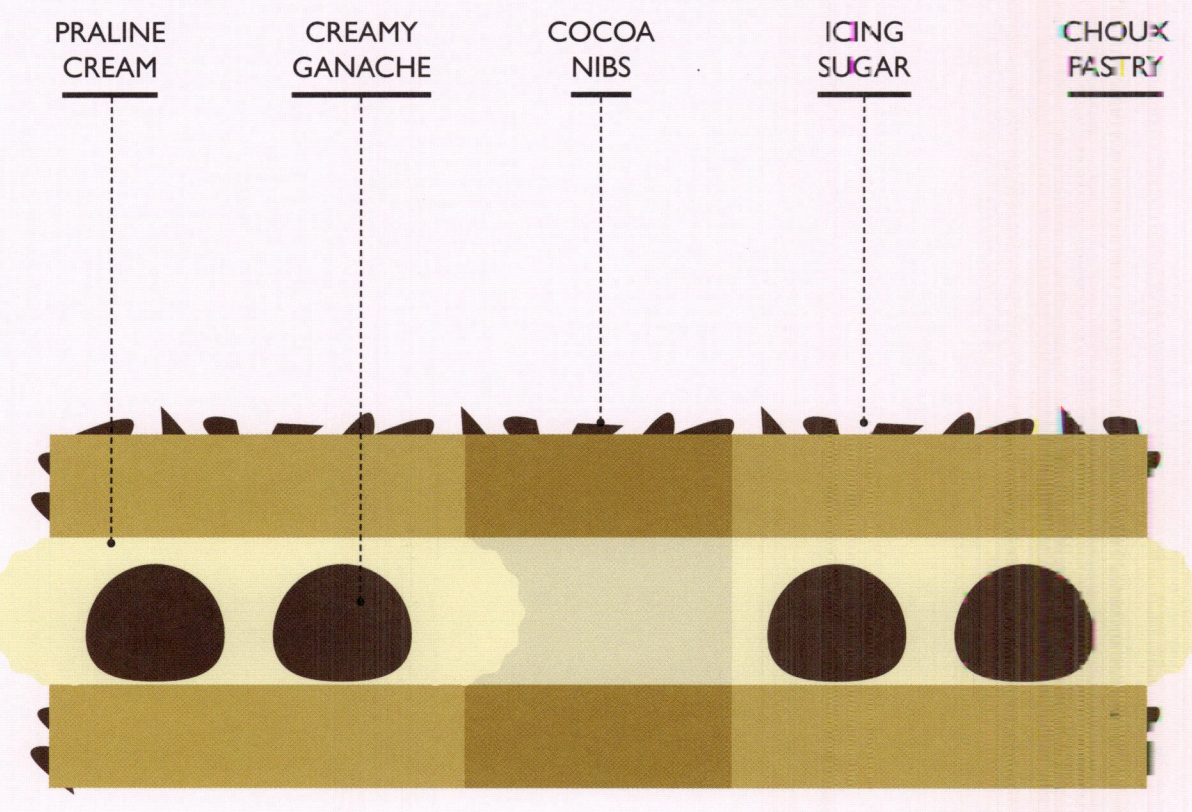

WHAT IS IT?

Choux pastry wheel with cocoa nibs, filled
with praline cream and creamy ganache.

HOW LONG WILL IT TAKE?

Preparation: 3 hours
Cooking: 40 to 50 minutes
Freezing: 4 hours
Refrigeration: 12 hours

EQUIPMENT YOU WILL NEED

Semi-spherical mould
16 cm (6 in) pastry ring
20 cm (8 in) pastry ring
Piping bag with grooved PF 12 nozzle
Paintbrush

VARIATION

All-chocolate Paris-Brest cake: replace the
praline with 50 g (2 oz) of pure cocoa paste.

SKILLS REQUIRED

Rehydrating gelatine (page 277)
Using a piping bag (page 278)

ADVICE

To make the wheel shape: put a 16 cm
(6 in) ring inside a 20 cm (8 in) pastry ring
and pipe out the choux dough between
the rings. Pipe out four rolls tightly
together, then 3 crosswise on top.

PLANNING AND PREP

Previous day
Ganache – praline pastry cream with gelatine
On the day:
Choux dough – cooking –
diplomat cream – assemble

Learn

SERVES 8

1 CREAMY GANACHE

125 g (4 oz) milk
25 g (1 oz) egg yolks (2 yolks)
25 g (1 oz) white caster (superfine) sugar
75 g (2 ½ oz) dark chocolate (66% cocoa)

2 PRALINE CREAM

For the pastry cream
250 g (9 oz) milk
50 g (2 oz) egg yolks (3 or 4 yolks)
60 g (2 oz) white caster (superfine) sugar
25 g (1 oz) cornflour (cornstarch)
25 g (1 oz) unsalted butter
80 g (3 oz) praline
4 g (2 sheets) sheet gelatine

For the diplomat cream
100 g (3 ½ oz) whipping cream

3 CHOUX DOUGH

100 g (3 ½ oz) water
100 g (3 ½ oz) milk
90 g (3 ¼ oz) unsalted butter
2 g (½ teaspoon) salt
120 g (4 oz) flour
200 g (7 oz) eggs (4 eggs)

4 DECORATION

30 g (1 oz) egg (½ egg)
30 g (1 oz) cocoa nibs
30 g (1 oz) icing (confectioner's) sugar

To make the Paris-Brest cake

1   Make the creamy ganache (page 42), pipe into the semi-spherical moulds (page 278) and freeze for at least 4 hours.

2   Make the praline pastry cream (page 52) by adding the praline and rehydrated gelatine at the same time as the butter. Cover with cling film (plastic wrap) and put in the fridge overnight.

3   Make the choux pastry (page 66). Preheat the oven to 230°C (450°F/gas 9). Put the dough in a piping bag and pipe into the 20 cm (8 in) wheel on a baking tray lined with baking paper (baking parchment) (page 277). Glaze with the beaten egg using a paintbrush. Sprinkle with cocoa nibs. Reduce the heat to 170°C (340°F gas 5) and put in the oven. Open the oven door briefly after 20 minutes to allow the steam to escape. Bake until evenly coloured (20–30 minutes more).

4   To finish the diplomat cream: whip the cream (page 280), and put in the refrigerator while whipping the pastry cream. Whip the pastry cream briskly to make it smooth, add one-third of the whipped cream and whisk. Add the rest of the cream and mix gently using a spatula.

5   Cut the choux wheel horizontally into two half-wheels using a serrated knife. Pipe out a layer of diplomat cream onto the base using the grooved PF 12 nozzle.

6   Unmould the ganache domes and place them on the layer of diplomat cream.

7   Cover with rosettes of diplomat cream using the grooved nozzle, put the top on and put in the refrigerator for at least 4 hours. Sprinkle with icing (confectioners') sugar and serve.

CHOCOLATE
TART

Understand

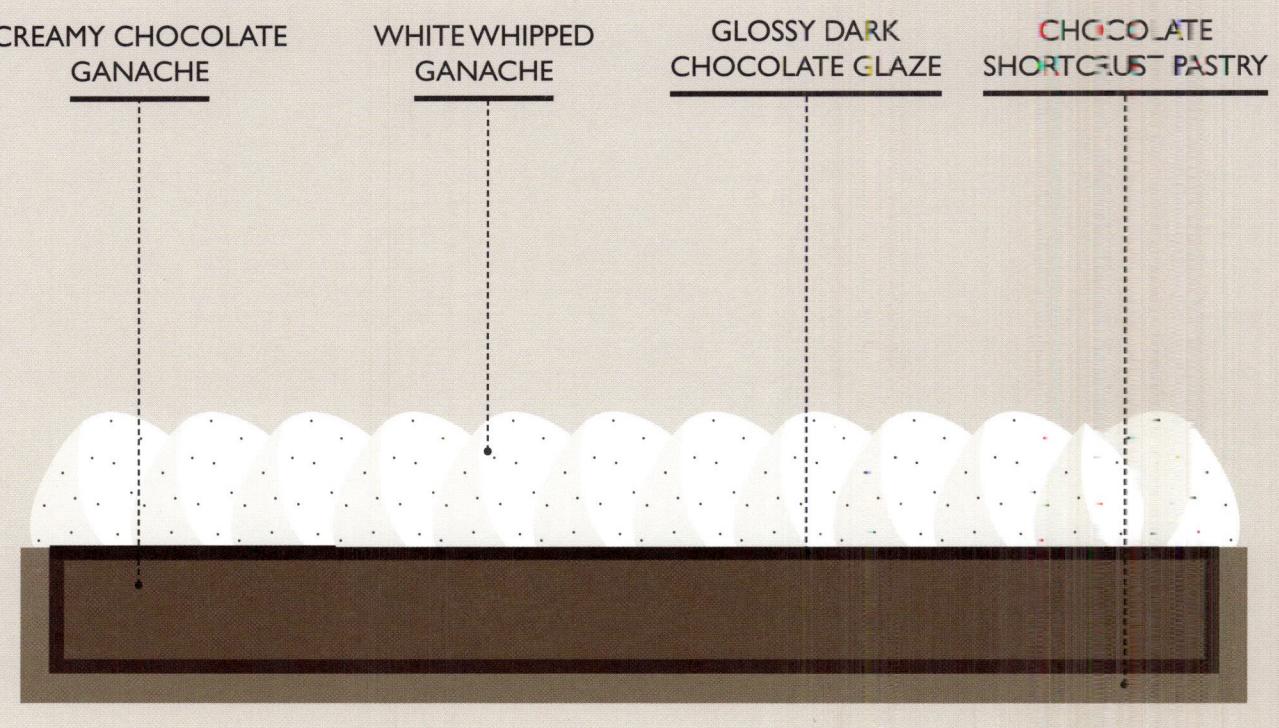

CREAMY CHOCOLATE
GANACHE

WHITE WHIPPED
GANACHE

GLOSSY DARK
CHOCOLATE GLAZE

CHOCOLATE
SHORTCRUST PASTRY

WHAT IS IT?

Chocolate shortcrust pastry base covered
with creamy ganache, dark chocolate glaze
and decorated with white chocolate ganache.

HOW LONG WILL IT TAKE?

Preparation: 2 hours
Cooking: 12 to 15 minutes
Freezing: 1 1/2 to 2 hours
Standing: 24 hours

EQUIPMENT YOU WILL NEED

24 cm (9 1/2 in) tart ring
Piping bag with 10 mm (1/4 in) nozzle
Piping bag with a St Honore tip nozzle

TRICKY POINT

Glazing

SKILLS REQUIRED

Spreading dough (page 284)
Lining a base (page 284)
Coating with a thin layer of
chocolate (chabloning; page 273)
Glazing (page 279)
Piping (page 278)

ADVICE

To check if the tart base is cooked, press
on the dough lightly with your fingertip:
it should be fairly firm but still a bit
soft, as it will harden on cooling.

PLANNING AND PREP

The day before:
Shortcrust dough – white
ganache – creamy ganache
On the day:
Cooking – chocolate coating
– glazing – finishing

Learn

SERVES 8

1 CHOCOLATE SHORTCRUST DOUGH

180 g (6 ¼ oz) flour
20 g (3¾ oz) cocoa (unsweetened chocolate) powder
70 g (2 ½ oz) unsalted butter
1 g (¼ teaspoon) salt
70 g (2 ½ oz) icing (confectioner's) sugar
60 g (2 oz) egg (1 egg)

2 CHOCOLATE COATING

40 g (1 ½ oz) dark chocolate, melted

3 WHIPPED WHITE GANACHE

330 g (11 oz) whipping cream
150 g (5 oz) white chocolate
4 g (2 sheets) sheet gelatine

4 CREAMY GANACHE

150 g (5 oz) dark chocolate (60% cocoa)
50 g (2 oz) egg yolks (3 to 4 yolks)
50 g (2 oz) white caster (superfine) sugar
250 g (9 oz) milk

5 GLOSSY DARK CHOCOLATE GLAZEE

90 g (3 ¼ oz) water
75 g (2 ½ oz) whipping cream
165g white caster (superfine) sugar
8 g (4 sheets) sheet gelatine
60 g (2 oz) cocoa (unsweetened chocolate) powder

To make the chocolate tart

1   Make the chocolate shortcrust dough the day before you plan to eat (page 58). Make the white ganache, heating only half of the cream (page 44). Make the creamy ganache (page 42).

2   After leaving to stand for the required time, roll out the dough (page 284) and make a base in the previously buttered tart ring (page 284) placed on a baking tray lined with a baking paper (baking parchment). Prick the tart base with all over with a fork. Put in the freezer for 1 hour. Preheat the oven to 150°C (300°F/gas 3), then bake for 12 to 15 minutes. Remove from the oven and leave to cool.

3   Lightly coat the tart base with a thin layer of chocolate when cold (page 273). Make the dark chocolate glaze and leave to cool (page 70).

4   Using a piping bag with a 10 mm nozzle, fill the tart base with creamy ganache spiralling from the centre outwards, up to 2 mm from the top of the ring. Freeze for 30 minutes to 1 hour.

5   Pour the dark chocolate glaze on the centre of the tart, then tilt and turn so that the glaze completely covers the top (page 279).

6   Whip up the white ganache, put it in a piping bag with a St Honore nozzle tip and pipe out onto the tart (page 273).

204

MILK CHOCOLATE
TART

Understand

GOLD POWDER

MILK CHOCOLATE GLAZE

MILK CHOCOLATE MOUSSE

DARK CHOCOLATE CRUMBLE

SHORTCRUST PASTRY

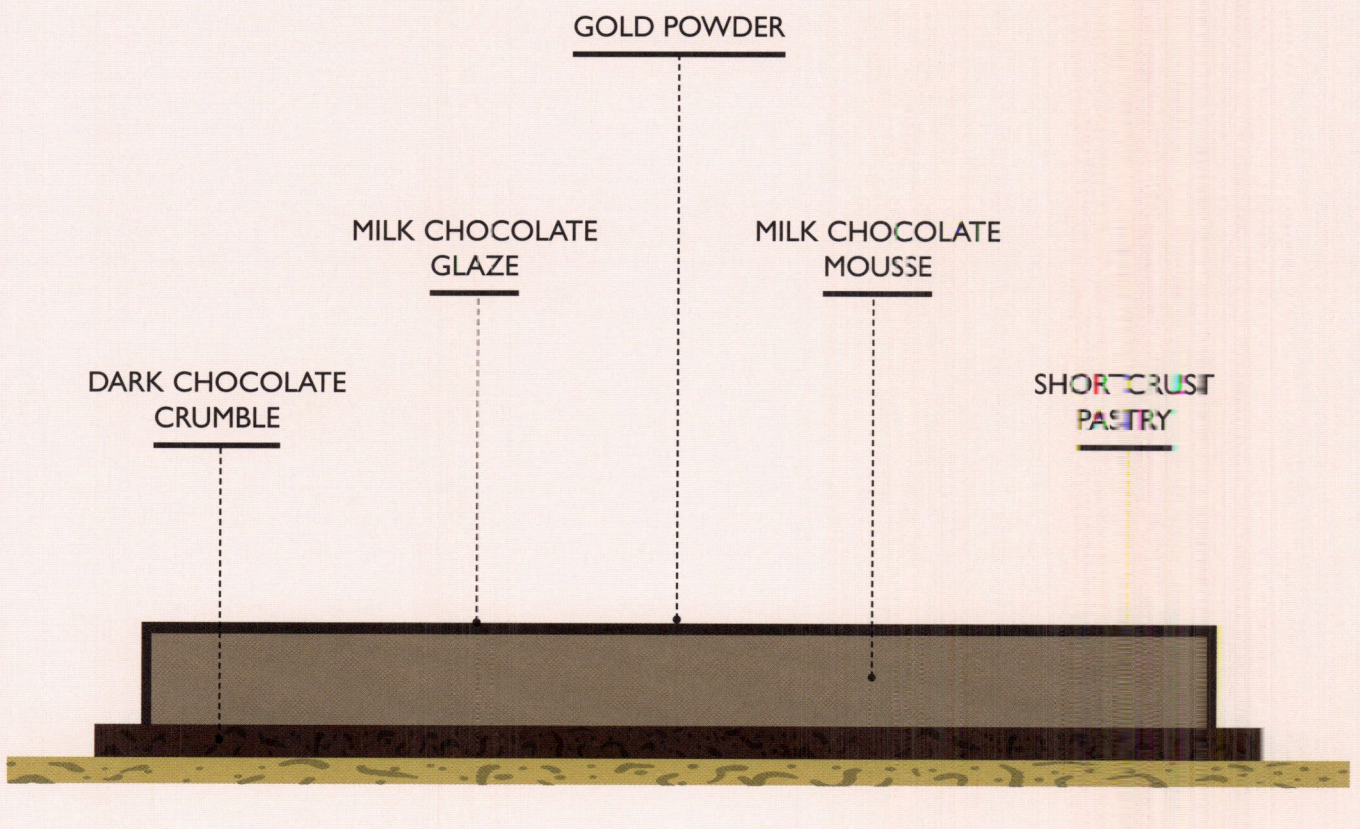

WHAT IS IT?

A hazelnut shortcrust base covered with dark chocolate crumble and topped with milk chocolate mousse and milk chocolate glaze.

HOW LONG WILL IT TAKE?

Preparation: 2 ¹/₂ hours
Cooking: 45 minutes to 1 ¹/₄ hours
Freezing: 7 hours
Refrigeration: 7 hours
Standing: 24 hours

EQUIPMENT YOU WILL NEED

Transparent acetate strip
20 cm (8 in) dessert ring
24 cm (9 ¹/₂ in) dessert ring
Kitchen blowtorch
Piping bag

VARIATION

For a 100% chocolate milk tart, replace the dark chocolate in the crumble with chocolate milk.

TRICKY POINT

Glazing the mousse disc

SKILLS REQUIRED

Using a double-boiler (page 276)
Rolling out dough (page 284)
Making a base (page 284)
Glazing (page 274)
Decorating (page 38)

PLANNING AND PREP

The day before:
Mousse – shortcrust dough – crumble
On the day:
Cooking – glazing – assembling – finishing

206

Learn

SERVES 8 TO 10

1 HAZELNUT SHORTCRUST DOUGH

180 g (6 ¼ oz) flour
40 g (1 ½ oz) ground (powdered) hazelnuts
70 g (2 ½ oz) unsalted butter
1 g (¼ teaspoon) salt
70 g (2 ½ oz) icing (confectioner's) sugar
60 g (2 oz) egg (1 egg)

2 DARK CHOCOLATE CRUMBLE

50 g (2 oz) unsalted butter
50 g (2 oz) white caster (superfine) sugar
50 g (2 oz) flour
50 g (2 oz) ground (powdered) almonds
100 g (3 ½ oz) dark chocolate

3 MILK CHOCOLATE MOUSSE

275 g (10 oz) milk chocolate
60 g (2 oz) whipping cream
60 g (2 oz) milk
15 g (½ oz) white caster (superfine) sugar
230 g (8 oz) whipping cream
30 g (1 oz) egg yolks (2 yolks)

4 MILK CHOCOLATE GLAZE

250 g (9 oz) milk chocolate
90 g (3 ¼ oz) dark chocolate
225 g whipping cream
40 g (1 ½ oz) inverted sugar or neutral honey

5 DECORATION

pinch of gold powder

To make the milk chocolate tart

1   Make the milk chocolate mousse (page 48). Wrap the outside of the 20 cm (8 in) ring with cling film (plastic wrap), holding it in place with elastic string. Place the transparent acetate strip inside the 20 cm (8 in) ring, pour in the milk chocolate mousse, transfer to the freezer and freeze for 6 hours.

2   Make the hazelnut shortcrust dough (page 58). After leaving to stand for the required time, roll out the dough 2mm thick (page 284) and cut out a disc using a 24 cm (9 ¹/₂ in) pastry ring. Put in the freezer for 1 hour. Preheat the oven to 160°C (320°F/gas 4) and bake for 20-30 minutes.

3   Make the milk chocolate glaze (page 74). Preheat the oven to 170°C (340°F/gas 5). Make the dark chocolate crumble: mix the cubed butter, sugar, flour and ground (powdered) almonds until the mixture becomes coarse and grainy. Cook for 15 to 20 minutes, stirring occasionally with a spatula. When the crumble is evenly browned, transfer to a baking tray and allow to cool. Melt the dark chocolate in a double-boiler (page 276). When it has melted, add the crumble and mix with a spatula.

4   Place the 24 cm (9 ¹/₂ inch) dessert ring on the circle of dough and spread an even layer of chocolate crumble on it. Put in the refrigerator for 1 hour.

5   Unmould the mousse disc by removing the film and slightly heating the ring using a kitchen blowtorch. Put it on a rack set over a rimmed tray. Pour the glaze over the mousse starting from the outside and working towards the centre. Remove the excess using a palette knife (reserve and set aside) and shake the rack to even out the glaze. Return to the freezer for 15 minutes.

6   Put the reserved glaze in a piping bag, cut a small hole in the bag and squeeze out thin lines of glaze onto the mousse disc. Place the disk on the crumble-covered tart base. Defrost for 6 hours in the refrigerator. Dust the top with gold powder.

SOUFFLÉ TARTLETS

Understand

COCOA
POWDER

CHOCOLATE
SHORTCRUST

SOUFFLÉ
MIX

CREAMY
GANACHE

WHAT IS IT?

Chocolate shortcrust pastry base
filled with creamy chocolate ganache
and a chocolate soufflé mix.

HOW LONG WILL IT TAKE?

Preparation: 1 ½ hours
Cooking: 25 minutes
Standing: 24 hours

EQUIPMENT YOU WILL NEED

eight 8 cm (3 inch) pastry rings
10 or 11 cm (4 inch) biscuit cutter
Piping bag with a plain 8 mm
nozzle
Piping bag

TRICKY POINTS

Making a pastry base (page 284)
Making a French meringue (page 69)
Mixing a soufflé mixture (page 276)

SKILLS REQUIRED

Using a piping bag with a nozzle (page 278)
Piping (page 278)
Coating with a thin layer of
chocolate (chabloning; page 273)

PLANNING AND PREP

2 days before:
Shortcrust dough
The day before:
Make the base – ganache
On the day:
Cook the tart bases – chablon
– piping – soufflé
15 min before serving:
Cooking the soufflé – decorate

Learn

MAKES 8

1 CHOCOLATE SHORTCRUST DOUGH

180 g (6 ¼ oz) flour
20 g cocoa (unsweetened chocolate) powder
70 g (2 ½ oz) unsalted butter
1 g (¼ teaspoon) salt
70 g (2 ½ oz) icing (confectioner's sugar)
60 g (2 oz) egg (1 egg)

2 CHOCOLATE COATING LAYER

40 g (1 ½ oz) dark chocolate (60% cocoa)

3 FOR THE RINGS

50 g (2 oz) softened unsalted butter

4 CREAMY GANACHE

100 g (3 ½ oz) dark chocolate (60% cocoa)
30 g (1 oz) egg yolks (2 yolks)
30 g (1 oz) white caster (superfine) sugar
140 g (4 ½ oz) milk

5 CHOCOLATE SOUFFLÉ MIXTURE

100 g (3 ½ oz) dark chocolate (60% cocoa)
20 g (¾ oz) cocoa (unsweetened chocolate) powder
50 g (2 oz) milk
75 g (2 ½ oz) egg yolks (4 or 5 yolks)

6 FRENCH MERINGUE

75 g (2 ½ oz) egg whites (2 or 3 whites)
55 g (2 oz) white caster (superfine) sugar

7 DECORATION

10 g cocoa (unsweetened chocolate) powder

To make the soufflé tartlets

1   Make the chocolate shortcrust dough (page 58). After leaving it to stand for the required time, roll it out (page 284) and cut out discs of dough using the pastry cutter. Place the rings on a baking sheet lined with baking paper (baking parchment) and put the dough discs inside them to make pastry bases (page 284). Cut off the excess dough (page 284) and put in the freezer. Make the creamy ganache (page 42) and set aside in the refrigerator.

2   Preheat the oven to 160°C (320°F/gas 4), then bake the tart bases for 12 to 15 minutes. Coat the tart bases with a thin layer of chocolate (chablon; page 273) and refrigerate for 15 minutes. Put the ganache in the piping bag fitted with an 8 mm plain nozzle then pipe it into the tart bases in spirals until it reaches halfway up the sides.

3   Remove the tartlets from the rings. Cut eight 4 × 25 cm (¼ in × 10 in) strips of baking paper, which should be twice the height of the tarts. Using a paintbrush spread the softened butter on one side of each strip. Place the strips in the circles, with the butter on the inside, then put the tarts back in the rings. This collar will allow the soufflé mix to rise evenly and unmould easily. Set aside in the refrigerator.

4   Make the soufflé mixture: melt the chocolate in the double-boiler (page 276). Whisk the egg yolks with the milk, then set aside. Make the French meringue (page 69). Put one-third of the meringue in the melted chocolate and whisk briskly. Add the sieved cocoa and whisk again.

5   Add the egg yolk and milk mixture. Mix well, then stir in the remaining meringue using a spatula.

6   Place in a piping bag, make a small hole in the corner then fill the tartlets with 2 to 3 cm (¾ in to 1 in) of soufflé mix. Set aside in the refrigerator.

7   Preheat the oven to 200°C (400°F/gas 7). Bake the tartlets for 8 to 10 minutes. Remove from the oven and leave to stand for 3 to 5 minutes. Carefully remove the tart rings and strips of baking paper. Sprinkle with cocoa (unsweetened chocolate) powder and serve immediately.

CARAMEL
TART

Understand

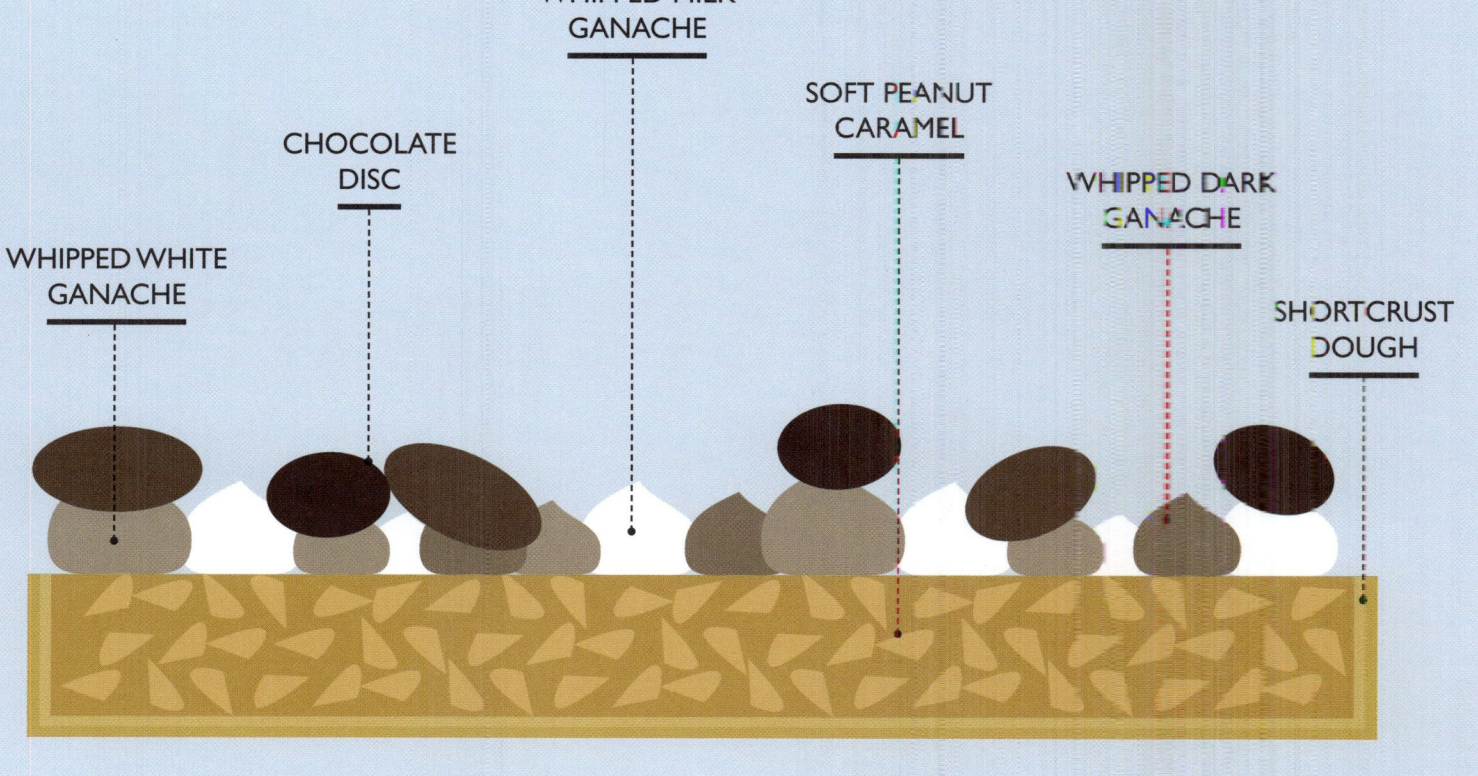

WHIPPED MILK
GANACHE

CHOCOLATE
DISC

SOFT PEANUT
CARAMEL

WHIPPED DARK
GANACHE

WHIPPED WHITE
GANACHE

SHORTCRUST
DOUGH

WHAT IS IT?

Shortcrust pastry filled with soft
peanut caramel and topped with
dark, milk and white ganache.

HOW LONG WILL IT TAKE?

Preparation: 2 hours
Cooking: 30 minutes
Freezing: 1 hour
Refrigeration: 2 hours
Standing: 24 hours

EQUIPMENT YOU WILL NEED

24 cm (9 1/2 in) tart ring
3 piping bags with No 6, 8 and 10 nozzles

VARIATION

Replace the peanuts with cashew nuts

SKILLS REQUIRED

Coating with a thin layer of
chocolate (chabloning; page 273)
Rehydrating gelatine (page 277)
Making dry caramel (page 282)

PLANNING AND PREP

2 days before:
Chocolate decorations
The day before:
Shortcrust dough – ganaches
On the day:
Make the base – cooking – caramel
– assemble – decorate

Learn

SERVES 10 TO 12

1 SHORTCRUST DOUGH

200 g (7 oz) flour
70 g (2 ½ oz) unsalted butter
1 g (¼ teaspoon) salt
70 g (2 ½ oz) icing (confectioner's) sugar
60 g egg (2 oz) (1 egg)

2 CHOCOLATE COATING LAYER

40 g (1 ½ oz) white chocolate

3 WHIPPED DARK GANACHE

120 g (4 oz) whipping cream
40 g (1 ½ oz) dark chocolate (60% cocoa)
1 g (½ sheet) sheet gelatine

4 WHIPPED MILK GANACHE

120 g (4 oz) whipping cream
40 g (1 ½ oz) mik chocolate
1 g (½ sheet) sheet gelatine

5 WHIPPED WHITE GANACHE

120 g (4 oz) whipping cream
40 g (1 ½ oz) white chocolate
1 g (½ sheet) sheet gelatine

6 SOFT PEANUT CARAMEL

100 g (3 ½ oz) white caster (superfine) sugar
50 g (2 oz) glucose syrup
140 g (4 ½ oz) whipping cream
70 g (2 ½ oz) unsalted butter
2 g (1 sheet) sheet gelatine
140 g (4 ½ oz) roasted salted peanuts

7 CHOCOLATE DECORATION

200 g (7 oz) dark chocolate (66% cocoa)
200 g (7 oz) milk chocolate

To make the caramel tart

1   Make the dark and milk chocolate discs
(page 38). Make the shortcrust dough (page 58).
Make the three whipped ganaches (page 42).

2   After leaving to stand for the required time,
roll out the dough 2 mm thick (page 284). Butter
the tart ring, place it on top of the dough, cut
about 3 cm ($^1/_8$ in) around the ring and then put
this circular base into the ring. Put in the freezer
for 1 hour. Preheat the oven to 160°C (320°F/gas 4).
Put the pastry base, in its ring, on a baking sheet
lined with baking paper (baking parchment) and
bake for 20 to 30 minutes. When the tart base has
cooled, coat it with a thin layer of the melted white
chocolate (chablon; page 273), using a paintbrush.

3   To make the soft peanut caramel: coarsely chop
the peanuts. Rehydrate the gelatine (page 277) in
cold water. Make a dry caramel with the sugar and
glucose syrup (page 282), stir in the previously heated
cream, boil for 30 seconds then take off the heat and
add the butter and drained gelatine. Stir and add the
peanuts. Leave to cool, then pour into the tart base
and leave to set for at least 2 hours in the refrigerator.

4   Whip up the three ganaches and put them
in the 3 piping bags with 3 different diameter
nozzles. Pipe out (page 275) random dome shapes
and ganache tips onto the soft caramel.

5   Decorate the tart with dark
and milk chocolate discs.

MILK CHOCOLATE
PECAN PIE

Understand

SHORTCRUST
DOUGH

CREAMY MILK
GANACHE

PECAN
PRALINE

MILK
GLAZE

CARAMELISED
PECANS

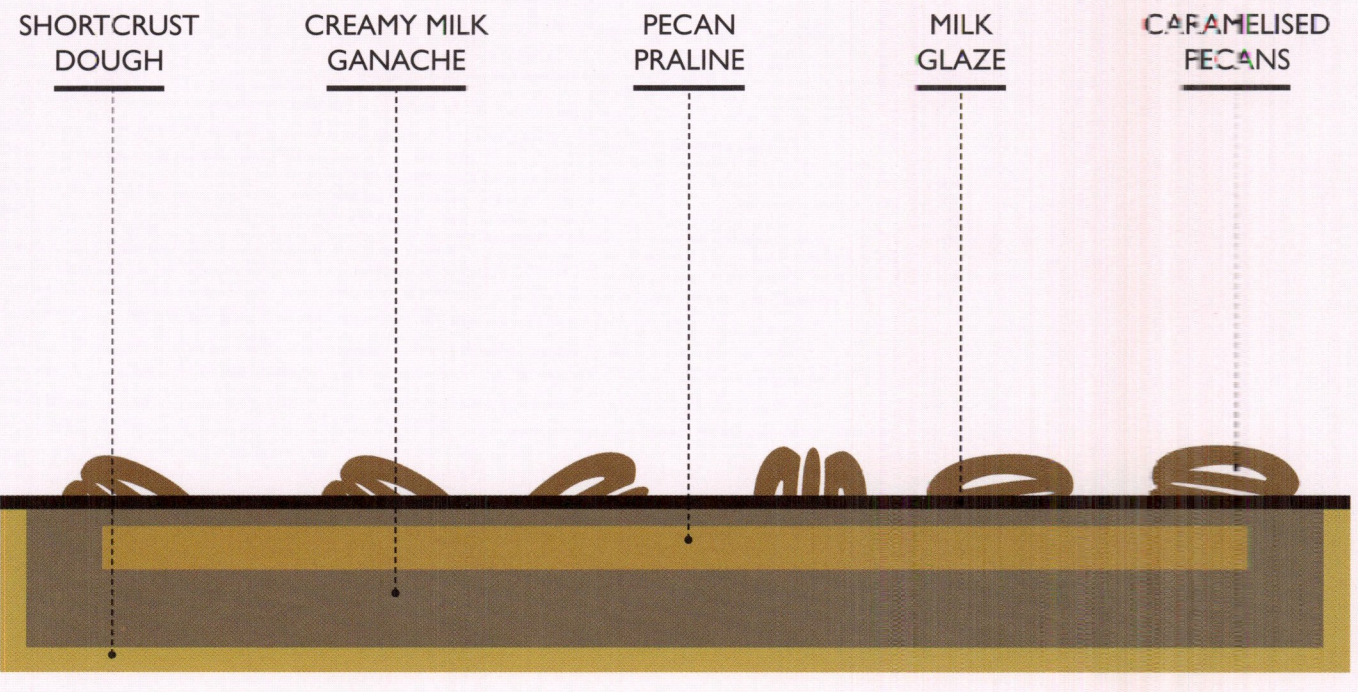

WHAT IS IT?

Shortcrust pastry filled with milk chocolate ganache and pecan praline, topped with milk chocolate glaze and caramelised pecans.

HOW LONG WILL IT TAKE?

Preparation: 2 ½ hours
Cooking: 30 minutes
Refrigeration: 3 hours
Freezing: 1 hour
Standing: 24 hours

EQUIPMENT YOU WILL NEED

24 cm (9 ½ in) tart ring
Piping bag
Thermometer

VARIATIONS

Replace the milk chocolate with dark chocolate and the pecans with almonds or hazelnuts.

SKILLS REQUIRED

Coating with a thin layer of chocolate (chabloning: page 273)
Piping (page 278)

ADVICE

Caramelising the nuts can be done on the previous day. In this case, keep the nuts at room temperature in an airtight box.

TIP

Instead of invert sugar use acacia honey.

ORGANISATION

Previous day:
Praline – shortcrust dough – ganache
On the day:
Make the base – cooking – assemble – glazing – caramelise the nuts – decoration

Learn

SERVES 10-12

1 SHORTCRUST DOUGH

200 g (7 oz) flour
70 g (2 ½ oz) unsalted butter
1 g (¼ teaspoon) salt
70 g (2 ½ oz) icing (confectioner's) sugar
60 g (2 oz) egg (1 egg)

2 CHOCOLATE COATING LAYER

40 g (1 ½ oz) white chocolate

3 PECAN PRALINE

200 g (7 oz) pecan nuts
200 g (7 oz) white caster (superfine) sugar
80 g (3 oz) water

4 CREAMY MILK GANACHE

250 g (9 oz) milk
50 g (2 oz) egg yolks (3 or 4 yolks)
50 g (2 oz) white caster (superfine) sugar
300 g (10 ½ oz) milk chocolate

5 MILK CHOCOLATE GLAZE

250 g (9 oz) milk chocolate
90 g (3 ¼ oz) dark chocolate (66% cocoa)
225 g (8 oz) whipping cream
40 g (1 ½ oz) invert sugar or neutral honey

6 CARAMELISED PECANS

75 g (2 ½ oz) white caster (superfine) sugar
25 g (1 oz) water
100 g (3 ½ oz) pecans

To make the milk chocolate pecan pie

1   Make the pecan praline (page 40) replacing the almonds and hazelnuts with pecans. Make the shortcrust dough (page 58). Make the creamy milk ganache (page 42), using milk chocolate instead of dark chocolate.

2   After the leaving to stand for the required time, roll out a 2 mm thick layer of dough (page 284). Butter the tart ring, place it on top of the dough, then cut the dough about 3 cm (⅛ in) around the outside of the ring. Put this circular base into the ring then transfer to the freezer for 1 hour. Preheat the oven to 160°C (320°F/gas 4), put the base on a baking tray lined with baking paper (baking parchment) and bake for 20 to 30 minutes, then leave to cool. When the tart base has cooled, remove the ring and coat with a thin layer of the melted white chocolate using a paintbrush (page 273).

3   Put the ganache in a piping bag and pipe out (page 278) a 5 mm (¼ in) layer over the tart base, working from centre and spiralling outwards. When you reach the side, double the thickness of the piping around the outer edge.

4   Put the praline in a piping bag and pipe it (page 278) onto the ganache, stopping when you get to the double thickness of ganache.

5   Cover the praline with ganache, being careful to stop 2 mm below the top of the tart to leave room for the glaze. Refrigerate for 2 hours.

6   Make the milk chocolate glaze (page 74) and leave to cool. To caramelise the pecans: put the water and sugar in a saucepan and cook until the syrup reaches 115°C (240°F). Remove from the heat, add the pecans and stir using a spatula until the syrup becomes grainy.

Return to medium heat and continue to stir for about 5 minutes, until the nuts are caramelised. Remove from the heat and pour out onto a baking tray lined with baking paper (baking paper), separating the caramelised nuts from each other. Leave to cool.

7   Pour the glaze onto the tart: start in the centre, tilting the tart slightly as you work so that the glaze flows gradually towards the edges. Leave to set in the refrigerator for at least 1 hour. Top with the caramelised pecans before serving.

220

PAIN AU
CHOCOLAT

Understand

CHOCOLATE
GANACHE

CHOCOLATE
CROISSANT DOUGH

PLAIN CROISSANT
DOUGH

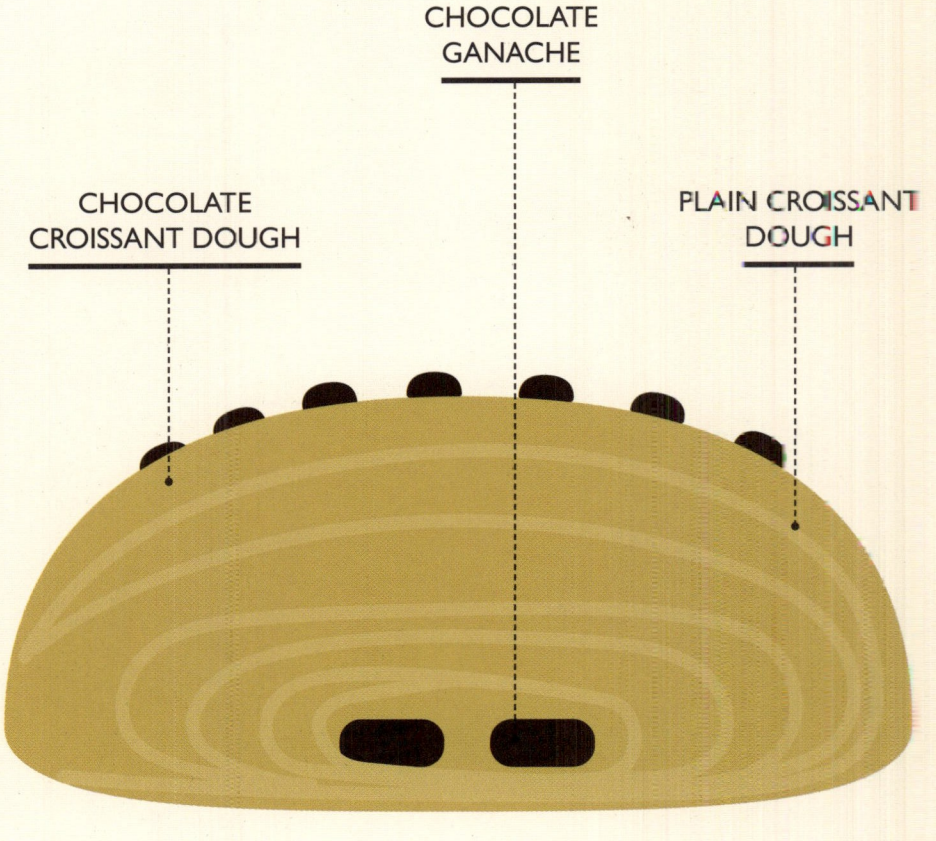

WHAT IS IT?

Plain and chocolate croissant pastries filled with chocolate ganache.

HOW LONG WILL IT TAKE?

Preparation: 2 ¹/₂ hours
Cooking: 20 to 30 minutes
Refrigeration: 30 minutes
Standing: 24 hours

EQUIPMENT YOU WILL NEED

Stand mixer fitted with a dough hook
Piping bag with a No 10 nozzle

TRICKY POINT

Incorporating the butter into the water-flour dough

SKILL REQUIRED

Folding dough (page 276)

ADVICE

Pain au chocolat can be prepared one day in advance and kept in the refrigerator. The following day, let them rise and bake. Do not exceed 3 folds for this type of dough, otherwise it may not rise properly. The more you fold the dough, the tighter the layers of pastry.

PLANNING, PREP AND STORAGE

The day before:
Ganache – water-flour dough
On the day:
Folding – assemble – raising – cooking
Uncooked pain au chocolate can be kept well-wrapped for 5 days in the freezer.

Learn

MAKES 10

1 CROISSANT DOUGH

Water-flour dough
23 g (¾ oz) fresh baker's yeast
190 g (6 ½ oz) water
200 g (7 oz) milk
750 g (1 lb 10 oz) flour
15 g (3 ½ teaspoons) salt
80 g (3 oz) white caster (superfine) sugar

Butter layer
275 g (10 oz) unsalted butter

Cocoa dough
15 g (½ oz) cocoa (unsweetened chocolate) powder

2 CHOCOLATE GANACHE

200 g (7 oz) chocolate (60% cocoa)
100 g (3 ½ oz) milk

3 EGG WASH

30 g (1 oz) egg yolk (2 yolks)
30 g (1 oz) milk

To make the pains au chocolat

1   To make the chocolate ganache, bring the milk to the boil, pour onto the chocolate, and stir after 1 minute. Put in the piping bag and pipe out two 40 cm (16 in) long rolls onto a sheet of baking paper. Put in the refrigerator.

2   To make the water-flour dough mixture, put the crumbled yeast, water, milk, flour, salt and sugar, in order, into the bowl of a stand mixer fitted with a dough hook then knead for 5 minutes at medium. To make the cocoa dough, take 400 g (14 oz) of the water-flour mixture and knead with the cocoa powder. Cover the dough with cling film (plastic wrap) and keep in the fridge until the following day.

3   To soften the butter, tap on it lightly using a rolling pin, working it into a 35 × 20 cm (14 × 8 in) rectangle. Roll out the plain water-flour dough to make a 50 × 20 cm (20 × 8 in) rectangle. Put the butter on

top of the dough. Bring the upper part of the dough halfway down the butter. Fold the lower part of the dough up over the previous part. Using the rolling pin, slightly widen the dough from the centre outwards. To make a double fold, turn the dough a quarter of a turn so the opening is on the right; with the rolling pin, press down lightly, 3 cm (1 in) from the ends to seal. Press down in the same way, moving towards the centre every few centimetres/inches. Roll out to make a strip 60 cm (24 in) wide. Fold 10 cm (4 in) from the bottom towards the top, seal by pressing down with the rolling pin. Bring the upper part back down to the previous part and seal. Bring the upper part back down to completely cover the lower, then widen slightly from the centre out. Refrigerate for 30 minutes.

4   Roll out both pieces into 40 × 30 cm (16 × 12 in) rectangles. Brush the plain dough with water and put the cocoa dough on top, then press down

gently with the rolling pin to make it stick.

5   Cut off the ends neatly. Cut in half lengthwise. With the tip of a knife, make oblique slashes along the length. Turn over so the plain side is towards you.

6   Put a roll of ganache on the side of the first rectangle and roll the dough around it. Repeat with the second rectangle.

7   Cut ten 10 cm (4 in) long rolls, transfer to a baking tray covered with baking paper (baking parchment), with the flap underneath. Press down lightly and glaze with egg yolk and milk wash. Leave to rise for 90 minutes to 2 hours at room temperature; they should double in size. Heat the oven to 210°C (410°F/gas 8). Egg wash a second time, put in the oven, and lower the temperature to 160°C (325°F/gas 4). Bake for 20 to 30 minutes.

BRIOCHE

Understand

COCOA BRIOCHE

WHAT IS IT?

A light and airy pastry made of raised plain dough and chocolate.

HOW LONG WILL IT TAKE?

Preparation: 1 ½ hours
Cooking: 45 minutes
Standing: 24 hours

EQUIPMENT YOU WILL NEED

Stand mixer with dough hook attachment
30 × 8 × 8 cm (12 × 4 × 4 in) cake tin

TRICKY POINT
Shaping the brioche

SKILL REQUIRED
Glazing with egg wash (page 281)

PLANNING, PREP AND STORAGE
The day before:
Dough
On the day:
Shaping – raising – cooking
Uncooked dough can be kept for 15 days in the freezer: shape the brioche, put it on a baking tray in the freezer and, once frozen, wrap it in cling film (plastic wrap) and store.

Learn

TO MAKE 1 BRIOCHE

1 BRIOCHE DOUGH

20 g (³/₄ oz) baker's yeast
250 g (9 oz) eggs (5 eggs)
400 g (14 oz) flour
10 g (2 ¹/₃ teaspoons) salt
40 g (1 ¹/₂ oz) white caster (superfine) sugar
200 g (7 oz) unsalted butter

2 CHOCOLATE PART

20 g (³/₄ oz) cocoa (unsweetened chocolate) powder

3 EGG WASH GLAZE

30 g (1 oz) egg yolks (2 eggs)
30 g (1 oz) milk

To make the brioche

1   Put all the ingredients in the refrigerator at least 4 hours in advance. To make the brioche dough: in the bowl of the stand mixer fitted with a dough hook, put the crumbled yeast, beaten eggs, flour, salt and sugar in that order. Turn on the mixer at low speed. Let it run until the dough no longer sticks to the side of the bowl: it should creep up along the hook, then a lump will separate, spin off against the side of the bowl and fall back several times into in the bowl. It will increase in elasticity but must not heat up.

2   Use a rolling pin to soften the butter by tapping it on the work surface. Take one third of the dough and make a rough mix with the butter on the work surface. Put it back into the bowl and knead with the hook until perfectly blended.

3   Take 350 g (12 oz) of dough and knead with the cocoa (unsweetened chocolate) powder. Wrap the two doughs in cling film (plastic wrap) and keep in the refrigerator until the following day.

4   Roll out the plain dough into a 40 × 30 cm (16 × 12 in) rectangle. Do the same with the cocoa dough. Brush the plain dough lightly with water using a paintbrush and place the cocoa dough on top. Roll it gently using a rolling pin to make it stick then trim off the ends to make the edges neat.

5   Make it into a roll, then cut it in half down the middle lengthwise.

6   Twist the two half-rolls together making sure that the cut surfaces are visible on top.

7   Place in the cake tin lined with baking paper (baking parchment). Prepare the egg wash: whisk the egg yolks lightly in a bowl with the milk. Brush the surface of the brioche once using a paintbrush (page 281). Cover the tin with cling film (plastic wrap) and leave to rise for 1 to 2 hours at room temperature until it doubles in size.

8   Preheat the oven to 200°C (400°F/gas 7). Glaze the brioche again with egg wash. Put in the oven, then lower the temperature to 160°C (320°F/gas 4) and bake for about 45 minutes. Remove the brioche from the oven wait 10 minutes and unmould onto a wire rack to cool.

BABA CAKES

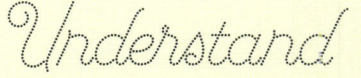

WHIPPED DARK
GANACHE

BABA DOUGH

COCOA
SYRUP

WHAT IS IT?

A yeast dough pastry that is baked, dried, then soaked in syrup and topped with whipped ganache.

HOW LONG WILL IT TAKE?

Preparation: 1 hour
Cooking: 1 hour
Refrigeration: 4 hours
Standing: 2 to 3 days

EQUIPMENT YOU WILL NEED

Stand mixer fitted with a
dough hook attachment
Two silicone moulds with six
5 cm (2 in) round holes
Piping bags

VARIATIONS

Add 30 g (1 oz) of rum to the syrup
Make a spice syrup using star anise, tonka bean, nutmeg, cinnamon and Szechuan pepper

TRICKY POINT

Squeezing the baba cake

TIPS

Dry babas can be kept for 1 month in a cardboard box in a dry place. To make baba cakes all the same size, put the moulds on weighing scales and weigh the dough when piping into the mould.

PLANNING, PREP AND STORAGE

3 days before:
Baba mix
The day before:
Ganache – chocolate decorations
On the day:
Syrup – soaking – decorate

Learn

MAKES 12

1 BABA DOUGH

15 g (½ oz) baker's yeast
130 g (4 oz) milk
100 g (3 ½ oz) eggs (2 eggs)
240 g (9 oz) flour
10 g (½ oz) cocoa (unsweetened chocolate) powder
5 g (1 ¼ teaspoons) salt
15 g (½ oz) white caster (superfine) sugar
75 g (2 ½ oz) unsalted butter

2 WHIPPED GANACHE

300 g (10 ½ oz) whipping cream
100 g (3 ½ oz) dark chocolate (66% cocoa)
2 g (1 sheet) sheet gelatine

3 SOAKING SYRUP

1 litre water (34 fl oz/4 cups)
500 g (1 lb 2 oz) white caster (superfine) sugar
40 g (1 ½ oz) cocoa (unsweetened chocolate) powder

4 CHOCOLATE DECORATIONS

200 g (7 oz) chocolate

To make the baba cakes

1   Put all the ingredients for the baba dough in the refrigerator at least 4 hours in advance. Put the crumbled yeast, milk, eggs, flour, cocoa (unsweetened chocolate) powder, salt and sugar, in that order, in the bowl of the stand mixer bowl fitted with a dough hook. Knead at medium power until the dough stops sticking to the side of the bowl and knocks against it. It should become elastic enough that when you hold up the dough between your fingers it should run out like a spider's web but not tear. It must not get hot.

2   Tap the cold butter on the work surface using a rolling pin to soften it. Take one-third of the dough and mix coarsely with the butter on the work surface. Put it back into the bowl and knead using the dough hook for about 5 minutes until perfectly blended.

3   Stop the mixer. Immediately transfer the dough to a piping bag, snip off the end and pipe the dough (page 278) into the buttered moulds. Between each cake, cut off the dough using scissors.

4   Leave the babas to rise at room temperature for 1 hour to 90 minutes until they double in volume.

5   Preheat the oven to 160°C (320°F/gas 4). Put the babas in the oven and bake for 30 to 45 minutes. Remove them from the moulds, put them on a rack, then switch off the oven and put the cakes back to dry for 15 minutes. Let them cool completely. They can be left to rest for 2 to 3 days in a dry place, ideally in a cardboard box.

6   Make the whipped ganache (page 44). Make the chocolate decorations (page 38). To make the syrup: put the water, sugar and cocoa in a saucepan and bring to the boil, then take off the heat. When the syrup is lukewarm, pour into a high-rimmed baking tray and put the babas in it. Place a slightly smaller tray on top to press down on the babas. After 15 minutes, turn them over and leave them to soak again. When you squeeze a baba cake, it should be soft throughout. Remove the babas from the syrup and squeeze them gently to remove the excess syrup, taking care not to break them. Put them in ramekins.

7   Whip up the ganache, transfer to a clean piping bag fitted with a star nozzle and decorate the babas with rose shapes, adding a chocolate decoration.

GALETTE
DES ROIS

Understand

COCOA PUFF
PASTRY

CREAMY
GANACHE

WHAT IS IT?

Two chocolate flaky puff pastry discs
filled with creamy ganache.

HOW LONG WILL IT TAKE?

Preparation: 3 hours
Cooking: 1 to 1 ½ hours
Standing: 9 hours

EQUIPMENT YOU WILL NEED

Stand mixer with dough hook
and flat beater attachments
24 cm (9 ½ in) pastry ring
Piping bag

VARIATION
Replace the dark chocolate with
350 g (12 oz) milk chocolate.

TRICKY POINTS
Making puff pastry
Assembling the galette

SKILLS REQUIRED
Making a pastry base (page 284)
Piping (page 278)
Scoring (page 284)

ADVICE
To help puff pastry to rise evenly, put 4
pastry rings in the corners of the baking
tray and place another baking tray on top.

TIPS
To cut the cake open without
breaking it, use a serrated knife and
move it on a piece of cardboard.

PLANNING AND PREP
2 days before: Make the dough –
prepare butter for the base
Previous day: 2 single folds – ganache – syrup
On the day: 2 double folds – leave to
stand – scoring – baking – filling

234

Learn

SERVES 8-10

1 PUFF PASTRY

Dough mixture
170 g (6 oz) water
15 g (3 ½ teaspoons) salt
10 g (½ oz) white vinegar
360 g (12 oz) flour

Base mixture
450 g unsalted butter
125 g (4 oz) flour
20 g (¾ oz) cocoa (unsweetened chocolate) powder

2 CREAMY GANACHE

250 g (9 oz) milk
60 g (2 oz) egg yolks (3 or 4 yolks)
60 g (2 oz) white caster (superfine) sugar
300 g (10 ½ oz) dark chocolate (66% cocoa)

3 GLAZING SYRUP

30 g (1 oz) water
40 g (1 ½ oz) white caster (superfine) sugar

4 EGG WASH GLAZE

30 g (1 oz) egg yolks (2 yolks)
15 g (½ oz) milk

235

To make the galette des rois

1   Make the cocoa puff pastry (page 54). The following day, make the creamy ganache (page 42) and set aside. Prepare the glazing syrup: bring the water and sugar to a boil, stir and leave to cool.

2   On the day, roll out the pastry 1 cm ($^1/_2$ in) thick, then leave to stand for 1 hour in the refrigerator. Preheat the oven to 180°C (350°F/gas 6). Cut out a 24 cm (9 $^1/_2$ in) disc and place on a baking tray lined with baking paper (baking parchment). To make the egg wash, mix the egg yolks and milk in a bowl, then use to glaze the surface (page 283).

3   Score the surface (page 284) of the pastry carefully using the tip of a sharp knife.

4   Put in the oven, then reduce the heat to 160°C (320°F/gas 4) and bake for 1 to 1 $^1/_2$ hours. When the pastry becomes crisp, remove from the oven and glaze with the egg wash immediately using a paintbrush.

5   When the cake has cooled, carefully slice in half using a serrated knife. Put the creamy ganache in a piping bag, snip off a corner, then pipe out a swirl pattern onto the bottom half, starting from the centre, then put the top back on. To serve, reheat the cake for 15 minutes at 150°C (300°F/gas 3) . Leave to stand for 30 minutes at room temperature and serve.

MILLEFEUILLES

Understand

CHOCOLATE
TOPPING

COCOA PUFF
PASTRY

CREAMY
GANACHE

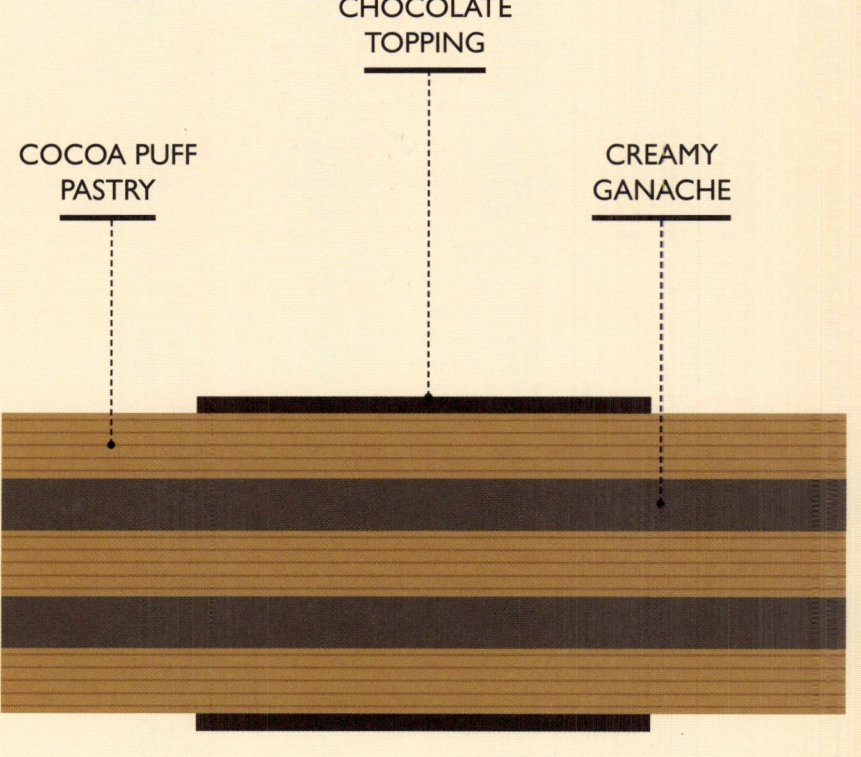

WHAT IS IT?

Rectangles of chocolate puff pastry
layered with creamy ganache,
and chocolate decorations.

HOW LONG WILL IT TAKE?

Preparation: 3 hours
Cooking: 1 hour
Refrigeration: 2 ¹/₂ hours
Standing: 2 hours

EQUIPMENT YOU WILL NEED

Stand mixer with dough hook
and flat beater attachments
Polyethylene sheet
Piping bag with a 10 mm (¹/₈ in) nozzle

VARIATION

Replace the creamy ganache
with pastry cream.

TRICKY POINTS

Making puff pastry
Assembling

SKILLS REQUIRED

Making a base (page 28)
Piping (page 27)

ADVICE

If the pastry rises too much during
baking, take it out of the oven, press it
down and put it back in the oven.

PLANNING AND PREP

2 days before: Make the dough –
prepare butter for the base
The day before: single folds – ganache
On the day: 2 double folds – leave to
stand – scoring – cooking – filling

Learn

MAKES 8–10

1 PUFF PASTRY

Dough
170 g (6 oz) water
15 g (3 ½ teaspoons) salt
10 g (½ oz) white vinegar
360 g (12 oz) flour

Base
450 g (1 lb) unsalted butter
125 g (4 oz) flour
20 g (¾ oz) cocoa (unsweetened chocolate) powder

2 CREAMY GANACHE

250 g (9 oz) milk
60 g (2 oz) egg yolks (3 or 4 yolks)
60 g (2 oz) white caster (superfine) sugar
300 g (10 ½ oz) dark chocolate (66% cocoa)

3 CARAMELISED TOPPING

50 g (2 oz) icing (confectioner's) sugar

4 CHOCOLATE DECORATIONS

300 g (10 ½ oz) dark chocolate (66% cocoa)
Mycryo powdered cocoa butter
(from specialist suppliers)

To make the millefeuilles

1 Make the cocoa inverted puff pastry (page 54).

2 The following day, make the creamy ganache (page 42) and set aside.

3 On the day, roll out the puff pastry into a 30 × 40 cm (12 × 16 in) rectangle 2 to 3 mm thick, then leave to stand for 30 minutes in the refrigerator. Preheat the oven to 170°C (340°F/gas 5). Put the dough on a baking tray lined with baking paper (baking parchment). Put another sheet of baking paper and a baking tray on top, transfer to the oven and bake for 30 to 40 minutes. Leave to cool.

4 Trim off the ends to make neat edges, then cut the flaky pastry into 3 strips of the same width using a serrated knife, then cut into 3 cm (1 1/2 in) rectangles. Preheat the oven to 220°C (430°F/gas 9). Sprinkle icing (confectioner's) sugar on top of the pastry, transfer to the oven and bake for 5 to 10 minutes, keeping a careful watch. When the top is evenly caramelised, remove from the oven and leave to cool.

5 Put the ganache in a piping bag. On a rectangle of dough, pipe out thin rolls of ganache packed close together (page 278), put on another rectangle of flaky dough, pipe out more ganache and finish with a rectangle of dough. Do the same with the other rectangles and the ganache. Keep the rest of the ganache for decoration.

6 For the chocolate decorations, temper the chocolate using the Mycryo method (page 30). Cut 6 cm (2 1/2 in) wide strips of polyethylene sheet. Spread the chocolate on them and cut every 8 cm (3 in). Place a millefeuille cake upright in the centre of each and fold the ends up over the cake. Refrigerate for at least 2 hours. Remove the polyethylene sheet before serving

MOELLEUX

Understand

SOFT DARK CHOCOLATE

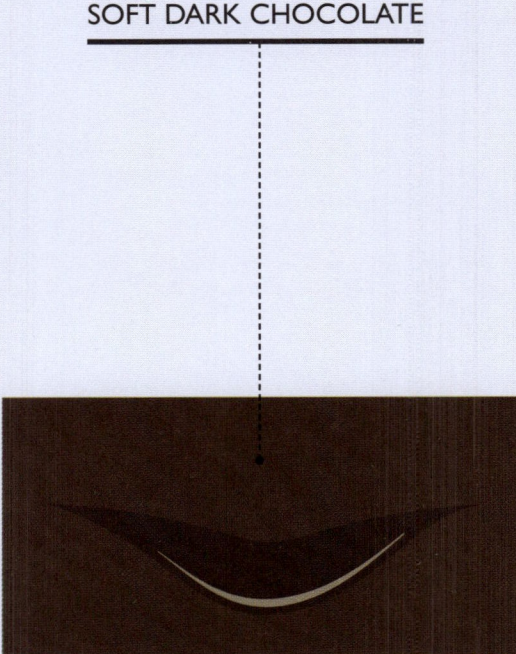

WHAT IS IT?

A small chocolate cake baked quickly so that the centre stays soft and runny, almost uncooked.

HOW LONG WILL IT TAKE?

Preparation: 15 minutes
Baking: 8 to 12 minutes

EQUIPMENT YOU WILL NEED

Five 7 cm (3 in) pastry rings

VARIATION

Soft white chocolate centre: insert a square of white chocolate into the centre of the dough before baking.

TRICKY POINT
Baking

SKILLS REQUIRED
Lining a pastry ring (page 277)
Using a double-boiler (page 276)

ADVICE
Continue baking for a few more minutes if the sides do not appear to be cooked enough.

TIPS

Use aluminium rings which transfer heat faster, making it easier to bake and unmould the cakes. They do not need lining with baking paper either, so just butter them a little. Buttering the rings before putting the baking paper in place helps the paper to stick to the sides

Learn

TO MAKE 5 MOELLEUX

150 g (5 oz) dark chocolate (66% cocoa)
150 g (5 oz) unsalted butter
150 g (5 oz) eggs (3 eggs)
110 g (3 ½ oz) icing (confectioner's) sugar
40 g (1 ½ oz) flour

1 Preheat the oven to 180°C (350°F/gas 6). To line the rings: butter them lightly, cut out strips of baking paper (baking parchment) that are slightly higher than the top of the rings and 1 cm (½ in) longer than the circumference so that the ends overlap. Put a strip inside each ring.

2 Melt the chocolate and butter in a double-boiler (page 276). Whisk the eggs in a bowl, then add the remaining ingredients onto the side of the bowl gradually incorporating them with a whisk to prevent lumps. Add the chocolate and melted butter.

3 When the mixture is well blended, pour it into the lined rings set on baking tray lined with baking paper (baking parchment).

4 Transfer to the oven and bake for at least 8 minutes. When they are cooked, the centres will be darker in colour and, when cut, should look like an 'eye'; the sides should be baked but the centre of the moelleux should still be soft and runny.

CHOCOLATE CHIP
COOKIES

Understand

CHOCOLATE
CHIPS

COOKIE
DOUGH

WHAT IS IT?

Shortbread cookies with chocolate chips and walnuts.

HOW LONG WILL IT TAKE?

Preparation: 15 minutes
Cooking: 10 minutes
Refrigeration: 2 hours

SKILL REQUIRED
Softening butter (page 280)

VARIATION
Replace the walnuts with macadamia nuts.

PLANNING, PREP AND STORAGE
Preparation:
Dough – cutting out – baking
Make the rolls of dough, wrap in cling film (plastic wrap) and keep them for up to 3 months in the freezer.

Learn

MAKES 24

120 g (4 oz) softened unsalted butter
60 g (2 oz) icing (confectioner's) sugar
80 g (3 oz) brown sugar
100 g (3 ½ oz) dark chocolate chips
100 g eggs (2 eggs)
200 g (7 oz) flour
1 g (¼ teaspoon) salt
2 g (½ teaspoon) baking powder
80 g (3 oz) walnuts, chopped

1 In a mixing bowl (or in a stand mixer using a flat beater), cream the butter until soft and smooth (page 280), then add the icing sugar and brown sugar. Break the chocolate into smaller pieces with a knife. Add the lightly beaten eggs. In another bowl, mix the flour, baking powder and salt and add half of this to the butter-sugar mixture, then mix. When the mixture is smoothly blended, add the rest of the dry ingredients, the chocolate chips and chopped nuts.

2 Make a roll of dough about 6 cm (2 ½ in) in diameter and wrap in cling film (plastic wrap). Leave to harden for 2 hours in the refrigerator.

3 Preheat the oven to 160°C (320°F/gas 4). Take the roll of dough out of the refrigerator and cut it into 1 cm (½ in) thick slices. Put them on a baking tray covered with baking paper.

4 Bake in the oven for about 10 minutes. The edges should be hard to the touch and the centre soft. Remove the baking tray from the oven and slide the sheet with the biscuits onto a worktop to halt the baking.

BROWNIES

Understand

DARK
CHOCOLATE

PECANS

ALMONDS

PISTACHIOS

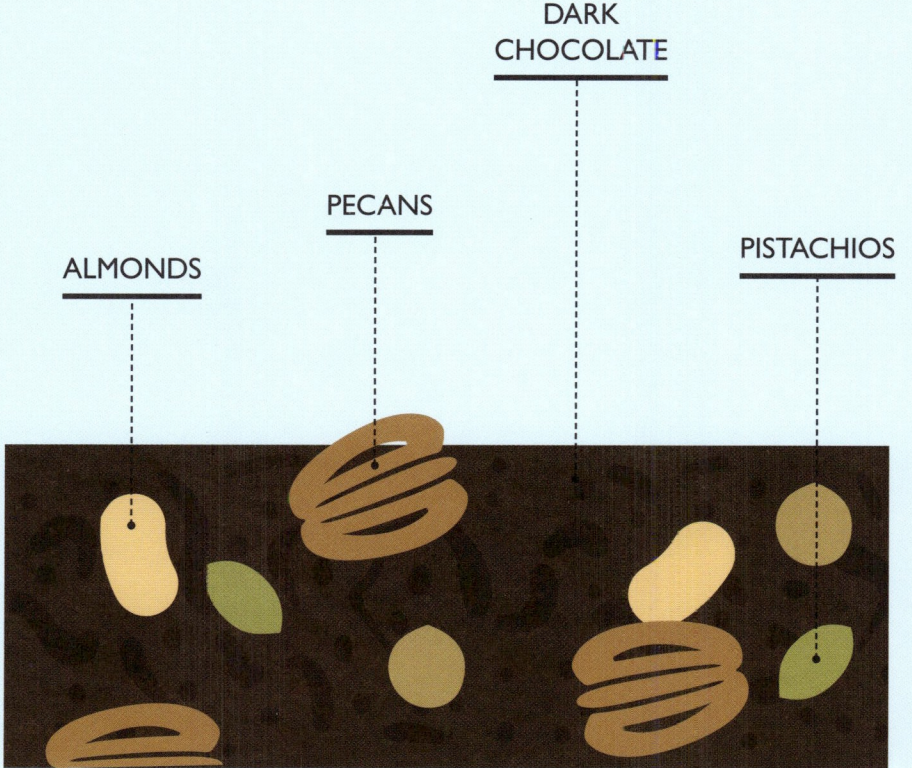

WHAT IS IT?

A brownie with a melt-in-the-mouth texture, with nuts and dried fruit.

HOW LONG WILL IT TAKE?

Preparation: 20 minutes
Cooking: 20 to 30 minutes

EQUIPMENT YOU WILL NEED

20 × 30 cm (8 × 12 in) deep baking tray

VARIATION

Replace the dried fruit with cranberries, dried blueberries, cashews, macadamia nuts, etc

TRICKY POINT

Baking

ADVICE

If used as the base for a dessert, increase baking time by 15 to 20 minutes.

PLANNING, PREP AND STORAGE

Preparation:
Cooking
The raw batter will keep for 3 months well-wrapped in the freezer.

Learn

MAKES 16

BASE

180 g (6 ¼ oz) unsalted butter
100 g (3 ½ oz) dark chocolate (66% cocoa)
150 g (5 oz) eggs (3 eggs)
200 g (7 oz) brown sugar
85 g (3 oz) flour

FILLING

180 g (6 ¼ oz) milk chocolate chips
40 g (1 ½ oz) hazelnuts
40 g (1 ½ oz) almonds
40 g (1 ½ oz) pistachios
40 g (1 ½ oz) pecans

1 Preheat the oven to 170°C (340°F/gas 5). Melt the butter in a saucepan, then add the dark chocolate and mix until evenly blended.

2 In a large bowl, lightly whisk the eggs and brown sugar together, then add the chocolate mixture and mix together. Sieve in the flour and mix again.

3 Cut the milk chocolate chips into smaller pieces. Chop the nuts.

4 Mix the chocolate and the chopped nuts. Add them gradually to the brownie batter. Line the baking tray with baking paper (baking parchment) then pour in the brownie batter.

5 Transfer to the oven and bake for 20 to 30 minutes. The centre should still be soft and squidgy.

CHOCOLATE TRUFFLE
CAKE

Understand

CHOCOLATE DOUGH

WHAT IS IT?

A melt-in-the-mouth chocolate cake.

HOW LONG WILL IT TAKE?

Preparation: 20 minutes
Cooking: 25 minutes

EQUIPMENT YOU WILL NEED

22 cm (8 ¹/₂ in) dessert ring
Stand mixer with whisk attachment

VARIATION
Add milk chocolate or white chocolate
chips before pouring into the ring.

SKILL REQUIRED
Using a double-boiler (page 276)

ADVICE
Take the butter out of the refrigerator
1 hour before starting to soften.
Make sure that the chocolate is not
too warm when mixing it in.

Learn

SERVES 6-8

250 g (9 oz) chocolate (66% cocoa)
250 g (9 oz) softened unsalted butter
125 g (4 oz) white caster (superfine) sugar
200 g (7 oz) eggs (4 eggs)
50 g (2 oz) flour

1 Melt the chocolate in a double-boiler (page 276). Whisk the butter and sugar in the bowl of the stand mixer until smooth and creamy. Add the eggs one by one, mixing slowly bewtween additions.

2 Add the flour. Whisk slowly to incorporate it, then add the melted chocolate and gently mix again.

3 Preheat the oven to 180°C (350°F/gas 6). Line the dessert ring with baking paper (baking parchment) and put it on a baking tray lined with more baking paper. Put the cake mixture in a piping bag, snip off a corner then pipe the mixture into the prepared ring, starting in the centre and working outwards in a spiral pattern.

4 Bake for 25 minutes. When the tip of a knife is inserted, it should come out slightly moist.

ROCK CAKE

Understand

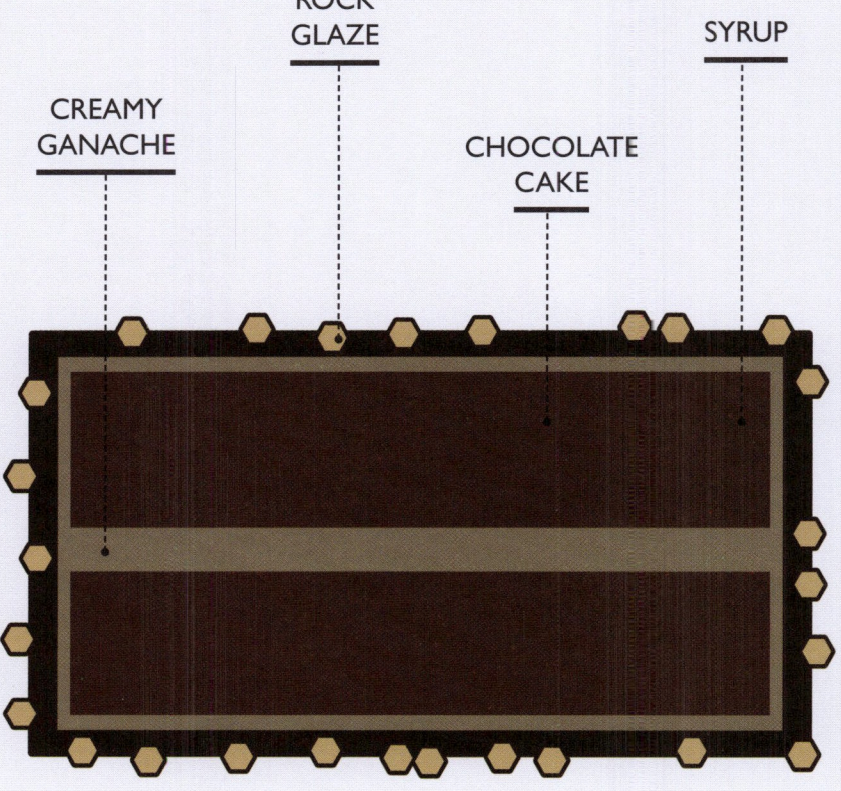

CREAMY
GANACHE

ROCK
GLAZE

CHOCOLATE
CAKE

SYRUP

WHAT IS IT?

A chocolate cake covered in creamy ganache and coated with rock glaze.

HOW LONG WILL IT TAKE?

Preparation: 1 ½ hours
Cooking: 40 minutes
Standing: 2 hr 40mins

EQUIPMENT YOU WILL NEED

Double-boiler
16 × 16 cm (6 ½ × 6 ½ in) baking frame
Paintbrush, Spatula
Piping bag with No 12 and basketweave nozzles

VARIATION

Add 30 g (1 oz) rum to the cake mix just before baking.

SKILLS REQUIRED

Using a double-boiler (page 276)
Chablon (page 273)
Piping (page 278)
Coating (page 279)

ADVICE

Soaking the cake when it comes out of the oven will make it softer and smoother.

PLANNING AND PREP

The day before:
Creamy ganache – soaking syrup
On the day:
Cake – assembling – glazing

250

Learn

SERVES 8-10

1 CREAMY GANACHE

250 g (9 oz) milk
50 g (2 oz) egg yolks (3 or 4 yolks)
50 g (2 oz) white caster (superfine) sugar
150 g (5 oz) dark chocolate
(60% cocoa minimum)
1 tonka bean (or half a vanilla pod (bean))

2 SOAKING SYRUP

80 g (3 oz) water
40 g (1 ½ oz) white caster (superfine) sugar

3 CHOCOLATE CAKE MIXTURE

75 g (2 ½ oz) unsalted butter
50 g (2 oz) dark chocolate (70% cocoa)
250 g (9 oz) eggs (5 eggs)
75 g (2 ½ oz) inverted sugar or neutral honey
125 g white caster (superfine) sugar
75 g (2 ½ oz) ground (powdered) almonds
120 g (4 oz) flour
8 g (½ tablespoon) baking powder
25 g (1 oz) cocoa (unsweetened chocolate) powder
120 g (4 oz) whipping cream

4 CHOCOLATE COATING LAYER

50 g (2 oz) dark chocolate (66% cocoa)

5 ROCK GLAZE

300 g (10 ½ oz) dark chocolate (66% cocoa)
260 g (9 oz) milk chocolate
160 g (5 ½ oz) chopped almonds
50 g (2 oz) grapeseed oil

To make the rock cake

1 Make the creamy ganache (page 42) adding the grated tonka bean/vanilla pod at the end. To make the soaking syrup: boil the water and sugar, stirring with a whisk and leave to cool.

2 Preheat the oven to 150°C (300°F/gas 3). To make the cake: melt the butter and chocolate in a double-boiler (page 276). In a mixing bowl, combine the eggs, inverted sugar/honey and the sugar, then add the ground almonds. Sieve the flour, baking powder and cocoa and stir them into the mixture. Add the cream, then the butter-chocolate mixture and mix well. Put the baking frame on a baking tray lined with baking paper (baking parchment). Pour the batter into the frame, transfer to the oven and bake for about 40 minutes. Remove from the oven, leave to cool for 10 minutes, then remove the frame.

3 Soak the cake with all the syrup using a paintbrush. Allow to cool completely. Using a serrated knife cut a few millimeters off the top of the cake to make it level.

4 Cut the cake in half lengthwise to make two 8 × 16 cm (3 × 6 in) rectangles. Turn one over and cover with a thin coating of chocolate (page 273). Gently rework the ganache with the spatula to soften it. Pipe out half of the ganache with a No 12 nozzle (page 278) onto the chocolate-coated rectangle, with the chocolate side underneath. Place the second rectangle on top and gently press down.

5 Put the rest of the ganache in a piping bag with a basket-weave nozzle. Coat the cake with ganache (page 279) and smooth using a spatula. Put in the refrigerator for 2 hours.

6 Prepare the rock glaze (page 72). Put the cake on a rack set over a baking tray, then pour the glaze over the whole length of the cake. Wait a few minutes, then put the cake on a serving dish and refrigerate for at least 30 minutes before serving.

MARBLE CAKE

Understand

LEMON CAKE   CHOCOLATE CAKE

WHAT IS IT?

A marbled, part lemon, part chocolate cake.

HOW LONG WILL IT TAKE?

Preparation: 45 minutes
Cooking: 1 hour

EQUIPMENT YOU WILL NEED

30 × 8 × 8 cm (12 × 3 ×3) cake tin
Stand mixer with whisk attachment
2 piping bags

SKILLS REQUIRED
Filling a piping bag (page 278)
Piping (page 278)

ADVICE
Dip the blade of a knife in a little oil and slash the cake down the centre lengthwise before it goes into the oven to help it rise when baking.

TIP
To check if the cake is ready, push the blade of a knife into the middle of the cake; it should come out clean.

SERVES 12

LEMON CAKE MIX

100 g (3 $^1/_2$ oz) egg (2 eggs)
60 g (2 oz) egg yolks (4 yolks)
215 g (7 $^1/_2$ oz) white caster (superfine) sugar
115 g (4 oz) whipping cream
50 g (2 oz) sunflower oil
170 g (6 oz) flour
4 g (1 teaspoon) baking powder
3 lemons

Learn

CHOCOLATE MARBLE MIX

50 g (2 oz) egg (1 egg)
30 g (1 oz) egg yolks (2 yolks)
125 g white caster (superfine) sugar
70 g (2 ½ oz) whipping cream
35 g (1 oz) sunflower oil
85 g (3 oz) flour
20 g (¾ oz) cocoa (unsweetened chocolate) powder
2 g (½ teaspoon) baking powder

1 To make the lemon cake mix: whisk the eggs, egg yolks and sugar in the bowl of the stand mixer bowl, then add the cream and the oil.

2 Sieve the flour and baking powder into a bowl, then add the zest of a lemon. Mix with a whisk, then add these dry ingredients to the lemon dough mixture. Mix everything together and put into a piping bag (page 278).

3 To make the chocolate marble mix: combine the eggs, egg yolks and the sugar in the cleaned bowl of the stand mixer, add the cream and the oil. Sieve the flour, baking powder and cocoa (unsweetened chocolate) powder in a bowl, then add these dry ingredients to the chocolate mixture. Mix everything together and put into a second piping bag.

4 Preheat the oven to 160°C (320°F/gas 4). Line the cake tin with baking paper (baking parchment). Pipe 230 g (8 oz) of lemon mixture into the bottom of the tin (page 278), then 200 g (7 oz) of chocolate marble mix in the centre. Add another 230 g (8 oz) of lemon mixture, then 200 g (7 oz) of chocolate marble mix in the centre. Finish with the lemon mixture. Transfer to the oven and bake for 1 hour.

TIGER CAKES

Understand

FINANCIER
CAKE MIXTURE

CREAMY
GANACHE

CHOCOLATE
CHIPS

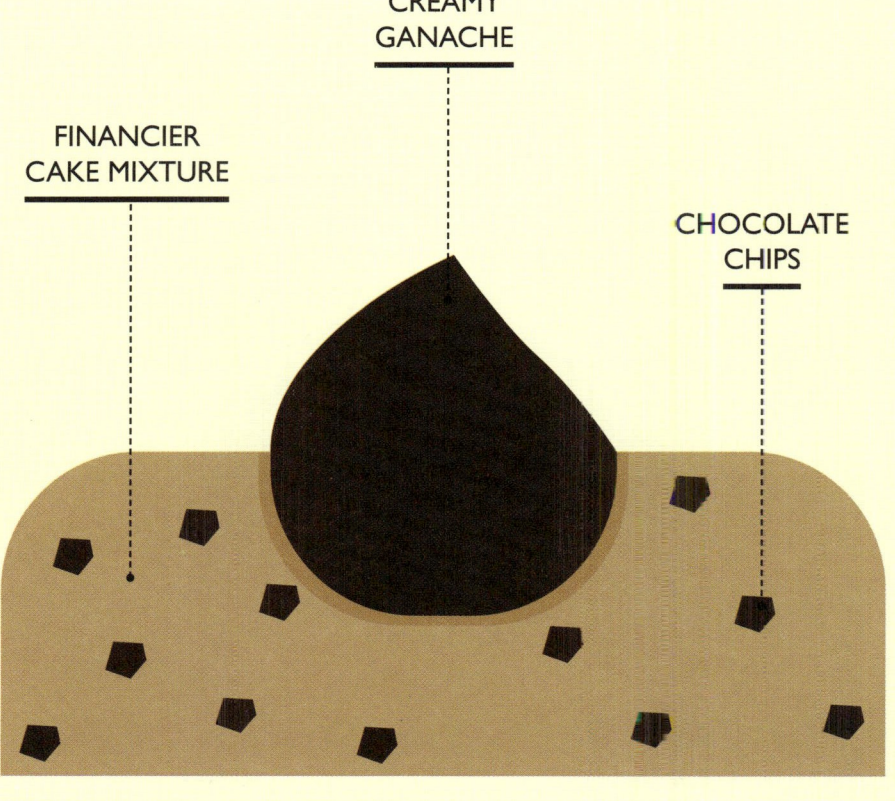

WHAT IS IT?

A soft cake made of ground almonds and
chocolate chips topped with creamy ganache.

HOW LONG WILL IT TAKE?

Preparation: 30 minutes
Baking: 20 minutes
Standing: 24 hours

EQUIPMENT YOU WILL NEED

Six 6 cm (2 ½ in) savarin cake moulds
Piping bag

TRICKY POINT
Adding butter

PLANNING AND PREP
The day before:
Ganache – financier cake mixture
On the day:
Baking – filling

Learn

MAKES 6

Financier cake mixture
120 g (4 oz) icing (confectioner's) sugar
60 g (2 oz) ground (powdered) almonds
40 g (1 ½ oz) flour
100g (3 ½ oz) unsalted butter
110 g (3 ½ oz) egg whites (4 whites)
80 g (3 oz) dark chocolate chips

CREAMY GANACHE

125 g (4 oz) milk
25 g (1 oz) egg yolks (2 yolks)
25 g (1 oz) white caster (superfine) sugar
125 g (4 oz) dark chocolate (60% cocoa)

1 Make the creamy ganache (page 42). Cover with cling film (plastic wrap) and leave in the refrigerator until ready to use. Make the financier cake mixture: mix the icing sugar, ground almonds and flour in a bowl. Heat the butter until it is lightly browned (see browned hazelnut butter; page 280), pour immediately over the ingredients and mix.

2 Gradually add the egg whites. Leave to cool, then stir in the chocolate chips. Cover with cling film (plastic wrap) and leave to stand until the following day.

3 After leaving to stand, take the financier cake mixture out of the refrigerator 30 minutes before use for it to soften. Preheat the oven to 170°C (340°F/gas 5). Fill the savarin cake moulds using a piping bag (page 278). Bake for 20 minutes. They should be lightly browned. Unmould when they are still warm.

4 When the cakes have cooled completely, fill the centres with creamy ganache.

MADELEINES

Understand

MADELEINE   DARK CHOCOLATE
COATING

WHAT IS IT?

Small, soft sponge cakes partly
coated with dark chocolate.

HOW LONG WILL IT TAKE?

Preparation: 45 minutes
Baking: 8 to 15 minutes
Standing: 24 hours

EQUIPMENT YOU WILL NEED

Madeleine cake moulds
Thermometer
Piping bag

VARIATIONS

Flavour the madeleine cake mixture by
adding the zest of a lemon or an orange.
Make a milk or white chocolate coating.

TRICKY POINT

Leaving the dough to stand long enough

SKILL REQUIRED

Tempering chocolate with Mycyro
powdered cocoa butter (page 30)

ADVICE

Do not pour the milk-glucose-vanilla-butter
mix into the madeleine cake mixture when
it is still hot or the heat will kill the yeast.

TIPS

Mycryo cocoa butter is useful to
temper small quantities quickly.
To unmould the madeleines more easily, first
place the mould in the freezer for 15 minutes.

PLANNING AND PREP

The day before:
Madeleine cake mix
On the day:
Baking – coating

Learn

MAKES 10

MADELEINE CAKE MIXTURE

25 g (1 oz) milk
1 vanilla pod (bean)
25 g (1 oz) glucose syrup
50 g (2 oz) unsalted butter
100 g (3 ½ oz) eggs (2 eggs)
75 g (2 ½ oz) white caster (superfine) sugar
25 g (1 oz) oil
125 g (4 oz) flour
3 g (¾ teaspoon) baking powder

COATING

200g (7 oz) dark couverture chocolate (66% cocoa)
2 g Mycryo powdered cocoa butter

1 Heat the milk, vanilla pod and glucose in a saucepan. When the mixture boils remove from the heat. Take out the vanilla pod and add the butter, then mix until smooth.

2 Whisk the eggs and sugar in a bowl. The mixture should foam slightly. Add the oil, then the milk-glucose-vanilla-butter mixture. Add the sieved flour and baking powder. Cover with cling film (plastic wrap) and leave to stand in the refrigerator overnight.

3 Preheat the oven to 210°C (410°F/gas 8). Grease the mould with softened butter. Pipe out a knob of mixture into the centre of each mould (page 278), stopping 5 mm from the top.

4 Transfer to the oven, then immediately lower the temperature to 180°C (350°F/gas 6). Bake for 8 to 15 minutes depending on the size of the madeleines; they should be lightly browned. Remove from the oven and quickly unmould onto a cooling rack.

5 Temper the couverture chocolate and the Mycryo butter (page 30). Carefully clean the imprints and wipe them dry with a clean cloth. Put the tempered chocolate in a piping bag and fill the madeleine imprints two-thirds full. Gently press the madeleines down into the moulds so that the chocolate rises between the edge of the mould and the cake. Leave to set for at least 2 hours at room temperature.

CHOCOLATE
MOUSSE

Understand

DARK CHOCOLATE
MOUSSE

CHOCOLATE
FLAKES

WHAT IS IT?

A light and airy dessert made of chocolate, cream and French meringue.

HOW LONG WILL IT TAKE?

Preparation: 30 minutes
Refrigeration: 6 hours minimum

EQUIPMENT YOU WILL NEED

Electric mixer
4-5 ramekins or small serving dishes

VARIATION

Add bergamot citrus zest to the chocolate

SKILL REQUIRED

Using a double-boiler (page 276)

ADVICE

To prevent lumps forming, do not put the egg yolks directly in contact with the chocolate, which tends to harden it. Take the desserts out of the refrigerator 15 to 20 minutes before serving.

PLANNING, PREP AND STORAGE

The day before:
Mousse
On the day:
Decorate – serve
Chocolate mousse can be stored for up to 3 weeks, well-wrapped, in the freezer.

Learn

MAKES 4–5

MOUSSE BASE

250 g (9 oz) dark chocolate (66% cocoa)
100 g (3 ½ oz) whipping cream
30 g (1 oz) egg yolks (2 yolks)

FRENCH MERINGUE

180 g (6 ¼ oz) egg whites (6 whites)
40 g (1 ½ oz) white caster (superfine) sugar

DECORATION

200 g (7 oz) chocolate (66% cocoa)

1 Melt the chocolate in the double-boiler (page 276). Warm the cream. Remove the melted chocolate from the double-boiler, pour cream over the chocolate and mix well to make a smooth emulsion.

2 Make the French meringue (page 69). Add one-third of the meringue to the chocolate-cream mixture and whisk briskly.

3 Add the egg yolks and whisk well. Add the remaining meringue and mix gently with a whisk. Finish mixing with a spatula.

4 Transfer to ramekins or small serving dishes and refrigerate for at least 6 hours, ideally overnight. Make the chocolate flakes (page 38) and sprinkle them on the mousse before serving (page 38).

MARQUISE

Understand

RICH CHOCOLATE
FONDANT

COCOA
POWDER

WHAT IS IT?

Chocolate fondant cake that
doesn't need baking.

HOW LONG WILL IT TAKE?

Preparation: 30 minutes
Standing: 24 hours

EQUIPMENT YOU WILL NEED

20 × 8 × 8 cm (8 × 3 × 3) cake tin
Spatula

SKILL REQUIRED
Using a double-boiler (page 276)

ADVICE
Serve with vanilla- or coffee-
flavoured crème anglaise

ORGANIZATION
The day before:
Make the cake
On the day:
Serve

Learn

SERVES 8-10

CAKE BASE

175 g (6 oz) softened unsalted butter
350 g (12 oz) dark chocolate (66% cocoa)
60 g (2 oz) egg yolks (4 yolks)

FRENCH MERINGUE

120 g (4 oz) egg whites (4 whites)
65 g (2 ½ oz) white caster (superfine) sugar

DECORATION

30 g (1 oz) cocoa (unsweetened chocolate) powder

1 Line the cake tin with baking paper (baking parchment). Take the butter out of the refrigerator in advance to soften. Melt the chocolate in the double-boiler (page 276).

2 Incorporate the softened butter into the chocolate in three stages using a whisk and mixing until smoothly blended.

3 Make the French meringue (page 69). Put one-third of the meringue into the butter-chocolate mixture and whisk briskly. Add the egg yolks and whisk well.

4 Add the rest of the meringue and whisk gently. Finish mixing using the spatula.

5 Pour into the mould, smooth with the spatula if necessary and refrigerate for 24 hours.

6 Unmould onto a serving dish and remove the baking paper. Sprinkle with cocoa powder and serve.

ICE CREAM

Understand

DARK CHOCOLATE
ICE CREAM

MILK CHOCOLATE
CHIPS

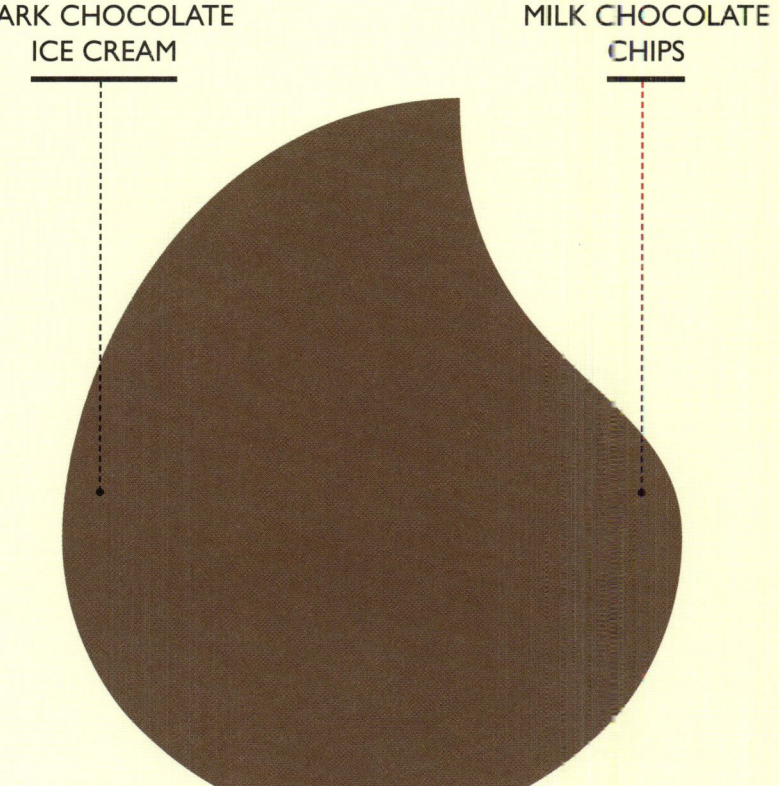

WHAT IS IT?

A rich, smooth crème anglaise-based chocolate ice cream.

HOW LONG WILL IT TAKE?

Preparation: 30 minutes
Ice-cream maker: around 45 minutes
Refrigeration: 24 hours

EQUIPMENT YOU WILL NEED

Ice-cream maker
Thermometer

TRICKY POINT
Cooking the crème anglaise

SKILLS REQUIRED
Using an ice-cream maker (page 269)
Beating egg yolks (page 281)

ADVICE
Put the mixture in the refrigerator overnight to allow the flavours to meld. To make it keep longer, add ice cream stabiliser during mixing, which will allow it to keep its creamy texture.

PLANNING AND PREP
The day before:
Chocolate crème anglaise
On the day
Ice-cream

Learn

MAKES 1 KG

200 g (7 oz) milk
200 g (7 oz) whipping cream
100 g (3 ½ oz) egg yolks (6 to 7 yolks)
80 g (3 oz) white caster (superfine) sugar
100 g (3 ½ oz) mascarpone
200 g (7 oz) dark chocolate (66% cocoa)

decoration
100 g (3 ½ oz) milk chocolate

1   To make the crème anglaise: bring the milk and cream to the boil in a saucepan. Meanwhile, beat the egg yolks and the sugar in a heatproof bowl (page 281). When the milk-cream mixture is just about to boil, pour half of it onto the yolk-sugar mixture and whisk well. When the mixture is smooth, pour it back into the saucepan. Return to medium heat, stirring constantly, until the mixture is thick enough to coat the spatula, at a maximum temperature of 85°C (185°F). Pour onto the chocolate, wait one minute, then stir.

2   Add the mascarpone and mix. Transfer to a bowl, cover with cling film (plastic wrap), allow to cool then put in the refrigerator overnight.

3   Chop the milk chocolate using a chef's knife. Process the ice cream (page 269) according to the manufacturer's instructions. At the end of the cycle, add the chopped chocolate and process for another 5 minutes.

CHAPTER 3
ILLUSTRATED GLOSSARY

UTENSILS 268

CHOCOLATE MOULDS

EQUIPMENT 270
KEEPING MOULDS CLEAN AND DRY 271
FILLING A MOULD 271
SCRAPING 271
UNMOULDING 271
JOINING TWO CHOCOLATE PIECES 271

CHOCOLATE PRODUCTS

WHITE/MILK/BLOND (CARAMELISED
WHITE) CHOCOLATE 272
DARK CHOCOLATE (60%, 66%, 70%) 272
RAW CHOCOLATE 272
COCOA BUTTER 272
MYCRYO BUTTER® 272
COCOA POWDER 272
COCOA NIBS 272
COUVERTURE CHOCOLATE 272

A CHOCOLATE GLOSSARY

COATING WITH A THIN LAYER OF
CHOCOLATE 273
TEMPERING 273
REMOVING A BAKING FRAME 273
STRAINING GLAZE 273

TIPS FOR MAKING CHOCOLATE

MAKING A PAPER CONE FOR PIPING 274
TEMPERATURE 274
'BLOOMED' CHOCOLATE 274
THICKENED CHOCOLATE 274
VISCOUS CHOCOLATE 274
SHRINKAGE OF GANACHES 274
KEEPING EQUIPMENT CLEAN
AND DRY 274

CHOOSING CHOCOLATE

ENJOYING CHOCOLATE 275
BUYING CHOCOLATE 275
HOW TO KEEP AND STORE 275

BASIC TECHNIQUES: MAKING

INCOPRPORATING USING A SPATULA ... 276
MIXING WITHOUT
INCORPORATING AIR 276
SCRAPING 276
USING A DOUBLE-BOILER 276
STRAINING 276

BASIC TECHNIQUES: PREPARING

REHYDRATING GELATINE 277
PREPARING A BAKING TRAY 277
LINING A BAKING RING 277
USING ACETATE STRIPS 277
SETTING UP FOR GLAZING 277

BASIC TECHNIQUES: PIPING

PIPING BAG 278
FILLING THE PIPING BAG 278
MAKING A TEMPLATE 278

BASIC TECHNIQUES: FINISHING

PIPING OUT A SPIRAL 279
COATING WITH A PIPING BAG 279
GLAZING A LOG CAKE 279
COVERING WITH FLAKES 279

INGREDIENTS: CREAM, BUTTER

CREAM 280
MAKING WHIPPED CREAM 280
FIRMING-UP WHIPPED CREAM 280
BUTTER 280
SOFTENED BUTTER 280
BROWNED 'HAZELNUT' BUTTER' 280

EGGS

EGGS 281
EQUIVALENT EGG WEIGHTS 281
BEATING EGG YOLKS 281
WHIPPING AND FIRMING UP
EGG WHITES 281
THE 'RIBBON TEST' 281
EGG WASH GLAZE 281

SUGAR, HONEY

SUGAR 282
MAKING A SYRUP 282
MAKING A CARAMEL 282
SOAKING IN SYRUP 282
HONEY 282
INVERTED SUGAR SYRUP 282
GLUCOSE SYRUP 282

FRUIT, FLAVOURINGS

ROASTING DRIED NUTS 283
DRYING FRUIT 283
ZESTING FRUIT 283
GOLD DECORATIONS 283
FOOD COLOURING 283

TIPS: DOUGH

ROLLING OUT DOUGH 284
MAKING A PASTRY BASE 284
CUTTING OFF EXCESS 284
KNEADING 284
MAKING A SHORTCRUST DOUGH 284
SCORING 284

TIPS: MACARONS & CHOUX PASTRY

MAKING MACARON MIXTURE 285
PIPING OUT MACARONS 285
COOKING AND STORING 285
DRYING CHOUX DOUGH 285
MAKING CRUNCHY CRAQUELIN 285
PIPING CHOUX PASTRY 285

UTENSILS

1 Whisk, spatula, bowl scraper

2 Palette knives, spatulas

3 Comb spatulas, brush

4 Paint brushes

5 Serrated knife, chef's knife, paring knife

6 Fork, dipping forks

7 Piping bags and nozzles

8 Baking tray, baking rack

9 Baking paper, transparent acetate strip tape, polyethylene sheets

UTENSILS

1 Scales, thermometer

2 Round bowls

3 Rings, pastry cutters

4 Baking frames

5 Log cake moulds, cake moulds/tins

6 Hand blender, stand mixer, attachments

7 Blender

8 Ice cream maker

CHOCOLATE MOULDS

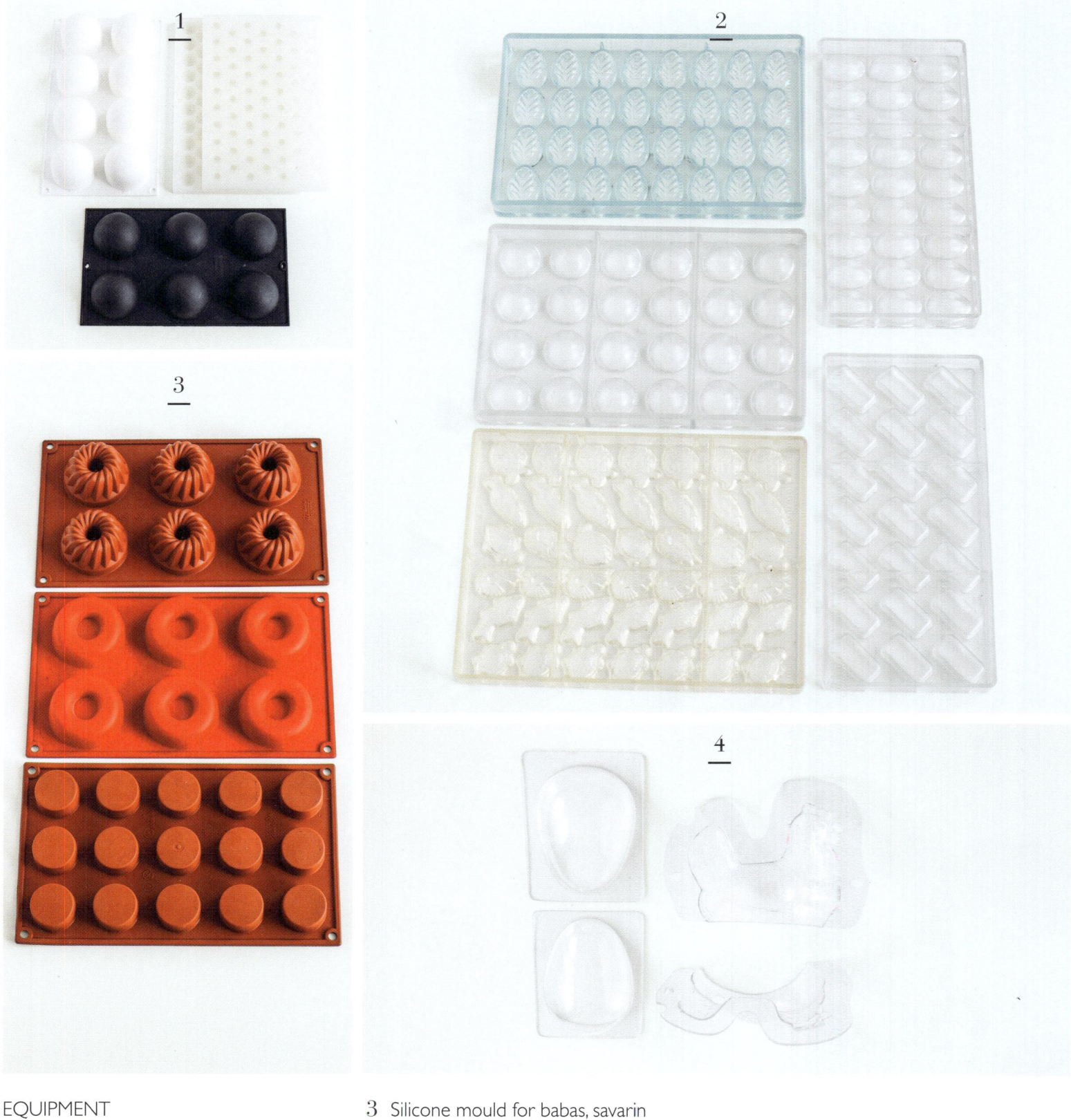

EQUIPMENT

1 Half-sphere silicone moulds

2 Chocolate moulds, polycarbonate mould with small fish imprints

3 Silicone mould for babas, savarin moulds, discs

4 Polycarbonate mould to make eggs and hens

CHOCOLATE MOULDS

1 KEEPING MOULDS CLEAN AND DRY

Wipe the mould imprints with a clean cloth before pouring the chocolate in to remove any trace of moisture or fat.

Hold moulds by their edges to limit hand contact. Body heat is higher than the temperature at which chocolate is processed, and the heat may cause white "bloom" on the chocolate after setting.

2 FILLING A MOULD

Fill the mould with chocolate, tap lightly on the side to allow air bubbles to escape, then turn it over to let the excess chocolate flow out. Wait a few minutes, then repeat the operation.

3 SCRAPING

When the chocolate has begun to set, run a palette knife over the surface of the mould to remove excess chocolate and make sweets with neat, smooth edges.

4 UNMOULDING

Twist the mould slightly, turn it over and tap on the side with the handle of a spatula.

5 JOINING TWO CHOCOLATE PIECES TOGETHER

Heat a baking tray on a double-boiler, put the first piece on the tray for a few seconds so that it melts slightly and then stick it immediately to the second piece. Leave to crystallise.

CHOCOLATE PRODUCTS

1 WHITE/MILK CHOCOLATE/ BLOND CHOCOLATE (CARAMELISED WHITE CHOCOLATE)

2 DARK CHOCOLATE (60%, 66%, 70%)

3 RAW CHOCOLATE

The cocoa beans for 'raw' chocolate in bars have not been roasted. Avoiding heat treatment means that a maximum quantity of natural ingredients has been preserved. Its nutritional quality is superior to more processed chocolate.

4 COCOA BUTTER

Vegetable fat from the cocoa bean used to make the chocolate more fluid when it is tempered and to give the tempered mixture more body.

5 MYCRYO BUTTER

Pure vegetable fat from the cocoa bean. This cocoa butter has a completely neutral taste.

6 COCOA POWDER

Unsweetened chocolate powder.

7 COCOA NIBS

Roasted and crushed cocoa beans, with a strong and rather bitter taste. They are used to add flavour and crunchiness.

8 COUVERTURE CHOCOLATE

Couverture chocolate is high quality dark, white or milk chocolate packed in slabs, discs or chips and is used by professional chocolatiers, chocolate-makers and pastry chefs. Bars of dark, milk or white chocolate come in 70 g (2 ¹/₂ oz) to 100 g (3 ¹/₂ oz) bars or individual squares.

Couverture chocolate is chosen when the product is to be used for melting and processing. It contains less sugar and more cocoa butter (31% minimum). When melted, it is more fluid, creamy and has good coating qualities. It has a good consistency when tempered. Bars of eating chocolate may also be used for making decorations that do not require melting.

A CHOCOLATE GLOSSARY

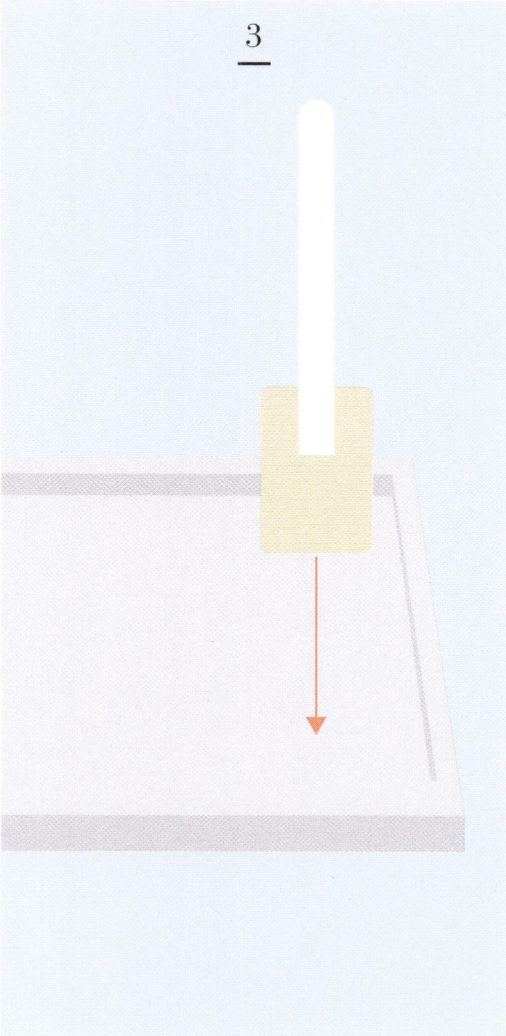

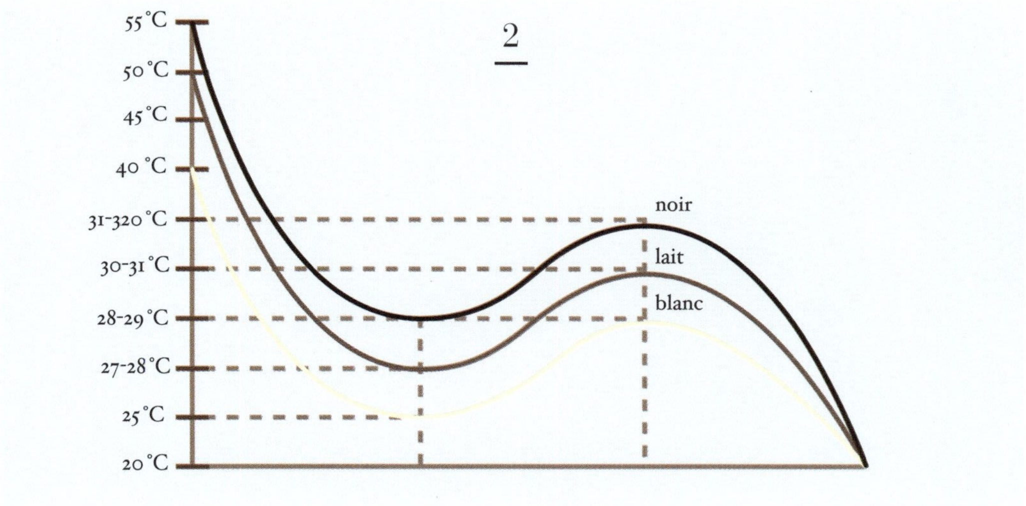

1 COATING WITH A THIN LAYER OF CHOCOLATE

Called 'chabloning' in French. Applying a fine layer of melted chocolate on a biscuit base, which hardens as it dries and prevents the biscuit from sticking.

Use regular baking chocolate, which does not require tempering. Melt it in a double-boiler, pour it over the biscuit base and spread as thinly as possible using a palette knife. Leave to harden. When assembling, place the chocolate side on the baking paper.

2 TEMPERING

Tempering is the process by which the fat contained in the chocolate changes from a liquid to a solid state. Once solid, the fat molecules interlock with each other, giving them rigidity and hardness.

Cocoa butter (the fat in the chocolate) is made up mainly of triglycerides which, depending on the temperature at which tempering takes place, can have up to five different crystal forms, each of which is stable at a particular temperature.. The process of tempering is crucial for giving chocolate its lovely sheen, and a texture that breaks with snap.

Temperature curves

Dark couverture chocolate: Melting temp: 55-58°C (131-136.4°F) /Tempering temp: 28-29°C/(82.4-84.2°F)Working temp: 31°-32 °C (87.8-89.6°F)

Milk couverture chocolate: Melting temp: 45°- 48°C (113°-118.4°F)/Tempering temp: 27°-28°C(80.6°-82.4°F)/Working temp: 29°-30°C (84.2°-86°F)

White couverture chocolat: Melting temp: 45°-48°C(113°F-118.4F°)/Tempering temp: 26°-27°C(78.8°-80.6°F)/Working temp: 28°-29°C (82.4°-84.2°F)

3 REMOVING A BAKING FRAME

Gently heat the outside of the frame using a kitchen blowtorch or run the hot blade of a knife between the ganache chocolate and the baking frame.

4 STRAINING GLAZE

Strain the chocolate glaze through a fine sieve in order to remove any impurities from the ingredients.

TIPS: MAKING CHOCOLATE

1 MAKING A PAPER CONE FOR PIPING

Cut out a right-angled triangle measuring 30 cm × 20 cm (12 × 8 in) from a sheet of baking paper. Holding the 30 cm (12 in) base in the middle and with the right angle on your right, bring down the tip opposite the middle of the base and start rounding the cone, turning it on itself until you reach the opposite tip. Bend the opposite point into the cone to hold it in position. Make sure that the tip of the cone is sharp. Fill the cone one-third full with the piping mixture,, fold down the top like a tube of toothpaste and cut off the tip to the required size.

2 TEMPERATURE

Use an accurate thermometer, ideally displaying one digit after the decimal point, to make sure that a dark couverture chocolate, for example, is between 31 and 32°C (87.8 and 89.6°F). To test the temperature, leave the thermometer in the middle of the mixture and stir until the temperature remains constant.

3 BLOOMED CHOCOLATE

There are several possible causes: moisture in the mould, cooling too quickly – this happens when you put the mould in the refrigerator– or the chocolate has been tempered incorrectly. Before using tempered couverture chocolate, dip a piece of baking paper into the chocolate mixture and leave the coating to set on the worktop. If after a few minutes, it hardens and breaks cleanly and does not melt instantly when touched, it can be used, otherwise you will need to start the process again.

4 THICKENED CHOCOLATE

If chocolate thickens during tempering, it will unfortunately never recover its fluid texture. It is best to set it aside and use for making ganache or mousse.

5 VISCOUS CHOCOLATE

If you let the temperature drop too far during tempering, the chocolate will begin to thicken and become viscous as it cools: unstable crystals have formed, having a negative effect on the texture of the chocolate.

6 SHRINKAGE OF GANACHE

It is best to leave ganache to set for 1-2 hours to prevent shrinkage when it is moulded or used for coating. Shrinkage produces air gaps, making the chocolate difficult to keep long-term.

7 KEEPING EQUIPMENT CLEAN AND DRY

Clean and dry the bowl thoroughly each time

CHOOSING CHOCOLATE

you use the double-boiler. Avoid washing your hands while working with chocolate to prevent moisture from getting into the couverture chocolate. Moisture will make the surface rough (a process called 'seizing') and may later cause the chocolate to form a white 'bloom' on its surface).

BUYING CHOCOLATE

When buying chocolate you should check:

Percentage of cocoa:

There should be a minimum of 30% cocoa

DECIPERING THE LABEL
In the UK and Europe, the term 'made from pure cocoa butter product' or '100% pure cocoa butter' guarantees that the finished product has no added vegetable oils other than cocoa butter.

The word '"origin..."' followed by the name of the country, means that the beans are wholly from the producing country indicated.

Chocolate bearing the AB label complies with the European CE directive. This directive refers to the organic production of agricultural products without the use of chemicals such as pesticides. At least 95% of the ingredients must be organically produced. The cocoa beans, cocoa butter, sugar, and other milk products used in the production of organic chocolate are from agriculture that complies with the European directive.

WHERE SHOULD YOU BUY CHOCOLATE?

BEAN-TO-BAR CHOCOLATE
Bean-to-bar chocolatiers are specialists in the craft of producing chocolate themselves, buying beans directly from growers and processing and producing the chocolate end-to-end. Buy direct from the producer, from reliable shops and online.

EATING CHOCOLATE
Bars of good-quality eating chocolate and baking chocolate are available from shops and supermarkets.

COUVERTURE CHOCOLATE
Can be bought in specialised professional shops or online, often in in 1kg (2.2 lb) to 3 kg (6.6 lb) bags.

HOW TO KEEP AND STORE

Chocolate should be kept out of the refrigerator away from light and heat. Put it in a dry place ideally between 16°C (60°F) and 18°C (64.5°F).

Ganaches should be eaten within three weeks after they're made, and bars of chocolate can be kept for up to 6 months.

BASIC TECHNIQUES: MAKING

1 INCORPORATING USING A SPATULA

Use a whisk to incorporate one third of the smoother, more runny mix into a second third in order to loosen it up. Then stir this mix into the remaining third using a spatula until you obtain a smooth, light mix.

2 MIXING WITHOUT INCORPORATING AIR

Push the stem of the mixer down to the bottom of the bowl and move it around gently in order to allow any air caught in the blades to escape, then mix without lifting.

3 SCRAPING

Scrape the sides of the bowl using a spatula or a bowl scraper to recover as much of the mixture as possible.

4 USING A DOUBLE-BOILER

The double-boiler makes it possible to heat ingredients, using steam, away from direct contact with a heat source. Because the heat is less intense, the mixture warms up and melts gently. This technique prevents burning chocolate or coagulating eggs.

Use a large saucepan and a larger diameter bowl so that you can rest the bowl on the saucepan without the bottom coming into contact with the water. Put water in the saucepan and heat it up to simmer but not boil. Put the mixture in the bowl and the bowl on the saucepan. The base of the bowl must not touch the water.

5 STRAINING

Using a round or conical sieve with a more or less fine mesh makes a mixture more fluid and/or eliminates lumps.

BASIC TECHNIQUES: PREPARING

1 REHYDRATING GELATINE

These recipes are made using sheets of dehydrated gelatine (for best results do not use powdered gelatine). Because it is so light, gelatine must be weighed carefully before use. For precision, measurements are in grams in this book. One sheet of gelatine usually weighs 2 grams but weights vary between brands. Gelatine must be rehydrated before it can be used for cooking. If it is not properly rehydrated, it will absorb further moisture from the mixture into which it is added and make it shrink.

Immerse the gelatine in a large bowl of cold water (it melts at low temperature). Let it soak for at least 15 minutes. Squeeze out the gelatine between your hands before adding it to the mix using a whisk.

Gelatine is used to help mixes stick together and give them body. Setting time is quite fast. Use the soaked gelatine as soon as possible so that the gelling power acts when the mixture is ready.

2 PREPARING A BAKING TRAY

Non-stick baking trays are available, but most trays must be covered with a non-stick surface: silicone cooking mats, baking paper (baking parchment). Silicone mats are perfect for working with chocolate but are not suitable for choux pastry. Baking paper is very handy, but less stable. Hold the corners in place with paper clips or put weights on the paper. Pipe out the mix then remove the weights when the piped mix is heavy enough to hold the paper down by itself.

3 LINING A BAKING RING

Lightly butter the inside of the ring. Cut out a strip of baking paper (baking parchment) slightly higher than the side of the ring and 1 cm (1/2 in) longer in circumference. Put the strip in the ring and stick it to the sides before pouring in the mixture.

4 USING ACETATE STRIPS

Transparent acetate strip (Le Rhodoid is a brand name to look out for) is flexible and very useful for working with chocolate. Cut the strip so that it is slightly higher than the top of the ring or frame. Insert the tape into each ring and pour out the mixture to set in a cool place. The tape prevents desserts from sticking to the ring; it also makes unmoulding clean and easy and protects against oxidation.

5 SETTING UP FOR GLAZING

Put the item to be glazed on a wire rack placed on a baking tray. Pour on the glaze. Smooth out the top with a palette knife to remove any excess, which you can collect in the tray for further use.

BASIC TECHNIQUES: PIPING

1 PIPING

A piping bag or pastry bag can be used without a nozzle to fill a tart base neatly or to make large round bases ensuring that the mixture is of even thickness. Fitted with a nozzle, the piping bag allows mixtures to be piped out very precisely or give a special shape to the preparation.

Hold the piping bag upright to press out discs or domes, lay it horizontally to shape éclairs. Squeeze with one hand, stabilise and guide the piping bag with the other. When there is not enough mixture left in your hand, push the dough down and rotate the piping bag a quarter turn.

2 FILLING THE PIPING BAG

Select a nozzle and insert it into the piping bag. Mark off where to cut so that the socket fits properly. Remove the nozzle and cut the end off the bag. Twist the nozzle firmly down into the bottom of the piping bag to prevent the mixture from leaking out during filling. Fold the top of the piping bag over the hand that holds it. Using a spatula, transfer the dough or ganache into the piping bag, scraping the spatula on the hand holding the bag. Fill the bag to a maximum of two-thirds full so that it does not overflow. Pull the top of the bag back up and give it a quarter turn, which pushes the dough down towards the nozzle. Remove the cap from the nozzle and twist the piping bag to push the dough/ganache out.

3 MAKING A TEMPLATE

To ensure regular sizes when piping, use a template as a guide. Using a pencil, draw circles of the required size on a sheet of baking paper. Turn the paper over and pipe out the mixture onto the drawn circles.

BASIC TECHNIQUES: FINISHING

1 PIPING OUT A SPIRAL
Pipe out a mixture spiralling from the centre outwards and squeezing the piping bag with continuous, equal pressure to ensure a regular shape without gaps or overlapping between each spiral of mixture.

2 COATING USING A PIPING BAG
Coat the chocolate or cake using a piping bag fitted with a basket-weave nozzle.

3 GLAZING A LOG CAKE
Put the cake on a wire rack placed on a rimmed baking tray. Pour out the glaze moving slowly from one end to the other. Gently shake the grid to remove excess glaze.

4 COVERING WITH FLAKES
Coat the chocolate using a piping bag, then roll it several times in the chocolate flakes.

INGREDIENTS: CREAM AND BUTTER

CREAM

1 THE PRODUCT

These recipes are made using fresh cream labelled 'whipping cream', which has a fat content of 36% (UK) and 35% fat (US). The cream used by French patissiers and chocolatiers has a similar fat content (30-34%).

There are various types of cream: raw (unprocessed), pasteurised (heated to 80°C/176°F) or sterilised (processed at a very high temperature).

It can come in liquid form or be thickened by adding lactic ferments. Pastry chefs and chocolate makers use cream with at least 30% fat because fat gives more body to the cream and adds taste. It is emulsified with melted chocolate to make ganaches, bringing smoothness and finesse.

2 MAKING WHIPPED CREAM

Cream is often incorporated whipped (whisked),to lighten pastry mixes. (Lightly whipped cream is also called 'chantilly cream'.)

Whip the cream briskly until it doubles in volume. It should become airy and firm as the fat globules in the cream enclose air and form bubbles. Use a food processor with a whisk, a cutter with a blade or an electric mixer.

3 FIRMING UP WHIPPED CREAM

To finish whipping up cream, increase the length and speed of movement to make it firm, smooth and evenly blended. The cream should lose some of its shininess.

BUTTER

4 THE PRODUCT

The butter used in these recipes is unsalted and is made from cow's milk. Use quality butter with a high percentage of fat (ideally around 82%). High-fat butter makes mixtures tasty, smooth and crumbly.

5 SOFTENED BUTTER

Working the butter to give it a creamy consistency before incorporating it into a mix helps to prevent lumps forming and gives smoothness. Cut the butter into small pieces, let it soften at room temperature or soften it at very low heat (without melting it), then work it with a spatula or a whisk.

6 BROWNED 'HAZELNUT BUTTER'

Put the butter in a saucepan and heat on a medium-low heat. When the crackling sound stops, the butter will have taken on a light, hazelnut colour, as the casein (protein) in the butter caramelises and colours. Browned butter has a rich, toasty flavour.

THE INGREDIENTS: EGGS

EGGS

1 THE PRODUCT
For pastry recipes it is best to weigh eggs.

Egg white contains proteins; egg yolk contains fat.

2 EQUIVALENT EGG WEIGHTS
One fresh egg: 50 g (2 oz) egg white: 30 to 35g (1 oz)

Yolk: 15 to 20 g ($^3/_4$ oz)

3 BEATING EGG YOLKS
Whisk egg yolks and sugar to make a frothy mixture. It should double in volume. The process takes several minutes and is faster if you use an electric whisk.

4 WHIPPING AND FIRMING-UP EGG WHITES
Use a food processor with a whisk attachment or a hand mixer to beat egg whites until they are firm and form peaks when the whisk is removed. Towards the end of whisking, increase the speed to make the whipped egg whites smooth and evenly blended. If necessary, add a little powdered sugar.

5 THE 'RIBBON TEST'
For egg yolks: The consistency of a mixture of egg yolks and sugar should be smooth and even so that it rolls off the spatula in a continuous stream without breaking, with a ribbon-like appearance.

For egg whites: when the bases of macaron halves are ready, there should be a 'ribbon' pattern.

6 EGG WASH
Coating pastry with egg wash provides colour during baking. It can be done with a whole egg, with just the yolk, or a mixture of both, and can include milk. Beat with a fork, then apply it to the dough using a paintbrush. Leave to dry then repeat the process, if necessary, before baking in the oven.

INGREDIENTS: SUGAR, HONEY

1 SUGAR

I THE PRODUCT

Sugar enhances the aromas, gives crispness, nourishes the yeast in leavened doughs and adds colour to baked cakes.

White caster sugar: refined powdered sugar, traditionally used in pastry making.

Icing (confectioner's) sugar: white sugar powder finely ground and enriched with starch to prevent solidification.

Brown sugar: raw sugar extracted from sugar cane.

Barbados: sugar made from the residual syrup from the refining of cane sugar.

2 MAKING A SYRUP

Use clean, dry utensils. Weigh the water and sugar, pour them gently without mixing. Clean off any splashes using a water-soaked paintbrush. Heat over medium heat keeping an eye on the saucepan.

3 MAKING CARAMEL

There are different ways to make caramel, depending on their use. Traditional caramel is made from sugar and water for sugar decorations and choux pastry glaze.

Dry caramel is made without water for the flavouring of mixtures that require a stronger taste.

4 SOAKING WITH SYRUP

Dip the paintbrush in the syrup and paint it on the biscuit base until it is fully soaked but not soggy. When you press down on the biscuit with your finger, the syrup should appear on the surface.

5 HONEY

A natural product from the beehive, bees' honey has a characteristic taste and is a powerful sweetener.

6 INVERTED SUGAR SYRUP

A mixture of glucose and fructose in equal proportions. It replaces sugar in some recipes because it has the characteristic of remaining soft and smooth without crystalising. Buy from specialist baking shops or online. If unavailable, use a neutral honey instead.

7 GLUCOSE SYRUP

A thick, colourless starch-based syrup made from corn or potato starch. It avoids the problem of crystallisation of sugar during cooking and is particularly used in glazes.

INGREDIENTS: FRUIT, FLAVOURINGS

1 ROASTING DRIED NUTS
Place them on a baking sheet covered with baking paper (baking parchment). Bake at 170°C (340°F/gas 5) for 15 to 25 minutes depending on their size. Roasting develops their aromas.

2 DRYING FRUIT
Cut thin slices of fruit. Preheat the oven to 90°C (200°F/gas ¼), place the slices on a silicone cooking sheet and dry in the oven for 1 ½ to 2 hours, turning them over halfway through keeping an eye on them all the time.

3 ZESTING FRUIT
The coloured, visible part of citrus fruit with an intense tangy taste. The pith is the bitter white part between the pulp and the peel and should not be used.

4 GOLD DECORATIONS
Edible gold for decorating food comes in powder, flakes or leaves. It is applied with paintbrush, does not have any particular taste but has a very fine, decorative effect.

5 FOOD COLOURING
These recipes use fat-soluble colouring powders. These should generally be mixed with white couverture chocolate at two 3-minute intervals to obtain the right shade of colour.

TIPS: PASTRY

1 ROLLING OUT DOUGH

Work on a floured work surface. To roll evenly, place 2 thin sticks on either side of the dough and roll out until the rolling pin rests on them. When rolling, press lightly on the rolling pin to gradually reduce the thickness of the dough bit by bit. If the dough no longer moves easily and begins to stick to the worktop, it needs to be covered with flour again.

2 MAKING A PASTRY BASE

Drape the dough carefully over the rolling pin and lay it on the buttered pastry ring, taking care not to apply any pressure, then cut off the excess dough. With one hand, lift the edge of the dough and start to bring it down the side of the ring. With the other hand, gently push the dough down into the corners to give a sharp edge to the pastry when it's cut. Using

your thumb, press the dough lightly and evenly into the sides of the ring without leaving marks.

Use tart pastry rings or rings (without bottoms) which allow the heat of the oven to cook the pastry from beneath..This is especially true for fruit tarts, to prevent cases where where the filling appears to be cooked while the dough is still raw.

3 CUTTING OFF EXCESS

Remove excess dough by placing a paring knife flat on the ring and gradually slicing it off, or run a rolling pin over the rim of the tart ring.

4 KNEADING

Knead the dough forwards pressing down with the palm of your hand to check its consistency, which should be smooth and regular. Repeat once or twice.

5 MAKING A SHORTCRUST DOUGH

Put small cubes of cold butter in the flour, rub together with your fingertips and then between your hands, without squashing. Or use a mixer at low speed, until you obtain a coarse, grainy consistency.

6 SCORING

Decorate the surface of a dough by scoring it with the tip of a knife, being careful not to go right through the dough.

TIPS: MACARONS & CHOUX PASTRY

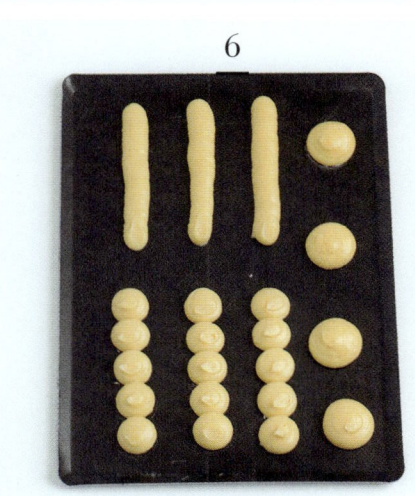

1 MAKING MACARON MIXTURE

Mixing Italian meringue and almond paste using a bowl scraper or spatula: stir one-third of the meringue briskly into the almond paste to start softening. Stir in the rest more gently, pressing the mixture down evenly to make a smooth blend.

2 PIPING MACARONS

Hold the piping bag vertically and press out discs. Do not lift the piping bag; the nozzle should be kept 1 cm ($^1/_2$ in) from the tray. Turn the piping bag a sharp quarter-turn to stop the mixture flow.

3 COOKING AND STORING

Macaron shells cook quickly (about 12 minutes) at a low temperature (150°C/300°F/gas 3). It is best to leave ganache-filled macarons to mature in a cool place for 24 hours the let the flavours intermingle: the ganache gives flavour to the top and makes it melt in the mouth more easily.

Macaron shells or ganache-filled macarons can be frozen after baking and stored for 3 months in an airtight container wrapped in cling film (plastic wrap).

4 DRYING CHOUX DOUGH

When making choux pastry, pre-cook the wet mixture before adding the eggs: when the dough is smoothly blended, flatten it out on the bottom of the saucepan and heat without stirring. Leave on the heat until it starts to stick to the bottom of the saucepan. Then, when you hear a crackling sound, shake it to check the bottom of the pan: if a thin film is sticking evenly, the dough is dry enough.

5 MAKING CRUNCHY CRAQUELIN

Craquelin is crisp, crunchy outer layer that makes choux pastry round, even and crunchy. Cut out discs and place them on the choux pastry before baking.

6 PIPING CHOUX PASTRY

Use a baking tray covered with baking paper (baking parchment) or a non-stick tray.

Choux pastry: use an 8 mm nozzle. Position it perpendicular to the tray and 1 cm ($^1/_2$ in) above it. Press until you have a 3 cm disc. Stop the flow of the dough with a sharp, quarter-turn movement, staying on a level with the choux pastry.

Éclairs: use a 14 mm nozzle. Position the piping bag at a 45-degree angle to the tray. Press with even pressure and move the piping bag along quickly. Stop the flow as for choux pastry.

LIST OF RECIPES

BASICS

ORIGINS OF CHOCOLATE

Pod..10
Fresh bean..11
3 varieties of cacao.......................................12
Fermentation...14
Processing the beans.....................................15
Crushing..16
Conching...17
Mass and powder..18
Cocoa butter...19
Sugar...20
Vanilla and milk..21
Dark chocolate 22
Milk chocolate, white chocolate..................23

CHOCOLATE BASICS

Tempering 24
Melting 26
Pre-crystallization 1: work-top method...........27
Pre-crystallization 2 :seeding method 28
Pre-crystallization 3: standing method............29
Pre-crystallization 4 :Mycryo method.............30
Keeping up to temperature and working.........31

CHOCOLATE SWEETS

Coating a sweet 32
Moulding a sweet..34
Decorating a sweet..36

DECORATIONS

Chocolate decorations...................................38
Chocolate decorations...................................39

CRÈMES ET MOUSSES

Praliné 50 % et Gianduja 40
Ganache crémeuse 42
Ganache montée blanche 44
Appareil à bombe 46
Mousse au chocolat sur appareil à bombe 48
Mousse au chocolat sur crème anglaise............50
Crème pâtissière..52
Crème diplomate...52

PÂTES

Pâte feuilletée
inversée chocolat...54
Pâte sablée 58
Biscuit à la cuillère 60
Biscuit au chocolat sans farine 62
Biscuit amande 64
Pâte à choux...66

MERINGUES

Meringue suisse 68
Meringue française..69

GLAÇAGES

Glaçage noir brillant 70
Glaçage rocher..72
Glaçage chocolat au lait................................74
Glaçage blanc...75

LES BONBONS ET LES PÂTISSERIES

LES BONBONS

Bonbons trempés ganache pure origine 78
Bonbons trempés noir ganache vanille.............82
Bonbons moulés choco lait & caramel.............84
Bonbons trempés ganache au miel 86
Bonbons trempés à la verveine 88
Bonbons moulés choco-menthe......................90
Bonbons trempés ganache framboise.............92
Bonbons moulés au Grand Marnier 94
Bonbons trempés noisette sésame..................96
Bonbons trempés praliné feuilletine 100
Bonbons moulés gianduja 102
Rochers praliné 104
Rochers vanille-coco 106
Fudge chocolat caramel 108

LES MOULAGES

Moulage œuf...110
Moulage poule 114
Moulage boîte 118
Fritures 122

À CROQUER

Plaques 124
Mendiants 126
Orangettes 128
Shortbread millionNaire..............................130
Truffes...132
Barres..134

LES ENTREMETS

Entremets macarons 138
Succès 142
Macarons au chocolat 146
Entremets meringué 150
Merveilleux 154
Chocolat-framboise feuillantine 156
Entremets au gianduja 160
Opéra..164
Poire-chocolat charlotte 168
Entremets combawa choco-Ananas..................172
Entremets choco-coco 176
Forêt-noire..180

LES BÛCHES

Bûche chocolat intense................................184
Bûche chocolat au lait passion 188

LES CHOUX

Éclairs...192
Choux dulcey
et cœur choco crémeux 194
Paris-brest...198

LES TARTES

Tarte au chocolat...202
Tarte choco-lait 206
Tartelettes soufflées 210
Tarte caramel 214
Tarte chocolat au lait pécan 218

LES INCONTOURNABLES

Pains au chocolat...222
Brioche 226
Babas...230
Galette des rois 234
Millefeuille..238

LES GÂTEAUX DE VOYAGE

Moelleux..242
Cookies 244
Brownie 246
Gâteau truffé 248
Cake rocher...250
Cake marbré 254
Tigrés 256
Madeleines...258

LES MOUSSES ET GLACES

Mousses...260
Marquise 262
Crème glacée...264

LE GLOSSAIRE

Ustensiles 268
Les moules chocolat.....................................270
Les produits du chocolat 272
Le lexique du chocolat 273
Les astuces du chocolat 274
Choisir le chocolat 275
Gestes basiques : réaliser.............................276
Gestes basiques : préparer 277
Gestes basiques : pocher..............................278
Gestes basiques : finition.............................279
Crème, beurre..280
Œuf..281
Sucres, miel...282
Fruits, aromatisation....................................283
Astuces pâte..284
Astuces macarons & choux...........................285

INGREDIENT INDEX

SPIRITS

Grand Marnier moulded chocolates . 94

ALMOND

Bars 134
Almond biscuit 64
Gianduja moulded sweets 102
Praline feuilletine dipped sweets 100
Brownies 246
Rock cake 250
Eclairs 192
Coconut chocolate dessert 176
Lime and pineapple chocolate dessert 172
Macaron chocolate dessert 138
Black Forest cake 180
Rock glaze 72
Macarons 146
Mendiants 126
Opera cake 164
Praline 50% Gianduja 40
Praline rock sweets 104
Milk chocolate tart 206

PEANUT

Caramel tart 214

BITTER COCOA POWDER

Baba cake 230
Biscuit without flour 62
Brioche 226
Intense chocolate log 184
Marble cake 254
Raspberry and chocolate feuillantine 156
Gianduja desssert 160
Lime and pineapple chocolate dessert 172
Black Forest cake 180
Galette des Rois cake 234
Glossy dark glaze 70
Marquise 262
Pains au chocolat 222
Success cake 142
Chocolate tart 202
Soufflé tartlets 210
Truffle chocolates 132

COFFEE

Opera cake 164

MILK CHOCOLATE

Bars 134
Grand Marnier moulded sweets 94
Milk chocolate and caramel moulded sweets 84
Mint and chocolate moulded sweets 90
Gianduja moulded sweets 102
Honey ganache dipped sweets 86
Raspberry dipped sweets 92
Hazelnut sesame dipped sweets 96
Brownies 246
Passion fruit milk chocolate log 188
Iced creme 264
Gianduja dessert 160
Macaron chocolate dessert 138
Fish moulded chocolates 122
Milk chocolate glaze 74
Slabs of chocolate 124
Caramel tart 214
Milk chocolate tart 206
Pecan pie with milk chocolate 218

WHITE CHOCOLATE

Mint and chocolate moulded sweets 90
Raspberry and chocolate feuillantine 156
Gianduja dessert 160
Coconut chocolate dessert 176
Black Forest cake 180
Fish moulded chocolates 122
White ganache 44
Hen moulding 112
Slabs of chocolate 124
Coconut vanilla rock sweets 106
Chocolate tart 202
Caramel tart 214
Pecan pie with milk chocolate 218

DULCEY® CHOCOLAT

Dulcey choux pastries with creamy chocolate centres 194

DARK CHOCOLATE 60 %

Intense chocolate log 184
Rock cake 250
Raspberry chocolate feuillantine .. 156
Dulcey choux pastries 194
Black Forest cake 180
Fish moulded chocolates 122
Creamy ganache 42
Box made of moulded chocolate .. 118
Egg moulding 110
Hen moulding 112
Mousse round bowl mix 49
Opera cake 164
Pains au chocolat 222
Chocolate Tart 202
Soufflé tartlets 210
Tiger cakes 256

DARK CHOCOLATE 66 %

Baba cakes 230
Bars 134
Caramel chocolate moulded sweets .. 84
Gianduja moulded sweets 102
Verbena dipped sweets 88
Raspberry ganache moulded sweets . 92
Vanilla dark ganache dipped sweets .. 82
Praline feuilletine dipped sweets .. 100
Brownies 246
Pear and chocolate Charlotte cake .. 168
Dulcey choux pastries with creamy centres 194
Biscuits 244
Iced creme 264
Eclairs 192
Gianduja dessert 160
Coconut chocolate dessert 176
Lime and pineapple chocolate dessert 172
Macaron chocolate dessert 138
Meringue dessert 150
Truffle cake 248
Rock glazing 72
Macarons with chocolate 146
Madeleine cakes 258
Marquise cake 262
Mendiants 126

Merveilleux cake 152
Millefeuille cakes 238
Moelleux dessert 242
Mousse with creme anglaise and chocolate 50
Mousses 260
Opera cake 164
Orangette sticks 128
Paris-Brest cake 198
Slabs of chocolate 124
Pralina 50 % gianduja 40
Praline rock sweets 104
Millionaire shortbread 130
Success cake 142
Caramel tart 214
Milk chocolate tart 206
Pecan pie with milk chocolate 218
Truffles 132

DARK CHOCOLATE 70 %

Single origin ganache dipped sweets . 78
Rock cake 250

FEUILLETINE

Praline feuilletine dipped sweets .. 100
Raspberry and chocolate feuillantine 156
Gianduja dessert 160

TONKA BEAN

Rock cake 250
Millionaire shortbread 130

FRESH FRUIT

Bars 134
Grand Marnier moulded sweets 94
Raspberry ganache moulded sweets . 92
Passion fruit milk chocolate log 188
Pear and chocolate Charlotte cake .. 168
Raspberry and chocolate feuillantine 156
Gianduja dessert 160
Coconut and chocolate dessert 176
Lime and pineapple chocolate dessert 172
Black Forest cake 180
Orangette sticks 128
Vanilla coconut rocks 106

CANDIED FRUIT

Mendiants 126
Orangette sticks 128
Slabs of chocolate 124

COCOA NIBS

Passion fruit milk chocolate log 188
Paris-Brest cake 198

MINT

Mint chocolate moulded sweets 90

HONEY

Honey ganache dipped sweets 86
Shortbread millionaire 130

HAZELNUT

Gianduja moulded sweets 102
Hazelnut sesame dipped sweets 96
Praline feuilletine dipped sweets .. 100
Brownies 246
Intense chocolate log 184
Dulcey choux pastries with creamy centre 194
Mendiants 126
Slabs of chocolate 124
Praline 50 % gianduja 40
Praline rock sweets 104
Vanilla coconut rock sweets 106
Success cake 142
Milk chocolate tart 206

WALNUT, PECAN

Bars 134
Brownies 246
Intense chocolate log 184
Biscuits 244
Slabs of chocolate 124
Pecan pie with milk chocolate 218

PISTACHIO

Brownies 246
Mendiants 126
Slabs of chocolate 124

PRALINE

Gianduja moulded sweets 102
Hazelnut sesame dipped sweets 96
Praline feuilletine dipped sweets .. 100
Intense chocolate log 184
Raspberry and chocolate feuillantine 156
Gianduja dessert 160
Paris-Brest cake 198
Praline rock sweets 104

SESAME

Hazelnut sesame dipped sweets 96

VANILLA

Vanilla and dark chocolate dipped sweets 82
Pear and chocolate Charlotte cake .. 168
Macaron chocolate dessert 138
Black Forest cake 180
Caramel and chocolate fudge 108
Madeleines 258
Vanilla and coconuate rock sweets . 106

VERBENA

Verbena dipped sweets 88

MÉLANIE'S ACKNOWLEDGEMENTS

Thanks to Pierre and Orathay for all the good times we had during the photo shoots.

Thanks to the Marabout team for producing this sixth book.

ANNE'S ACKNOWLEDGEMENTS

Thank you to the entire Scinnov team, to the various artisan chocolatiers we interviewed, and to all the authors of scientific publications that we have read; they have participated directly or indirectly in the production of this work.

Thank you to Marabout for working with me once again.

PIERRE'S ACKNOWLEDGEMENTS

Thanks to Mélanie and Orathay who are incredible professionals, and wonderful people.

EMMANUELLE'S ACKNOWLEDGEMENTS

Thanks to Robert Linxe, chocolatier, creator of Maison du Chocolat, who passed on his passion for 'the art of chocolate' to me.

To Claude Lebey, one of the founders of the Club des Croqueurs de Chocolat, French journalist, columnist and food editor, who taught me everything about 'the art of tasting'.

To Marabout for this incredible chocolate collaboration.

And to my three children who had only chocolate cakes, chocolate mousse, chocolate tarts or other ganaches for desserts throughout their childhood ... that's what we call transmission!

A big thank you to Valrhona, the partner of chocolate artisans since 1922, and the best chocolate manufacturer, for graciously providing us with Caribbean, Guanaja, Jivara, Dulcey, Ivory and praline cover chocolate to create the recipes in the book.

First published in 2019 by Hachette Livre (Marabout)
This English language edition published in 2021 by Hardie
Grant Books, an imprint of Hardie Grant Publishing

Hardie Grant Books (London)
5th & 6th Floors
52–54 Southwark Street
London SE1 1UN

Hardie Grant Books (Melbourne)
Building 1, 658 Church Street
Richmond, Victoria 3121

hardiegrantbooks.com

All rights reserved. No part of this publication may be reproduced, stored in a retrieval system or transmitted in any form by any means, electronic, mechanical, photocopying, recording or otherwise, without the prior written permission of the publishers and copyright holders.

The moral rights of the author have been asserted.

British Library Cataloguing-in-Publication Data. A catalogue record for this book is available from the British Library.

The Ultimate Book of Chocolate
ISBN: 978-1-78488-379-9

10 9 8 7 6 5 4 3 2 1

For the French edition:

Author: Mélanie Dupuis
Photography: Pierre Javelle
Illustrator: Yannis Varoutsikos

For the English edition:

Publisher: Kajal Mistry
Commissioning Editor: Eve Marleau
Translator: David Slack
Typesetter: David Meikle
Copy-editor: Susan Low
Proofreader: Gregor Shepherd
Production Controller: Nik Ginelli

Colour reproduction by p2d
Printed and bound in China by Leo Paper Products Ltd.

MIX
Paper from
responsible sources
FSC www.fsc.org   FSC™ C020056